BETWEEN A HEART AND A ROCK PLACE

BETWEEN A HEART
AND A ROCK PLACE

A MEMOIR

PAT BENATAR

WITH PATSI BALE COX

wm WILLIAM MORROW *An Imprint of* HarperCollins*Publishers*

HarperCollins books may be purchased for educational, business, or sales promotional use. For information please write: Special Markets Department, HarperCollins Publishers, 10 East 53rd Street, New York, NY 10022.

FIRST EDITION

Designed by Jamie Lynn Kerner

Library of Congress Cataloging-in-Publication Data has been applied for.

ISBN 978-0-06-195377-4

10 11 12 13 14   OV/RRD   10 9 8 7 6 5 4 3 2 1

For PD, Bina, and Boo Boo, you make my heart sing

CONTENTS

PROLOGUE

1979

I KNEW THE SOUND wasn't right.

As I sat there, listening to the playback from my first-ever recording session, I knew that something was off. It wasn't that the speakers were bad or the mics were low. It wasn't that my voice sounded wrong or the drummer was off the beat. It was more subtle than all that, but also much worse—not something that could be fixed by a simple equipment change. The problem was that I sounded like Julie Andrews trying to sing rock.

Part of the issue was that the musicians whom the producers had hired were very precise players. Everything sounded perfect—so perfect it was bland. It wasn't working. It wasn't rock and roll. I knew it, the producers knew it, and the record company knew it. But still everyone kept shoving me in the same direction.

For my first record deal, I'd signed with a label called Chrysalis Records. I'd been knocking on doors in New York for a couple of years when Chrysalis offered me a deal. My manager, Rick Newman, was a comedy club owner with no music experience. He'd discovered me while I was performing at Catch a Rising Star, a club in New York, and he believed in me enough to take on management duties. Early on, what he lacked in music knowledge, he made up for in passion, and he'd been fantastic in presenting me to labels. His enthusiasm was infectious. But though he was my biggest cheerleader and the greatest guy, he had to rely heavily on our attorneys, business manager, and the record label for advice. Chrysalis had signed a chick singer, and a chick singer was what they expected me to remain. The result was the all-too-perfect sound of my first session.

I didn't set out to be a solo artist. My dream was to be the singer in a rockin' band, like Robert Plant was to Led Zeppelin or Lou Gramm to Foreigner. I wanted a partnership, like Mick Jagger and Keith Richards had—an unrelenting back-and-forth between talented musicians. The sound I heard in my head was raucous, with hard-driving guitars speeding everything forward. I was a classically trained singer with a great deal of musical knowledge, but I had no idea how to make that visceral, intense sound happen. I had to evolve, but I didn't know how to make that evolution happen. And apparently, my record label didn't either.

It wouldn't be enough just to have a backing band who could play it looser. Deep down I knew that I needed a partner, somebody who understood where I wanted to take my music. Somebody to help me get there and be an equal and integral part of the band, a partner in every step we took. Somebody whom I wouldn't have to sit around and try desperately to explain my sound to, but who would just hear my voice and instinctively know. Make no mistake: I was looking for a music partner, *not* a boyfriend. I was separated from my first husband but still legally married. I'm far too traditional to have shrugged that detail off. The truth is, I didn't want any man in my life right then, except for a musical partner.

For its part, Chrysalis had no interest in bringing some dude into the act, except as a backup musician. At first, I didn't know how to react to the record executives, so I listened to them, and for a while, I followed along. I'm opinionated and strong, but not really confrontational. I don't pick fights with people unless they're necessary. When you're young, you tend to let people run your show, especially when those people have been successfully running a lot of other people's shows. But even as they kept pushing me to fall in line, I knew their way was wrong.

Thankfully, I trusted my instincts. That's probably the single most important thing anyone can know: *trust your gut*. It's especially important for young people because there are always going to be older folks hanging around explaining why they know best. I was young and inexperienced when I started out in music, and there were times I bought into the other people's *I know best* routine. And when I went against my gut, the decisions turned out to be wrong every time. Somewhere deep inside, you know which is the right path and which is the wrong one. The problem is that so many times we start doubting ourselves, questioning, second-guessing. My advice? Get over it. Remember that this is your career, and you don't get too many shots. If you go with what you believe, you will almost always be a step ahead of the game.

Now, if you do *not* believe your gut is trustworthy, then find some people whose intuition you do trust. Surround yourself with a few people who inspire confidence and run your ideas past them. As irritating as it was to have conflict with my label, I not only trusted my gut, but I had a few people around me who did as well.

Not being a music man, Rick may not have completely understood my thinking, but he knew that I wasn't going to back down. One fellow at Chrysalis Records understood what I wanted and why—my A&R man, Jeff "Buzzard" Aldridge. A&R stands for "artists and repertoire," and those are the staff members who deal directly with the artists and their music. The A&R guy is your guy. Everyone else is the record company's guy. Buzzard was our day-to-day person, the one I usually dealt with and the one I trusted.

The only problem with A&R representatives is that they are not usually the decision makers. They are not the people who will be marketing and selling your music or setting your promotion budget. Those are the suits, and they could make or break careers, including mine. And musically, those guys weren't getting it.

Luckily, after those first misdirected recording sessions, Buzzard convinced the suits to bring in one of the top producers in the business, Mike Chapman. He'd been working with Blondie at the time and didn't even think he'd be able to produce a whole record. Still, he'd work on a couple tracks with us. I'd heard talk that Chapman was difficult, something of a Svengali, because he was very controlling, but his success working with Blondie had Chrysalis foaming at the mouth. Though not a musician himself, Chapman was a very instinctual producer. He wasn't necessarily going to find the sound himself, but he might be able to connect me to people who could.

Initially Chapman was the only person who understood what I was going for, and he navigated a way to get it accomplished. He listened to me explain what I wanted, and started looking around for somebody who fit the picture. I could hear the guitar I wanted, the one that would bring alive what was only in my mind at that point. I'd been trying to come up with a partner and a sound for months, to no avail. My frustrations were rising on a daily—maybe hourly—basis. But I knew that Chapman was talented and smart. I want people who work with me to either be smarter than me or be willing and able to work harder than I do. (That's critical, because I am a working dog.)

Chrysalis set up a time to audition some players at SIR rehearsal hall on Thirty-seventh Street in Manhattan. After they got the initial lineup booked, Chapman had another thought, a twenty-two-year-old kid who had been touring with Rick Derringer.

"I think this is the one, Pat. His name is Neil Giraldo. He's perfect—just what you've been looking for."

"Okay, bring him in to audition."

"Well, I didn't tell him he's coming to an audition as such. I just told him to stop by so you could meet him. He's a genius, Pat."

That certainly grabbed my attention. "Genius" wasn't a word that Chapman used often. Chapman wasn't going to be at the audition, but Buzzard made the arrangements for Neil to meet with us. And so as the time went by that day, I got more interested in meeting this genius. Then I was told that Buzzard had arrived with the guitar player.

"Oh, cool," I said, nonchalantly.

I was talking to Rick Newman, with my back to the door, and didn't turn around immediately. When I did, Buzzard was talking to this guy Neil. He stood there looking like Adonis, hair to his shoulders, the most drop-dead gorgeous man I had ever seen in my life. Somewhere in the distance the "Hallelujah" chorus was playing. Luckily he didn't look at me in that moment, because I froze in my tracks. Something shot through my entire being. Every nerve ending in my body lit up like the Fourth of July, and every hormone in my body went insane. I felt like someone had hit me in the face with a two-by-four.

I thought, *Girl, you have just seen the father of your children.* (Did I mention that I was *not* looking for a boyfriend?)

When Neil finally turned around, I honestly felt like time slowed down. It's corny. It's a cliché. But that's exactly how I felt, like he was walking toward me in slow motion.

"Hi, I'm Neil Giraldo."

At that point I finally noticed that he didn't have a guitar. Here was a musician who was looking for a new gig until Rick Derringer went back out on tour, and though he wasn't auditioning, he hadn't even brought his instrument along. That endeared him to me all the more. I gave him the snappiest greeting I could think of:

"Hi."

I couldn't say anything else, so finally Neil sat down at the piano.

"What's the hell is the matter with you, Pat?" Newman asked. "You barely spoke to this guy."

I shrugged. My brain was going *gong, gong, gong!*

I finally whispered. "Newman, I don't care if this guy can't play a note. We'll get him lessons. He's in the band."

Newman looked a little sick.

When the gonging quieted down enough for me to hear the piano, I snapped out of it, then felt a bit let down. My hormones might have been roaring, but I am, after all, a Capricorn, and capable of getting down to business. As much as I wanted this to be perfect, the piano wasn't getting to me. He played brilliantly, but I just couldn't feel it. Was it possible that this guy was the love of my life but not the music partner I wanted? *What a drag.* He finished playing the piece, and then he turned to the group of guys waiting to audition.

"Man, could I borrow your guitar?"

One of the musicians handed him a guitar. He turned around, leaned over, and fastened the strap. Then he turned back, fiddling with the tuning, his hair still down over his face. I wish I had that moment on film. When he hit the first chord, I nearly fell to my knees. It was amazing—the very thing I'd had in my head and never once heard anybody play. His playing was so passionate, so intense. Of course he had the gig.

CHAPTER ONE

THE LITTLE ANDRZEJEWSKI GIRL WHO COULD SING

I WAS NEVER JUST a girl's girl. I grew up wanting to do boy things. Nail polish and baby dolls weren't enough for me. I wanted to be making a fort or climbing a tree. Boys seemed to have all the fun. They got to use a hammer and nails. They got to sneak into abandoned houses and go exploring. They were out riding in go-karts. All that was right up my alley.

And the boys I hung around made me tough. At first they were merciless—they never cut me any slack. You want to be on the baseball team? Use this thin mitt that hurts your hands so badly you have to bite your cheek not to cry. You want to hang out in our clubhouse? Get ready to have earthworms squished onto your bare legs. It was trial by fire, but in the end, I wouldn't have been caught dead crying over a skinned knee. All this made me fierce, and soon they realized that I was "okay for a girl," which was just fine with me, because I had a plan. I just needed them to let me in, which, of course, they did.

My plan was this: I also loved being a girl. Loved it. There wasn't enough makeup on the planet for me to play with and I lived in the pages of fashion magazines. But I was absolutely boy-crazy, and that's where my plan came in. I wouldn't be a typical tomboy; I would push the envelope in my neighborhood and bridge the gap between "girl stuff" and "boy stuff." I didn't want to be a boy, I wanted to be a girl who could do everything boys could. I thought the whole thing out: If I played boy-type games and did boy-type things, I could run around with the boys plus have all the fun they did. I got to both be them and be near them. It was the best of all possible worlds.

And that particular world started out in Greenpoint, Brooklyn—an ethnic area first populated by the Germans and Irish in the mid-nineteenth century, followed by the Poles and Italians some years later. Greenpoint was a culturally diverse neighborhood where everything from the foods to the traditions changed from block to block. You could guess the ethnicity of a street by the smells coming out of the kitchen windows. But even though their histories were wide-ranging, the people were close.

We were the Andrzejewski family, and we lived on the Polish block. Ethnically, we were a mixed family. Andrew, my father, was Polish and his family was new to America. Mom, Mildred, was Irish and Dutch with some Native American added in. I always used to say that my mother's ancestors came over on the *Mayflower*. They didn't really, but they had been in America for many generations when I was born in 1953. The Van Kuykendall and Douwes families had come from Holland to America in 1645.

When I was two years old, the family moved from Brooklyn to North Hamilton Avenue in Lindenhurst, on the South Shore of Long Island. We were not alone in this exodus from the city; quite a large group on the Polish side of the family moved to Long Island, including my father's sister as well as many cousins on my mother's side. It represented a different way of life—away from the concrete and toward the water. In Brooklyn, people lived in brownstones with everyone literally and figuratively close. That proximity to everyone you loved was terrific, but my parents wanted a "better" life for their family, a fresh start away from the immigrant neighborhoods. Out on the Island, we had space. We had real yards where you could hold barbecues and family reunions. Our house even had an aboveground pool, a luxury by anyone's standards.

Looking back on it now, life in Lindenhurst was like an episode of *Happy Days*, complete with white picket fences and picturesque churches, but it was very much a blue-collar town full of factory workers, carpenters, and fishermen. I think the only "professional" I knew was the dentist. He was also the man who owned one of the only three Mercedes I saw until I was out of high school. There was nothing fancy or pretentious about Lindenhurst. It was the kind of place where you could play outside after dark and go berry picking when you weren't clamming.

We went to the beach a lot, although it wasn't as romantic as you might think. This wasn't a beach like you'd find in Florida or California. Lindenhurst was a fishing town, and our local beach was affectionately nicknamed Crud Beach. Located on the South Bay, our waters were dark, with a reedy, sandy floor. They were also very shallow. You could practically walk across the bay. All of us kids hung out there until we were old enough that our parents allowed us to go to the "real" beaches on the Atlantic. Most of my friends' fathers were fishermen, so we had great access to boats—not the smart speedboats, but clam boats.

The clam boats were fishing vessels, flat, with a little steering house. We'd pile on and hold on for dear life; if we got hungry, we'd stop and dig up some fresh clams out of the bay. When we got older, we'd sneak out some beer, and, well, that was a perfect afternoon. Boats were like cars where I grew up, and of course, my parents never wanted me out on anyone's boat. But that never stopped me. One time, I went out on one of my friends' father's clam boat, and we were horsing around with another boat and managed to ram them into each other. We ended up losing power and needing a tow in from the Coast Guard. I was four hours late for dinner, and my parents thought I was dead. When I got home, believe me, I wished I was.

Our home on North Hamilton Avenue was a little twenty-four-by-twenty-four-foot Cape Cod, with four rooms on the main floor: a living room, kitchen, and two tiny bedrooms. The second floor was actually an attic with a pitched roof. There, we had two more tiny and much-needed bedrooms. My parents were in one of the bedrooms on the main floor, and my brother, Andy, and I shared the other. My grandmother May Prey Knapp, whom we called Nana, and her children—my mother's younger sister, Ruthie, and her younger brother, William Jr.—lived on the top floor. It was a full house to say the least.

My parents had not been planning on having us all under one roof, but shortly after we moved out to Long Island, my mother's father died. At the time, my grandmother was a young housewife in her forties, with no job skills. In the wake of his passing, there was no question that she, along with Ruthie and William Jr., would move in with us on Long Island. That was when families stayed together during difficult times, and my parents were not about to leave my mom's family in Brooklyn to fend for themselves.

Before my grandfather's death, my parents' plan for their new life on Long Island had been for my mother to stay home with me and my newly born baby brother. That vision of Long Island life was dashed once my parents had three new mouths to feed. There was no way that my father could support everyone on his own, so my mom went to work, something that terrified me at the time. I wasn't ready for her to leave me. Without her around all the time, I was forced to create a sense of independence, an emotional armor that helped me protect myself. For her part, my mom wasn't ready to leave either. Even though she knew that she'd done the right thing by taking her family in, she felt robbed of her chance to be the stay-at-home mom she'd always envisioned.

Both my parents worked in factories, Dad as a steelworker, Mom at an electronics company. I wasn't a latchkey kid, but I became self-reliant early on. My grandmother May was also there to help, keeping house, cooking the meals, caring for me and my younger brother, but I never felt she was the adult in charge. My parents were still the parents, and she was my grandmother, a different kind of adult. She had a great sense of humor—she was a "cutup," as they used to say, the kind of woman who'd get down on the floor and play with my brother and me—but she was also really strict. She'd wash your mouth out with soap in a heartbeat. You'd say one wrong word and she'd grab that soap and clamp you between her knees. Suddenly, that soap was in your mouth and you were spitting bubbles, wishing you'd kept quiet in the first place.

Though she may not have always been parental, my grandmother was definitely a hard worker. We had one of those old-style wringer washers, where you can smell the soap and see the steam rising out of it. She was constantly pulling hot sheets through that wringer, her muscled arms toned and looking more like a longshoreman's than a grandmother's. Along with my mother, my grandmother also took care of the yard work and daily house maintenance. I don't believe I ever saw my father with a screwdriver in his hand. He did backbreaking manual labor all day at work, and he was not climbing a ladder or mowing the grass when he got home. So that was left to the females, mainly my mother and grandmother.

I suppose some people would question having your mother-in-law living in your home, but I think my father really appreciated it. The man was a saint, one of the most easygoing people I've ever known. And he adored my mother; as long as she was happy, he'd make any sacrifice. Besides, Nana was easy to have around. You'd never think of her as one of those cartoonish meddling mothers-in-law. She was too busy washing, ironing, and doing yard work.

Living in the attic with my grandmother were my aunt Ruthie and uncle Billy. When we moved to Lindenhurst, Ruthie had graduated high school and was working, but she drove my mom crazy. She was a wild one. Boys were coming by in cars, honking their horns. Ruthie would run out to meet them wearing her pointy stuffed bras and tight sweaters, a little scarf tied around her neck, and bright red lipstick. Ruthie had a boyfriend named Bill whom I just loved. He was handsome and drove a big blue convertible. He'd pull up in front of the house and we'd hear *honk, honk, honk.* And out she'd run waving a cigarette. I remember a few times when Ruthie came home late and my mom was so mad that she backed Ruthie up against the wall and grabbed her by that neck scarf.

"You better straighten up, Ruthie Knapp! Coming home in this shape."

I'm not exactly sure *what* she had been doing, but whatever it was didn't sit well with my mother. My grandmother didn't have any idea what to do with Ruthie. Ruthie was a force of nature.

When I was about six years old, Ruthie got married, and the couple moved into the basement of our house. Unfortunately, she did not marry my hero, Bill with the blue convertible. The guy she married was an idiot who drank too much. Now instead of just one rebellious teenage girl causing trouble, we had an angry, abusive drunk living in the basement. You could hear him downstairs raising hell at Ruthie at all hours. It was like an asylum.

One day it all came to a head. After we'd heard them fighting for a while, there was a great commotion, and they ran up the stairs. Ruthie burst out of the basement door and ran across the room toward the front door. Her husband came right up after her waving a butcher knife and looking like a madman. My mom, who had been standing in the kitchen, swung into action. She grabbed an iron skillet and cracked him over the head.

"That's it! You get out of my house right now!"

I have not seen my mother as angry before or since. I don't think I fully appreciated it in the heat of the moment, but that took balls—taking a frying pan after a drunken man with a knife. Not exactly everyone's first instinct, yet that's the kind of woman that my mother was.

My reaction to the whole thing was shock. I was stunned that people would chase each other around with knives and speechless that my mother could be pushed into fits of temper. Ruthie and her husband moved out, but eventually she came to her senses and got a divorce. She remarried, this time to a darling man named Ralph, with whom she began a fine family and turned over a new leaf.

If Ruthie was Mom's outrageous sibling, her younger brother, Billy, was the quiet one. Uncle Billy was sixteen when we all moved in together, and I had a mad childhood crush on him. I thought he was my personal Prince Charming. He'd sit at the kitchen table doing his homework and looking so handsome, and I'd swoon. When his girlfriend, Marilyn (who's now my dear aunt Marilyn), would come over, I'd be sure to sit between them or on Billy's lap to make sure she understood who the alpha female was in this relationship. At four, I was absolutely convinced that he was going to marry me and I couldn't understand why she was wasting her time there.

My little brother, Andy, was also a sweetheart—gentle and funny, but tall and overweight as a child, as chunky as I was skinny. He was teased mercilessly as a kid too, and it upset me to see it hurt him so deeply. Being something of a target contributed to a general sense of worry that seemed to follow Andy everywhere, exacerbating a natural tendency he inherited from my mother.

Mom was the biggest nervous Nellie I ever saw. It's no wonder that

Andy was so often afraid, because Mom found danger at every turn. She worried that my father would be in a terrible accident at work or on the road home. If my father was twenty minutes late getting home, she was on the phone to the police. She was sure that one of us kids would walk across the street and get hit by a car. She lived in fear that someone would kidnap us. If she was with us at a park or playground she was sure we were going to get hurt on the equipment.

She was right to worry about Andy. My little brother got hurt so much when he was a kid that I called him Frankenstein—he'd been sewn back together that much. I worried about him incessantly and felt incredibly responsible for him. In my mind, with my mother working, accountability fell to me. He was my little brother, my duty. Sometimes it was the school that had to make the call to Mom's work. "Mrs. Andrzejewski, this is Daniel Street Elementary. Can you come get Andy?"

It was worse if he got hurt at home. Then Nana had to make the call, and she made everything into an apocalyptic event.

"Mildred, you better get home. I think Andy might need to go to the emergency room."

Hysterics!

"Is he bleeding? Is anything broken?"

I was terrified every time it happened, not so much because of Andy but because of my mother's reaction. In my head, everything was on me, as though I was the adult when Mom was gone. Whether it was real or imagined, that left me, an eight-year-old, to handle things. Of course, I was totally overwhelmed and ill equipped to deal with such circumstances, yet even at that age I thought of myself as the one in charge. My grandmother was a sweet, kind woman, but not someone you could rely on to take charge of a situation. My parents' lives were overloaded with work, and though they sacrificed so much for us, they, through no fault of their own, couldn't be there for us all the time. My dad worked constantly, and loving as he was, he was perpetually exhausted. When he came home the only thing he wanted to do was sit down, watch the ball game, eat dinner, and relax. My mom wanted to be there for us, but the practical realities of her job made that difficult.

Sometimes I think that's what caused Mom to overreact to things. Because she couldn't pay attention to every detail of our lives, when something did happen, it was both shocking and expected. She became fatalistic about every bad thing imaginable. Some horrible evil lurked right outside the door, and it was waiting for us. It drove me nuts. But her fears had an effect on me just like they did on Andy. I grew up watchful, scared that somebody *might* try to grab me off the streets. In my pursuit of independence I became guarded—ready for anything. I tended to arm myself with a stick or something, *just in case*. Of course, my mother hated that, too.

"You're gonna put your eye out!"

I tried to stay away from the house as much as possible. I knew there was a peaceful world out there with adventures that were exciting without being fatal.

THE CONVERSATION USUALLY STARTS this way: I'll meet someone who asks me how I seem so grounded, so normal. Maybe they'll tell me about an encounter they had with a rock star who acted like a complete asshole. The truth is that the way I am now is the way I've always been. People who get rich and act like idiots were always that way—only now they have money.

I've always described myself as a very common person. I grew up without a lot of angst or internalized problems. I didn't sneak out after dark to raise hell and cause my parents any sleepless nights. No drinking. No drugging. You will never see my name in some scandal sheet. It's just not gonna happen. I've never done anything in my life that would excite a tabloid reporter. In fact, if you knew me now you'd never take me for a rock star. I'd be the mom driving her daughter to high school, the one who shops for her own groceries and carries them inside when she gets home, too. As Julia Roberts once said, "I'm just an ordinary person with an extraordinary job."

After thirty seconds of talking to me, people will sense all that, and they'll ask me how I've been able to stay myself.

"You are who you are" is the only response I have for them. I know who I am. And I understand just what a stretch it was for me to end up where I did.

Moving out to Long Island was considered moving on up, but despite our idea of upward mobility, we were in far worse shape financially in the years after our move. Even two incomes couldn't make up for the added expense of having Ruthie, my uncle, my grandmother, my brother, and me all under the same roof. Consequently, we were always broke. Nobody talked about it, and my parents certainly didn't resent Nana and her two younger children. But the situation left us poor, and my mom and dad were perpetually worried. You could see it on their faces and hear it in my mother's stifled sobs when it came time to pay bills.

Every month like clockwork, I'd stand in the doorway, peer into our dimly lit kitchen, and watch as my mother sat at the table with a pile of envelopes, a pad of paper, and a pen in front of her. She'd make notes and scribble down numbers. She'd keep a handkerchief on the table and use it to wipe the tears from her eyes. If she knew I was watching her, she didn't acknowledge it, and neither did I. I never said a word, just backed away and went to bed.

Going to the grocery store with Mom was awful, because her choices always involved penny-saving decisions. She never bought anything extra, no backups, no luxuries—we were always on a strict budget. We never bought more than two rolls of toilet paper at a time. Not three, *never* four. Just two. You worried all the time that the toilet paper would run out before payday. I hated that. Seriously. (Seeing my pantry today, you'd think I have a Costco franchise. In fact, Costco is one of my favorite places in the world, because I can look at all those items lined up and picture them in my pantry. I bet I own enough toilet paper to last a family of four for a year. I'm the same way with *everything*. I have stacks of frozen food in freezers, multiples of canned goods lined up on shelves. Friends and family could do their grocery shopping at my house, and they sometimes do. I feel secure knowing that I will never run out of anything, that my kids won't ever worry about not having school supplies for a project and that there will always be enough goddamn toilet paper.)

Partially because of our financial struggles, my family became a very tight group. My parents were easygoing, kind, and good-hearted. Strict without being disciplinarians. The worst I ever got growing up was a quick swat on the butt. The amount of love that my brother and I felt from my parents was intense, and to an independent girl like me, it sometimes felt more like smothering. Despite our closeness, they tried to insulate Andy and me from all the stress and hardship. I never saw them argue or ever be unkind to each other; they showed a unified front at all times. They were in love, and despite the shitty hand they'd been dealt, they were happy (except at bill-paying time). When everyone was together at night, we would talk about our days without discussing the serious issues that they had to contend with.

The two of them met when they were just fourteen years old. They dated until Dad went into the army, then married as soon as he got out. Mom was a wonderful opera singer and had performed with the All-City Chorus when she was young. I believe she might have turned professional if she hadn't got pregnant with me. Mom has always had a big personality—very excitable and constantly talking. She has opinions, and she won't hesitate to tell you about all of them. My dad was the opposite—quiet, thoughtful, and reserved, more of a loner. In that way I took after my father. I wasn't shy, but I was a bit of a loner, too.

My mother was a perpetual optimist; good fortune was always just around the corner, and she was hell-bent on having fun until it arrived. Even if things were horrible, all could be fixed by a drive to Amish country or cutting out sandwiches with cookie cutters or making crafts. One time when we were on vacation in Florida, my brother and I fell in love with a capuchin monkey in a pet store. We begged my mother to let us get it and she shockingly she said yes. Anything that was fun was allowed and encouraged. We bought the monkey and drove him 1,100 miles in a Dodge with my parents, my grandmother, my brother, and me. We named him Jo-Jo and he lived with us for sixteen years until he died. The crazy thing was that I never thought it was odd to have a monkey. It was only after I began telling the story to people that I came to realize how unusual it was.

I always loved this positive outlook and spontaneity, but I didn't appreciate it enough when I was a kid. It seemed flippant and irresponsible; I didn't want road trips and craft projects, I wanted her to buckle down and fix everything. What I couldn't see was how selfless her behavior actually was. She couldn't see a way out, so she made the best of a bad situation. Her only concern was her children's well-being, protecting us from the harsh realities that she and my father faced.

Even though I was young, I was already far too pragmatic to appreciate her approach. I loved both my parents, but I viewed the way they ran their lives as flighty. That, combined with the fact that I'd grown up forcing myself to feel too much responsibility, created a detachment from them that drew out my solitary qualities and toughened me up. I'd assess my problems and fix them on my own. When something was wrong with me, it was my job alone to pick myself up and dust myself off. I became self-sufficient and determined, motivated by our problems with money and by my own belief in myself. Watching my mother try to pay bills made me a driven person, determined to never be in that same situation.

I don't want to overstate things. We never went hungry. The heat and water stayed on. I had a great childhood with overworked but loving parents and a tremendous extended family. But the reality was that we were what people today call "the working poor." We lived on the edge of poverty, and I hated living on that edge. I hated it for my mother and my father, for my little brother. Oh, and I *really* hated it for me.

So, despite all these money concerns, I had a good childhood. Our school was only a few blocks from our house, and I liked to hang around the school playground in the afternoon. It was always a good time with my friends around, but it was even better when everyone else went home and I was alone, with no one around to tell me not to swing too high or stand up on the monkey bars. So that's when I climbed up on the slide and stared at the sky, thinking about things, dreaming, picturing a world where dads weren't overworked and moms didn't sit and cry late at night over money, where people worked hard and *didn't* live on the edge of financial disaster.

Reading fueled my fantasy world. I was a voracious reader—books, magazines, and newspapers, anything in print. I loved to read about historical figures, about people who had done great things, about places far removed from North Hamilton Avenue. I started making up my own stories, putting characters and plots together, creating great adventures for my made-up cast. The great thing about coming from a multiethnic neighborhood was that you had all kinds of traditions and rituals to work into your tales.

In my dreams, I was Italian, not Polish-Irish. I don't know where it came from, but I *felt* Italian. One thing I loved about Italians was the food. Most of my friends were Italian and I tried to eat at their houses as much as possible. My mother and grandmother were Americanized, and they were also Depressionized. When my mom did feel up for cooking, she knew what she was doing. She'd learned the traditions of Polish cooking from my dad's mother, and she could make some pretty amazing pierogis. But because my grandmother did the day-to-day cooking, most of the time we ate very bland food—roast and potatoes, bread, macaroni and cheese. (I don't want to sell my nana short when it comes to mac and cheese. She made her own pasta with a creamy sauce, and it was spectacular.)

The Italians, however, did not see food as mere sustenance; they saw it as an art form. Mom knew that every time I went to play with one of my Italian friends, I was going to eat. She'd ask me what I had been eating, and maybe I would say, "Snails in red sauce."

"Shhhkeeve!" my mother would exclaim. That's what Italians said for "yuck." And wherever I ate, she used that language to tell me I had just eaten something she considered yucky.

So there I was, a Polish-Irish girl who wanted to be Italian and whose best friend, Brenda Cherney, was from one of the three Jewish families in the area. When I wasn't building forts with the boys, I was playing paper dolls with Brenda. She was my outlet for all things girlie. Together we were starstruck little girls who worshiped glamour. We loved all the movie stars—Claudette Colbert, Cyd Charisse, Barbara Stanwyck, Doris Day, Judy Garland, and Katharine Hepburn. I thought that Maureen O'Hara was just the most beautiful woman in the world, that Sophia Loren was perfect and *so* Italian. But my absolute favorite was Audrey Hepburn, with her striking looks and high-fashion image in her films. No one looked like those people where I grew up. I obsessed over movies from the thirties and forties, admiring the women of that era for their grace and strength. What I didn't like was their passivity. I thought if you could combine being beautiful and being capable you could rule the world.

Brenda was one of the first people whom I listened to "popular" music with. We loved listening to 45s on my Victrola, and I kept the records in a little case with a poodle on it. The first song I remember buying was "The Twist" when I was about five or six. But I listened to all kinds of music. When we were a little older, we got into the Beatles, and became obsessed. The only fight we ever had was over the fact that she knocked my imitation leather "John Lennon" hat into a mud puddle. I loved Tony Bennett and Frank Sinatra, not to mention big band music and show tunes. My family's selections were not always to my taste. They loved Jerry Vale (I heard "Volare" every day), and my mom and Ruthie listened to Perry Como, Andy Williams, and Louis Prima. I adored Louie Prima even then, but even though I wasn't as sold on their choices, I learned to appreciate all sorts of styles.

And of course, since Brenda and I were both boy-crazy, we talked nonstop about boys. I remember having a little friend, Bobby Leto, in the first grade, kissing him by the fountain, and then running off giggling about it. That was about the extent of what boy-crazy meant in those days. Kisses and giggles. But my second boyfriend was important, because he was my first great Italian love, Vincent Pizzello. Oh, how I loved him, with that black hair and those sparkling dark eyes.

Because of our neighborhood, I developed a great respect for other people's religions. Brenda's mother, Ida, taught me how to keep kosher, and I loved Hanukkah as well as Christmas. I enjoyed the traditions of both religions and the traditions of the various ethnic groups, the Germans, Polish, Irish, and Italians. In Lindenhurst, you embraced everyone's heritage, and I loved that diversity. There wasn't an issue about any of it. I'm not saying there was no prejudice, because I doubt you can ever completely get away from that. But for the kids, differences were simple and often about food or who owned the rarest baseball card. You ate poppy-seed cakes at your Polish friends' homes, potato pancakes with your Jewish friends, and good bread and pasta with the Italians.

Whether it was celebrating Christmas or Hanukkah, I *loved* the holiday season. I came by Christmas madness as naturally as Andy came by his anxiety—by following Mom's lead. Christmas was one time when she threw caution to the wind. All year long we worried about running out of toilet paper, and then came Christmas. There were presents for everyone, wonderful foods, visiting with the family in Brooklyn. A similar phenomenon happened every summer. Suddenly we had money to take a wonderful vacation to a hotel with a pool or near a beach.

It was only years later, when they finally moved from the Lindenhurst house, that I found out these summer trips and Christmases were financed by constant loans they'd taken out against their home. By the time they moved, the loans had built to over $45,000 on a house that had originally cost them $7,000 because they had borrowed against it so many times. So not only had they not paid off a dime of the original house note, they were deep in the hole. For years they'd given us vacations and presents, never thinking about what the consequences would be down the road. This simultaneously endeared them to me and drove me crazy. Personally, I could've done without a week in Florida for a little more peace at home, but it made them happy to give us these things.

And so twice a year they'd given the family a big time. That's what my parents were like. They worked and worried all year, then sunk themselves in debt in hopes of giving us kids some great memories. When you think there's no chance of things ever really getting better, you go for anything you can and hope for the best.

THE WHEELS THAT WOULD ultimately pay off my parents' house and allow us to buy more than two toilet paper rolls at a time started turning when I was pretty young. I was always something of a ham, singing little songs and dancing around when I was a kid, entertaining the family and getting rewarded with a hug. I usually initiated the show. The Brooklyn relatives would be on Long Island for one of our barbecues, and I'd be pestering everyone.

"Let me sing a song! Watch this!"

The older folks would say, "Okay, okay. Sing us a song."

I'd show off, and everyone would clap. "That's great, Patti!" I even sold concessions, buying penny candies at Brenda's uncle's candy store and selling them to my relatives and neighbors during the performance. Then the uncles and aunts would give me hugs, and I'd run off with the cousins to play.

But in the fourth grade music went from being a sideshow to being a major part of my life. That was the first year I was old enough to sing in the grade school choir. On the first day of choir that school year, the teacher had everyone sing so she could assess our vocal ranges. After I sang, I noticed the choir teacher looking at me with an odd expression. After choir, she approached me.

"What's your name? I want to call your mother."

Oh no. I thought I was in trouble. I never got in trouble at school. Breaking into a thinly veiled panic, I went with her to the phone, and while I held my breath in one of those horrified Doris Day–movie moments, the teacher dialed Mom at work.

"Do you know about this child?" she asked my mother.

What in the world? I was paralyzed with fear. I couldn't imagine causing a problem for my parents. My aunt Ruthie, with her smoking and sneaking out with boys, was the troublemaker in our house. What had I done?

"Patti has a wonderful voice, Mrs. Andrzejewski. A great voice. I think she should be encouraged in music."

Whew, it was the *opposite* of trouble. Instead I was actually having someone validate what I believed to be true: I knew how to sing.

My parents were thrilled with this news. My mother already knew that I could sing, but she'd never interfered, never wanted to impose her views on me. By this age I was fiercely independent, and she was always careful to give me my space. But from then on everybody was all over me like the plague when it came to music. I was groomed to represent the school at all the local and regional competitions. I spent extra hours after school working with the choir teacher on voice training. I loved it. I was that little Andrzejewski girl who could sing. I practiced all the time in my upstairs bedroom with the window open, much to the frustration of a boy named Joey who lived across the street. He would throw rocks at my screen and yell up to me, "Andrzejewski, shut up!" Of course, I only sang louder.

Maybe it was to help encourage my new interest in music, but the year I was ten my parents got me a red transistor radio for Christmas. Even I couldn't have dreamed up as fine a gift as that red radio, and I couldn't wait to open it—for the second time. By this time I knew that Santa wasn't the one delivering presents on Christmas morning, so I usually went on a hunt to find where Mom was hiding the packages. That year they happened to be under her bed. I got the present out and carefully opened it when she was at work.

I gasped so loud that I'm surprised my grandmother didn't hear me and rush into my parents' bedroom. There it was: a bright red plastic transistor radio. My hands were shaking so hard with the excitement of it that I could barely get the radio wrapped back up. But I did, and she never had a clue (or at least she never let on) that I'd been into her stash of gifts. Of course, that made the time before Christmas drag so much I thought it would never come. But it did, and I acted my part perfectly—shrieking with surprise. The "ohhh"s and "ahhh"s. I was so sneaky. That radio opened up whole new worlds of music to Brenda and me. Suddenly the Stones and the Beatles were a turn of the dial away.

My parents didn't like their music quite that loud. And for quite a while in 1964, all they heard was the Beatles blasting out of my room. I would hear Dad say, "Make her stop that!" Finally Mom would shout: "This is ridiculous! I know all the words to those songs! Shut your door."

Listening to those bands was mind-blowing for me. They were like nothing that I was being trained to sing and nothing that I'd studied. I knew no one who was involved in rock music. No guitar players, no one rehearsing in a garage. I knew about shows that played in New York City, because sometimes the school took us on musical outings. I knew about being in plays, about glee club, about choral groups at the school. And it was through one of those grade school performances that I met a woman who would become almost a surrogate mother to me, most assuredly my musical mentor.

She walked up to me after my solo performance during the spring concert when I was in sixth grade.

"Do you know who I am?" she asked.

"No," I said, although I knew she must be *somebody* because she had a definite air of authority, of importance.

"My name is Georgia Ruel. I'm the high school choir director, and in four years you are *mine*."

Her words alone scared me to death; I couldn't imagine what she meant. As it turned out, what Georgia Ruel meant was business. She took it upon herself to see that I was classically trained, that I had the scholarships and grants for lessons my family couldn't afford. She didn't wait for high school, either. She started helping me get the money for private lessons right away, and for the next six years I received training that was as good as anyone could buy.

The woman who took immediate charge of my training, Emma Foos, was kind of a stern taskmaster. She was German and could barely speak English. She reminded me of those old black-and-white movies where women of a certain age have boobs that hang right down to the waistline of their housedresses. But she understood classical voice training, and she kicked my butt. Emma had a pointer that she waved around for emphasis and direction. She also used it to whack my diaphragm if I wasn't giving the exercises my all. She was dead serious about music, and she reminded me of this fact every single day.

For the most part, things went on like that for a few years. Thanks to Georgia Ruel I learned and progressed, while things at home stayed pretty much the way they had always been. That is, until I was fourteen and my only real childhood trauma began to take shape: my parents split up.

At the time my brother and I were completely in the dark about any troubles. Of course, there were always the money problems, and my father was more exhausted than usual. But Andy and I were living in a vacuum, clueless about any storm brewing. There was no fighting, not even an argument that I heard. Everything was just as it had been for years. They worked, came home, and collapsed. I didn't have any idea anything was wrong until I watched my dad walk out the front door carrying two suitcases. I was in a complete state of shock when he left. I just stood there with my mouth open and watched him drive away. And when I finally got myself together enough to demand an answer, Mom's explanation was short.

"Your dad and I are getting a divorce."

The words seemed so foreign it took me a few minutes to realize she'd actually said them out loud. I couldn't believe it. I didn't know what was happening. Not only was I shocked, I was angry.

Perhaps even more shocking was that thirty days later they were back together. They'd gotten a divorce, and then suddenly my dad was back in the picture. He moved home, they remarried, and my mother acted as if nothing had happened. If anything she was a little dismissive about the whole ordeal, and it was never something that we spoke about. I, however, was livid, with the kind of righteous anger fourteen-year-olds are particularly good at. (I should note that my parents then stayed happily married until my father's passing in 2009.)

I WAS JUST STARTING school at Lindenhurst High when my parents divorced and remarried. Instead of using all my pent-up anger as an excuse to act out, I turned more and more to music. Basically, I started high school pissed off and singing for Georgia Ruel.

Of course, when I wasn't singing, I was still completely boy-crazy. My first great teenage love was named Shaun Lynam. He carried my books; we held hands in the hallway and gazed at each other. We were such an item in junior high and the early years of high school. We spent every evening together doing our homework; we went to the movies, went ice-skating, and of course, went to Crud Beach. I went to all the ball games to watch him play basketball, and he came to watch me sing at school events.

We were hot for each other—we did everything imaginable except "the deed." When we finally broke up it was because we both knew we were on the verge of taking our relationship farther, and at fourteen, neither of us wanted to take that step yet. If we kept on seeing each other, it would only lead to trouble, so we both agreed to cut it off.

I liked having one boyfriend at a time, and I wouldn't have been out slutting around for *anything*. But I didn't mind tarting up my image. I started high school in disguise, dressing in what I'd call provocative preppie. I loved those pleated plaid skirts and the madras shirts. Underneath it all, I was closer to Sally Field in *Gidget* or Marlo Thomas in *That Girl,* but I swaggered through the halls looking more like Britney Spears in her first video.

We had a dress code at Lindenhurst High, so I couldn't leave the house looking like that. I had to leave my skirt down below my knees until I got to school. Then I'd be in the bathroom rolling that sucker up as high as I thought I could get by with. (At Lindenhurst, the seniors always gave the freshmen gifts at the end of the school year, and that year the senior boys gave me a pair of bloomers because I wore such short skirts. Mission accomplished.) It wasn't that I was fishing for attention, because I wasn't; I just had my own look. Even though people would have described me as cute, I was skinny and flat chested with thin hair—nothing like the Italian goddesses who were my friends and populated the school like beautiful ripe figs.

The halls were patrolled by the Matron, a woman who watched

us like a hawk, checking to see who'd been rolling up their skirts and demanding we roll them back to a respectable length. If someone had not rolled up her skirt, if it really *was* too short, the Matron swung into action. You had to kneel down in front of her, and if your hem didn't touch the ground, she pulled a seam ripper out of her pocket and let out the hem herself! Then you walked around the rest of the day ragged but right.

Bangs were another sore point with the Matron. I wore them just the way she hated them, right down over my eyelashes. I loved those long bangs that the English models had and thick eyeliner like Sophia Loren wore. I spent most of my time in the halls looking around to see if she was coming so I could brush my bangs to the side. If the Matron thought your bangs were hanging too low, she had another weapon in her pocket: a pair of scissors! She made you stand up against the lockers while she cut your bangs into Mamie Eisenhower territory. No way was I going to let that happen, so I was watchful at every turn. (Can you imagine what would happen today if some adult hall monitor ripped out the hem of a girl's skirt or whacked off her bangs?)

My entire mission with this look was, of course, to make the boys take notice. And they did, especially in choir. When you first walked into the choir room, the singers were lined up in this order: basses, tenors, altos, and sopranos. So I had to parade in front of everyone to get to my spot. I'd start the walk, my short skirt flipping, and the basses and tenors would start with the catcalls: *Andrew-eski*. They were actually yelling "Andrzejewski" except that they couldn't really pronounce it. I'd bat my nicely made-up eyelashes and look sassy.

My high school experience was split up into two parts. Boys were pretty important. I loved to flirt and tease, but I wasn't a backseat type of girl. And then there was music. While I did try sports here and there, Georgia Ruel was having none of it. Swim class? Forget it. The pool might be too cold and I might get a sore throat. Cheerleading? No way. Yelling outside in cold weather might damage my voice.

Georgia also helped to keep me in line when it came to drinking and smoking. My mother was pretty in the dark about what other kids were doing, but Georgia, she knew what was up. I would have been dead if she found out that I'd smoked even just one cigarette, but I wasn't really interested in smoking. Similarly I never had more than a beer or two, because drinking never appealed to me. With the memory of Ruthie's first husband fresh in my mind, I couldn't see the fun in being wasted—only the danger. Georgia reinforced my natural inclinations. With the exception of an occasional highball on New Year's Eve, neither of my parents drank or smoked. Despite being a teenager, my responsible nature just had a way of kicking in when it came to stuff like that. The one time Brenda and I got drunk it was a disaster. It was New Year's Eve, when we were fourteen. I was spending the night and Brenda's parents when out to a party. We managed to consume half a bottle of Seagrams 7, and then spent the remainder of the night alternately trying to stop the room from spinning and throwing up. After that my drinking days were over. Of course, I had friends who did those things, and that was fine, but I knew it wasn't for me.

With no sports, drinking, or smoking, boys and music mostly summed up high school—though there was more music than boys. Every possible minute was devoted to music. Georgia saw to that. She envisioned me becoming a classical singer or going into musical theater. Even though I loved rock music, we never even talked about it. It wasn't just Georgia Ruel's traditional outlook that caused us to avoid the topic of rock; I couldn't envision myself ever singing rock because my voice was all wrong for it.

The great thing about being in the music program at Lindenhurst was that we made trips to the city to see some musical productions and to hear the symphony and opera—trips that I never would have been able to afford were it not for the school. I sang the solo at a lot of the school programs, and we had an amazing choir. I also sang in the All-State chorus that won prizes throughout the state and kudos from big-time critics. That was all due to Georgia and her brilliant direction. She always pushed me to be better than I was, to work harder than I thought I could, creating a strong work ethic within me. There was no coddling, no cutting me any slack. She knew better than I did what I was capable of doing. And I was lazy. Singing well came easily to me, requiring hardly any effort on my part at all. This was not something I could take credit for; it was just the gift that was given to me. But to reach my potential, I had to work—hard. God and nature had blessed me with raw talent, but it needed to be honed and refined.

And of course, I participated in the school's musical productions, including playing Queen Guinevere in *Camelot*. Because of copyright laws we couldn't always afford to do the biggest productions, and instead we put on vintage shows like *Plain and Fancy* and *Little Mary Sunshine*. We did everything, and it was a good learning experience. I had to learn an Amish accent when I played Hilda Miller, Barbara Cook's part in *Plain and Fancy*. In *West Side Story*, I played Anita, which is hilarious. Anita is the Hispanic girl who has racial insults thrown her way. I am about the whitest person you'd ever meet.

All of this was done with one clear goal: to attend Juilliard and continue my training. But while track never got in the way of my music, boys did.

One boy in particular.

I met Dennis Benatar when I was in the tenth grade, and I thought I was deliriously in love. We dated for the rest of high school, and I did believe this was the *big one,* my great love. What did we have in common? What led me to believe that this was my chance at love? Well, what does a sixteen-year-old girl know about love? I was just another girl who wasn't worldly enough to make a sound choice.

There's a misconception about me that I turned down a scholarship to Juilliard because of Dennis. The fact is, I didn't even go to the audition. To be accepted into Juilliard, you have to go through a lengthy process. You have to learn a lot of pieces, fill out tons of paperwork, make sure all the i's are dotted and the t's crossed. Georgia Ruel walked me through the whole thing. Months went by, and with Georgia's help I was ready. When I started my senior year, the time to audition for Juilliard drew near, but in September of our senior year, the unthinkable happened. Dennis enlisted. Remember, this was 1971, and the Vietnam War was still going on.

The Juilliard audition was coming up in November, yet all I could think of was Vietnam. I thought Dennis would be sent to war and he would be killed. It may have been Mom's old fatalistic worldview, but I know a great many young people went through those exact same emotions back then. Everything just exploded, and I didn't think I could do anything except stay with him until we got through this nightmare. Every time I brought it up, Dennis pleaded with me to stay with him, to just blow off the audition, asking me not to go. And so I didn't.

I would almost have rather done anything in the world but face Georgia Ruel with the news of my decision. She was my closest confidant, as good a friend as any I had in high school. Over the last several years, I'd spent most of my free time with her. If I wasn't in a class, I was in the choir room with Georgia. She gave me the dynamics and the fundamentals of my music, but she also had become an older sister. She was my mentor, my teacher, and my friend.

"I've decided not to audition for Juilliard."

Georgia looked sick. "You can't mean that."

"Yes. Dennis may have to go to Vietnam. We're going to get married."

"You haven't thought this through," Georgia began. She went on and on, eventually breaking down into tears and trying in vain to convince me to think over my decision. But for me that was the end of it. My mind was made up. Everything I'd worked for since I was ten years old was about to be thrown out the window. I would stick with Dennis, who might be sent to Vietnam to fight and die.

Not long after I'd made my decision, I began to second-guess why

I'd ever even thought I could make it at Juilliard in the first place. I tried to justify and rationalize my choice. *What was I thinking? How could a kid from a blue-collar family with two working parents fit in at a place like Juilliard? I probably wasn't good enough anyway. I might not have been accepted. In fact, it's almost a certainty that I wouldn't have been accepted.* Before it was over, I had convinced myself that this was the very best move I could have made. And I was being loyal to my great love.

After graduation, Dennis went to basic training and I decided to live at home and attend the State University of New York at Stony Brook. I took health education and sex-ed classes, thinking I'd become a teacher, but my attendance was short-lived and I quit during my first semester to take a job waitressing at Friendly's. I needed to save money for the wedding, which I knew my parents would not have been able to afford and I never would have asked them to pay for. Music faded into the far past, something I'd done in another life. Dennis and I had planned on getting married in November, but in September he was sent to Vietnam. That rolled the wedding date to the following summer, 1972, when he was to return.

Much to both of our surprise, he was back in three months and changed a great deal, now facing long bouts of depression. I didn't know any of the details of why he only stayed three months, but I assumed it was because of the depression and anxiety. This has been such a pattern, soldiers coming back from war suffering from post-traumatic stress. In the old days they called it shell shock. Without professional help, it does not get better. One of the most tragic aspects of PTSD is that instead of getting therapy, so many of these young men self-medicate with drugs or alcohol. And that is what Dennis did. I smoked pot a few times with him. I wanted to help him, support him, and show him that I understood what he was going through. It was an act of solidarity, but it just wasn't me. I hated being stoned, so I stopped smoking, but he did not.

But while his life had changed dramatically, mine was staying the same. I had been at home, in our town, working to pay for the wedding. The chasm between us had widened, but I didn't see it. I was too blinded by missing him and wanting to leave my home and get out into the world. The marriage seemed like an exit. Because it was obvious that our lives had split in two different directions, I should have put the wedding on hold until we knew whether we were still suited for each other. But I didn't. The wedding was still scheduled for the end of July 1972.

I knew the day we wed that I was making a terrible mistake.

I can still remember that feeling when the church doors opened and I set my foot down on the carpet. I looked up and saw the man I thought I wanted to marry and suddenly my brain said, *Run!* But there I was putting one foot in front of the other walking down that aisle. *No, no, no!* my brain kept screaming at me.

The next thing I knew I was reciting my vows. Then he was kissing the bride. And I spent the next eight years in and out of a bad marriage.

I've told both my daughters to watch for that feeling and trust it. I don't care how many people have been invited to the wedding, or what relatives drove for half a day to get there, or what kind of wine you ordered. If you start down that aisle and something says, *Don't do this,* turn around and run.

"I'm giving you my permission right now," I've told them. "You have my permission to stop it at any point, and I don't care about the circumstances."

The way I figure it, the band will already be there, the food will already be there. We'll all be dressed up. Why not simply have a party and call it a big day?

I wish I'd done that.

CHAPTER TWO

I CAN DO THAT

THE MARRIAGE WAS OFF and on from the beginning.

For the next few years, Dennis and I split up about once a year, and for about six months at a time. While this was happening, we also moved around quite a bit because he was still serving in the military. First we moved to Massachusetts, where he was stationed at Fort Devon. We then went on to Fort Jackson in South Carolina and Fort Lee, near Richmond, Virginia. Throughout these moves, we kept separating but always decided to "give it one more try."

Those were tough years on both of us. There was no doubt he'd been through a trauma and it had marked him. We really struggled during our marriage, and as a result, I was essentially on my own a lot of the time. Though I worked and tried to take classes whenever I could, sadly, I stayed away from music.

It was while we were in South Carolina that I found a job at the Citizens and Southern Bank. Being so compulsive, I liked the order to the setup at a bank, with all those stacks of neatly bound packets of money and organized files. I had no experience working in a bank, but the funny thing was, the bank hired me precisely because I didn't have any experience. They were switching over to a new check processing system, and the bank officials decided to start fresh with someone who had never worked with the old one. That way there was no "unlearning" necessary. It worked out so well that they sent me to school to be a trainer for other branches. I went from branch to branch, training lovely little blue-haired ladies on the new system while they kept telling me, "Ah don't know why Ah have to learn this, darlin', the old way was just fine." I had the best time, and I really did love those ladies.

However, some of the older male customers weren't so sure about me.

I worked as a trainer for a couple of years before being promoted to head teller at my own branch. All those elderly men with their Confederate-flag lapel pins would raise their eyebrows at my leopard-print dresses and peer at the name tag that read PATRICIA BENATAR, HEAD TELLER.

"Ben-ay-ter. That's not a local name, is it?"

"No, sir, it is not."

"Where are you from, little lady?"

"New York," I'd say, laying on my thickest New York accent and watching them recoil in surprise.

"I think Ah'll go to the next winduh . . ."

In the end, I learned to love the South and appreciate it. I was comfortable there. I think one of the main reasons I related to those people was that their ways were so genteel. There was a softer edge to what they did, and they truly were the salt of the earth. These were people who got up every morning, went to work, went to church, fed their children, and tried to do the best they could. It was blue-collar, working-class, and felt incredibly comfortable for me. Even if some of the older men were taken aback by my leopard-print dresses, they were like me in so many ways, very down-to-earth. Just regular folk.

When we made the move to Virginia, my banking skills paid off, and I was hired at the F & M Bank in Hopewell. Maybe it was working around all that money and seeing the paltry paycheck at the end of the month that did it, but I finally realized that I could not spend my life in a bank, even if I kept getting promoted. There was a limit to where I could go, and I knew it. I was aware that in too many jobs, I'd need a college degree, and I didn't have one. I often kicked myself for quitting school just to jump into the wrong marriage, but ultimately I knew I had to make a change.

Then one day in 1973, after we had moved to Virginia, something miraculous happened. Some gay friends who worked at the bank with me asked me if I wanted to go with them to see a Liza Minnelli concert at the Coliseum in Richmond. I was not a huge fan of hers, but I loved *Cabaret* and adored her mother, so I thought, *Why not?* I figured that with everything basically in the dumper, a great music spectacle would lift my spirits. I hadn't sung for two years. That's what the new life was doing to me. The thing I loved most had slipped away from me. I kept thinking that I had really messed up somewhere along the way. I knew that there were people like Georgia Ruel who had seen great things in my future. All those plans, all that promise, and what was I doing? Counting other people's money.

The Coliseum in Richmond was a great venue, comparable to the Forum in L.A. (now the Staples Center). As I sat there, watching Liza sing, loving the showmanship and taking in the entire performance, I looked around at the people in the audience, the lights, the stage, and thought: *I can do that. This is ridiculous. I'm a better singer than she is. Sure, she's a great performer, but with practice, I can definitely do this. I want to perform again, only this time, on a stage like the Coliseum.*

Sound crazy? Maybe it was. And maybe we should all follow some crazy idea when our gut tells us it's right.

I did *not* mess around. The very next day I went to the bank and gave my notice. I found a little music paper—a *Village Voice* sort of thing—and started looking through it for anything that seemed like a singing opportunity. I stumbled across an advertisement for a singing waitress at a dinner theater in Enon, Virginia, called the Roaring Twenties Café, where the performers doubled as the waitstaff. I applied and got the job, complete with a flapper dress and a garter.

In twelve hours I had changed my life.

The Roaring Twenties Café was a funny place. You'd be serving a baked potato one minute and have to jump on the stage the next, with or without blue cheese dressing on your costume. They didn't serve alcohol, so the customers brown-bagged it. It was a cabaret-style show, a revue. I did a lot of Judy Garland songs, sang in some ensembles, and in one portion of the show I was in a Sonny and Cher sketch. After a couple of music-free years, I began to feel like myself again, quickly becoming close friends with the other performers. We were really just Muzak live, but career-wise it was a step ahead of being a bank teller.

And the clientele who frequented the Roaring Twenties Café? Lots of traveling businessmen, but couples came too. The middle-aged men who were away from their families always behaved the worst. Most were these rotund old Southern boys with their big cigars. That was when you could still smoke everywhere. They'd be puffing those stogies and then reach out and slip a finger down around your garter.

"Why don't you sit down here, darlin'? Let's talk about a few things."

"How about I punch your eye out?"

Once in a while that comeback didn't work and somebody would still hang on to that garter. So I'd have to say, "I don't think so, fellas. I'm from New York, and *you're* an asshole!"

They'd sit there roaring with laughter, bellies shaking, saying things like, "That little Yankee girl is cute *and* feisty."

But they got the message, and usually, they took it fine. They were just a bunch of good old boys, and they'd back off as soon as I put them in their place. It wasn't exactly the big time, but it was something of a start.

The real beginning came when I met Phil Coxon, who played piano at the Roaring Twenties Café. I started singing with his band, Coxon's Army, and and we played at local clubs like a place called Sam Miller's. In 1974, we got to be such a famous regional act that we were the subject of a PBS special. We even had a radio hit in Richmond with "Day Gig" on Trace Records. Between Coxon's Army and singing a few local ad jingles, I was making a huge amount of money for the time, over a $1,000 a week, an enormous sum considering that the rent on the apartment I shared with Dennis was only $100 a month.

During this time, Dennis and I split up a few times, and it was becoming less and less clear where our relationship and my career were headed. Then in 1975 I had another one of those moments. One morning I read an article about open-mic club nights in the *New York Times,* saying that this was a big scene in the city, where singers and comics could build a following and possibly be discovered. Open mics were a great equalizer, a way that anyone could be heard by people who mattered in the entertainment industry. I thought about the potential for about five minutes, then decided to pack up and head to New York. The response from my Richmond friends and colleagues was across the board negative.

"What? But you're making so much money here!"

"Why would you do that? You own this town!"

"Why spoil the good thing you got goin' here?"

They were right, but I knew that Richmond was only going to take me so far. I was never going to seriously go anywhere if I couldn't do this on the biggest stage of all.

"If I really want to make it, I've gotta be in New York," I explained to them with the air of confidence that only a twenty-two-year-old can pull off. "I'm never going to really get ahead, to do any better than I am already. Good money or not, I'm stuck."

"You'll be back," they all told me.

"No, I won't."

❧

IT TOOK ME ABOUT a day to gather my things and head for New York. I'm no fool. I didn't jump into the middle of New York City and use up all my savings renting an apartment. I moved back to North Hamilton Avenue with my parents and started singing every place I could, trying to get a break. Dennis ended up following me, and eventually we moved to the city, taking a little East Side one-bedroom apartment on Eighty-first Street. My husband decided that he was going to try to manage me, which was a ridiculous idea, but for whatever reason it made sense to him. What it really meant was that we had but one income: mine.

One of the places I started going to was considered a real star maker, a club called Catch a Rising Star on First Avenue between East Seventy-eighth Street and East Seventy-seventh Street—not too far from our apartment. Catch a Rising Star was the reason I'd come to New York in the first place—the article had mentioned it specifically as a place where upcoming talent could be discovered. People who kick-started their careers at Catch over the years include Jerry Seinfeld, Billy Crystal, Ray Romano, Ellen DeGeneres, David Brenner, Whoopie Goldberg, Eddie Murphy, and my dear friend Richard Belzer. It had only been in business since 1972 but already had legendary status in entertainment circles.

I was scared to death the first time I sang there. Early that afternoon, I'd gone to the club and waited outside with all the other hopefuls to get a number. It was first come, first served—the number you got determined when you went on. I got number 29, which meant that I wouldn't go on until nearly three A.M. Luckily the club had a good late-night crowd. When it was finally my turn, I sang a cover of Judy Garland's "Rock-a-Bye Your Baby with a Dixie Melody." I was so nervous I had to hide my shakes. After I'd sung the final note, I closed my eyes, terrified to open them and see the crowd's reaction. The next sound I heard was everyone in the joint going absolutely crazy. I was in total shock.

While I was singing, Rick Newman, the club owner, had been drinking with some of his friends in the bar at the front of the club, not paying much attention to the contestants. When he heard the audience cheering for me he burst through the doors as I was exiting the stage.

"Who are you and where did you come from?" he asked with a smile. I don't know what reaction I was expecting from my performance, but that was not it. I laughed and told him my story. Newman was a big, tall guy—very seventies with his open shirts and gold chains. He had curly dark hair and a big mustache that made him look like he was wearing one of those fake noses with glasses. (Richard Belzer even poked fun at him about it in his act: "Hey, does that nose go with the glasses?") My performance made Newman an instant fan, and he offered to do anything he could to help me get started. That at least meant more performances at Catch a Rising Star.

It didn't take me long to become a fixture at Catch, and hanging out there became one of my favorite things to do, whether I was performing or not. The comics weren't just funny onstage. They were "on" most of the time. We would stay up all night and then go for breakfast at a local coffee shop called the Green Kitchen. Between Richard Belzer and the other guys, I think I had coffee and milk shooting out of my nose every fifteen minutes. I finally figured out that Belzer waited until I had just taken a big gulp of my coffee to jump in with a one-liner. Then, of course, I looked like an idiot for all to see. The best part though was nobody thought you looked like an idiot.

I loved to play poker, and on some nights, I'd stay there with the comedians until five in the morning in a card game. With the exception of a few times when some girlfriend of Newman's played with us, I was the only woman in those games, but it wasn't something that ever really occurred to me. In my mind I was just laughing with the boys—John Belushi, Chevy Chase, John DeBellis, The Untouchables. I learned everything about humor, timing, and swearing from these guys, hence my extensive collection of obscenities. The whole scene was just fun, and I fit right in.

Those became some of the happiest times of my life. Everyone was trying to make it, and in the process we were a family. We were all working toward the same end. We cheered each other's successes and stood by each other when auditions went badly. It didn't matter that you didn't have any money or that your name wasn't on any marquee yet. Everyone was more or less in the same position, with some closer to the brass ring than others but everyone trying. When you find creative people who are all trying to do similar things, so often resentment and competition overtake everything. It's so rare to find people who are confident enough in themselves and their own talents that they're able to honestly be there for one another. But that was precisely what we had. It was a close-knit community, with all of us encouraging and supporting each other. You didn't find much negativity there. It was tough in New York; Catch was a safe haven.

But while Catch was good fun and good exposure, it didn't pay anything, and I needed a paycheck at least once in a while. One day I was talking to a good friend named Mel Pralgo, who was a partner in a band that played weddings and bar mitzvahs, and laid it on the line.

"Shit, Mel! I'm dying here. I need to make some money!"

He shrugged. "Why don't you come sing with me? We'll do parties, weddings, and bar mitzvahs. You won't get rich. It pays a couple of hundred at a time. But it's something."

And so I did. I decided something was a lot better than nothing, and off we went every weekend. I sang "The Way We Were" and "Feelings" so many times I'd probably do something requiring jail time if I ever had to sing them again. One night, we were playing a party in Huntington, Long Island, and I was sitting in a local club when in walked Harry Chapin. He was truly one of the most casual stars ever, basically a modern-day troubadour. That night, he looked like he'd just rolled out of bed. After I got to know Harry, I realized he always looked like that. His hair was always messed up, and he couldn't have cared less what he wore. He also never, ever, carried any money on him. Even that first night I met him, he had to ask the bartender to spot him.

Harry and I started talking about a play that he was doing at a local theater.

"I think you'd be perfect for this one part."

I hesitated, because I hadn't done any theater work since high school.

"Why don't you just come audition and see?" he said.

So that's what I did, and I landed a role in his rock musical, *The Zinger,* which played at the Performing Arts Foundation for a month. It was a thrilling opportunity, especially because I got to work with Christine Lahti and Beverly D'Angelo. I was a step behind them professionally. They were on their way up, while I was pre—on my way up. I didn't expect this gig to be the big break I hoped for, but I did see it as a wonderful learning experience, a way to be onstage with pros. (Most of all I got to know Harry and his darling family. When he died, it absolutely broke my heart.)

The best part about all this was that I had the freedom to experiment. I was trying to make it, but I wasn't limiting myself. New York offered endless ways to experiment musically and push the envelope. I just had to find those opportunities and take advantage of them. In the process, I ended up doing a lot of different things and meeting cool people. Meanwhile I was singing anywhere and everywhere that I could—always looking to get in front of a crowd. I ran in different circles because that was a good way to meet people, but I didn't think that every single thing I did would result in the big time. That goal was first and foremost in my mind, but I also wanted to experience all that New York City had to offer. I was driven but I was also having fun.

And when I wasn't on performing or trying to line up my next gig, having fun meant hanging out with my friends. New York was an insane place to be in the late seventies, and while I didn't participate in the drug scene, I was definitely around it all the time. You'd show up at parties and there would just be mounds of coke, and, of course, pot was everywhere. But none of that was my thing. Now, I'm not saying I was an angel, but that stuff really didn't interest me. I wanted to be in control of the situation, and in my experience, that control was usually the first thing drugs made you relinquish. Doing drugs would've produced so much anxiety that it wouldn't have been worth it. (Thanks, Mom, finally a situation where those scare tactics paid off.) Besides, I always worried that I'd hurt my throat or ruin my face or eat too many M&M's. I was too responsible to let go like that.

Eventually it just became a given that although I was cool being around people who were wasted, I didn't indulge personally. I had a lot of druggie friends (some of the comedians I hung around were notorious drug users), but the bulk of my close friends were laypeople or musical theater people, both of which were much more benign. The choice to not spend a lot of time with the hard-core rockers was mine. For me, it was about the music; for a lot of them it was a lifestyle. I was a nice girl, a little square and cautious perhaps, but with an edge. Still, I would not be a casualty. I had a plan to succeed and not succumb.

After I'd been living in the city for a bit, I started looking for a manager, and I decided to take a chance on a semi-well-known guy named Jeff Nicholas who wanted to represent me. When I told Newman about him, he was skeptical, but he told me to give it a try.

"Just don't sign anything" were his only words of caution.

I began working with Nicholas, and at first, things were okay. He seemed interested in my career and we seemed to have a similar vision of what I needed to do. I spent most of my time hanging around Catch with the gang, always keeping Newman informed about what I was up to. One afternoon, Nicholas set up a meeting with a songwriter he wanted me to meet. The guy lived on Central Park West, and the plan was for me to meet him at his apartment by myself so that we could start talking over ideas. Walking up the pristine avenue across from the park, it occurred to me that with this address, this songwriter had to be a big shot of some kind. Clearly this meeting was a good one for me to take. When I arrived at his door, I saw he was in his midforties with a thin comb-over on his shiny, balding head. At first, he seemed nice enough, but there was an anxiety to him that seemed off. For one thing he had several locks on his door, which was odd given the neighborhood and the fact that this was a doorman building. I quickly found out why.

I spent the next hour being chased around the piano—literally. At every turn the guy kept trying to put his hands all over me, refusing to let me out of the apartment. I finally began to cry, and with the tears, he seemed to realize how green and young I was. He took pity on me and let me leave, but the damage had been done. I rode the crosstown bus back to the East Side, shaking and crying the whole way home. I went straight to the club and told Newman what happened. Instantly his paternal instinct for me kicked in. He sent some people to Nicholas's house to convince him that he should gracefully walk away from any relationship with me.

That was where my association with Jeff Nicholas ended. I had always been cautious about the people I trusted, but after that run-in, I came to see just how guarded I needed to be. As open and progressive as the music business was supposed to be, it was still very much a man's world. Men held the power, and they weren't afraid to wield it in order to get what they wanted.

The whole experience left me feeling demoralized. As great as my support system at Catch was, none of those guys ever had to deal with something like this. It was Newman, though, who was able to lift my spirits, when he and I began to discuss the possibility of him managing me. He was hesitant because he'd never managed a music act before and had absolutely no experience in the music business. But neither of us let that stand in the way. We both believed I had the goods necessary to make it. Whatever we didn't know, we'd figure out as we went. We were taking baby steps. How hard could it be?

Once he started repping me, I got thrown into Newman's world headfirst. I'd always known that Newman had some colorful friends, and when we'd first started working together, I had periodic run-ins with some of these guys, many of whom were total characters.

One morning, before I'd signed with Chrysalis, I was meeting Rick at a restaurant-bar called Friar Tuck where he was going to introduce me to a prospective agent. The restaurant was closed during the day, so only a skeleton staff was there prepping for the evening. I was sitting at the bar and waiting for Newman, but since it was eleven A.M. I wasn't drinking. However, there was an older gentleman who was also sitting at the bar, and he *was* drinking. We sat there a long time, not speaking and occasionally smiling politely at each other.

When it became clear that Rick was officially very late, the gentleman finally spoke. "Hey, doll, whattaya doin' here?"

"I'm waiting for my manager—we're having a meeting," I told him.

"Oh, are you waiting for Ricky?" he asked.

"Yes." I was surprised he knew Rick. He shook his head.

"Now that's wrong. It's rude to keep a pretty girl like you waiting so long. Whatsamatter with him? Me, I got an excuse, I've been hit in the head a lot of times." He smiled and went on eating his meal. I later found out that the gentleman was legendary boxer Rocky Graziano.

Another time, Rick and I went out for some Italian food at a restaurant called Jilly's in midtown. Jilly Rizzo, the owner, was a longtime friend of Frank Sinatra, and right as we were walking in, Frank was walking out. He stopped to say hello to Newman, and looking at me he said, "Who's this little girl?"

"Frank," Newman said, "her name is Pat Benatar and she's an amazing singer. You'd love her voice."

Frank smiled, those famous blue eyes twinkling, and then pinched both my cheeks. "With this doll face, she'll have no problem. Good luck, kid, maybe I'll see ya around."

Then he was gone, and the only thing running through my head was, *Oh my God, did Frank Sinatra really just pinch my cheeks and call me doll face?* Newman and I may not have known where we were going together, but at least with him it was never a dull moment.

IN 1977 I ACCIDENTALLY hit on my stage image thanks to an old science fiction movie and a Halloween party.

It was a 1953 D-movie titled *Cat-Women of the Moon* that inspired me to dress up in black spandex with a lot of eye makeup. It's pretty shocking that Ed Wood didn't have a hand in making this movie. It's that bad. But I was a junkie for terrible sci-fi and horror flicks, so I knew it well. There was something about the campiness of their outfits that was too good to pass up—especially for Halloween.

That night, I carried a ray gun and wore black tights, short black boots, and a sheer black top—not to mention lots of eyeliner. A bunch of us dressed up and decided to go to the Village to see all the outrageous costumes. With a large gay population, most of whom made dressing up for Halloween an art form, the Village was the only place to be. We all entered a costume contest at Café Figaro on Bleecker Street, and given the competition, I figured there was no way my Cat-Woman of the Moon outfit would win. Unbelievably, it did. After the contest, I had to go back uptown for a show at Catch, and to celebrate, I decided to perform in costume. So, there I was, in this crazy getup, singing the same songs I'd been singing for months, only this time I looked like I stepped out of a fifties sci-fi flick.

That night, though, something changed. I don't know if it was because I felt like I was playing a role or I simply removed my personal shell, but I had newfound bravado, a sexual swagger that wasn't there before. The notes were the same, but they had an attitude to them, an aggression. In the years since, I've returned to that night countless times, and even now, I'm not totally sure what prompted the change inside me. I'd been on that stage for months, and I'd had the spotlight on me for years; never before had I owned the stage like I did that Halloween.

The audience ate it up. They stood and applauded, yelled and stomped—not exactly the reaction I was used to. Don't get me wrong, I usually got a good reception, especially at Catch, but this crowd was going crazy. As I took in the moment and looked around the packed, costumed room, I tried to piece together just what had happened. It didn't take long for me to figure it out.

Now, I may have been a newbie, but I was no dummy. I decided to wear the outfit again the next night (minus the ray gun), and the crowd had the same reaction, even bigger than the night before. That was all the proof I needed. From that moment on I wore variations of that outfit every time I played. My stage persona was born. Later on when people asked my mother about my skimpy outfits, she quipped that she was relieved I was wearing clothes at all because she'd been worried I would end up a stripper. (When one journalist was obviously fishing for a negative comment from her about my stage outfits, her response was simply, "If I had her shape I'd dress like that too!")

Riding the wave of my newly energized live show, Newman got some demo tapes together that were beautifully produced—but that was precisely the problem. They didn't sound like rock and roll. My attitude, which I honed through performing, was solid, but my vocal delivery was still too controlled, too trained. Because I sang a lot of other singers' music, I tended to emulate their voices when I was performing their songs. Part of the blessing of having a wide vocal range was also a curse: I sang songs too closely to the sound on the actual recording, making it hard to hear *my* voice.

I could see this was creating a problem, so I sought out songwriters with original material that I could put my own vocal stamp on. This proved to be the right move, and when we had enough original songs, we made more demos. Newman and I were both convinced a record deal was right out there waiting for me. For a long time it seemed like we spent every spare minute trying to get a name of some record label rep who would let us drop off a tape. Sometimes we didn't have a name. We just dropped the tape off at the front desk. Everybody passed.

I shared the demos with people I knew, and while everyone agreed they were wonderful, the tapes were still missing something only I could hear. Never one to give up, I went back to performing live, figuring that was where I needed to be in order to work toward the sound I heard in my head. I stopped playing at cabaret clubs like Gypsy's, Goodtimes, and Dangerfield's, and I moved into rock venues. Through singing original songs, my voice began to emerge, and though it still wasn't quite what I wanted, it was getting closer all the time. My stage persona was growing by leaps and bounds; it became sensual, aggressive, and on occasion I was compared to Jagger. I was beginning to have control over an audience in ways I'd never had before.

It was exciting, but even then I knew a huge part of what I wanted to achieve was absent. While I loved bands and singers from every genre of music—the Beatles, Linda Ronstadt, Simon and Garfunkel, Dylan, and all things Motown—none of those were how I envisioned myself. I wanted that amazing, blistering guitar player, a partner to play off. Musically, I wasn't getting that monstrous chordal "bed" I was looking for. Zeppelin, the Stones, the Clash, Foreigner—all had that intense, guitar-driven sound. I was well aware that this was new territory for a woman, but that made it all the more attractive. I had listened to Grace Slick and Janis Joplin, and I admired them. But neither of them had the sound I wanted. I wanted to be Robert Plant.

The success of my live shows highlighted that whatever was working live clearly wasn't coming across in those demos. Finally Newman decided that it was time to showcase me for labels, to let them see the onstage energy I projected. We held it downtown at one of the city's best-known clubs, a place called Tramps, on Fifteenth Street. It was the kind of place where up-and-comers debuted and established players went to showcase new material. Newman ran around getting people to promise that they'd be there, and every friend and relative I had showed up. The showcase would be for two nights, and I should have felt tremendous pressure about the whole thing—not only were we paying for the show but sometimes in the music business, you get one shot. If you pull those label people out, you better be prepared to deliver. But I knew that I would put on a good show. It wasn't arrogance. I had worked for three years for this day and I was confident I was ready.

The first night my set list ranged from Roy Orbison's "Crying" to the Rascals' "You Better Run" to a reggae version of "Stairway to Heaven." The crowd ate it up, partially because the entire room was filled with my friends and family. The one label representative I met that night was Jeff "Buzzard" Aldridge from Chrysalis, who loved it. And one music critic in attendance *really* loved it. This will tell you the power of the press back then: Carl Arrington from the *New York Post* wrote a rave review about the show—the kind of accolades normally associated with parental adulation or eulogies. The next night people were lined up around the block for my set. It was insane. On that second night of the showcase, five different record labels came to the show, all because of the *Post* review. Buzzard was back, and after the show he brought Terry Ellis and Chris Wright, the founders of Chrysalis Records, backstage to meet me. Suddenly all of the record companies who had passed were interested.

The very next day I started meeting with record labels. But having already met Terry, Chris, and Buzzard, I really felt like I wanted to sign with them. It was a smaller label, which was very appealing to me, since it meant I might get more personal attention than at the giants.

After one meeting with Terry and Chris, I was signed to Chrysalis, unprepared but on my way.

What I didn't know was that the contract I signed practically made me an indentured servant. Because Newman hadn't managed a singer before, he didn't know what to be on the lookout for. As a result, neither one of us really knew what was necessary to protect me. From the day I first signed on that dotted line, I felt like I was playing catch-up, learning on the fly as I tried to follow the record label's rules.

At that first meeting with Terry and Chris, I explained what I wanted to accomplish, trying to describe for them the hard-rock sound that I'd been working to articulate but had yet to achieve. Though they'd liked what they'd heard and seen at the showcase, they were intrigued by my idea. The thought of having a female front person who could compete with male rockers, filling arenas, selling massive amounts of records, was unheard-of. Female pop singers, yes, of course, but a solo female rocker? There wasn't anything like that out there. The cash registers in their heads were chiming.

The fact that they'd had such success with Blondie only made them salivate more, and oddly enough, one of the first things they threw my way after signing with them was the chance to take a small part in an independent movie called *Union City* that Debbie Harry was also in. I showed up on the set, and over the course of making it, Debbie and I ended up spending a few days together. From the start, I really liked her. She was everything I wasn't—quirky in the best sort of way and definitely part of the New York art crowd, a group I admired and whose libertine lifestyle I enjoyed vicariously. She was crazy yet sweet as could be. The movie itself was a bizarre little thing, and I'm only really in it for a minute, but the whole experience just made me bat my wide eyes in disbelief at where I was standing. I was hungrier than ever to find that sound, my sound.

As it turned out, Chrysalis desperately wanted me to find that sound too, and they thought they knew how to get it. They assembled a group of New York's finest session players, Paul Shaffer (later of David Letterman's band) among them, and hired a successful producer named Ron Dante. With this pedigree, everyone thought we were off to a great start. The label had given me a song called "Heartbreaker" that we were pitched through the Chrysalis A&R department. It was written by a couple of British guys, Geoff Gill and Clint Wade, and though it was obviously a strong starting point, the original lyrics had too many English colloquialisms that an American audience wouldn't understand. The record label worried that it wouldn't fly with American listeners and asked me to rewrite some of the lyrics.

In spite of these promising beginnings, the sessions were a disaster. Everything was wrong. The tracks were played technically well, but they had no soul, no passion. The music was so uninspiring that I couldn't conjure any fire in the vocals. We had "Heartbreaker," for God's sake! But the recordings were a fiasco. I cried for days, saying that I was finished before I'd even started.

After listening to the sessions, Chrysalis determined that they'd been a little hasty jumping on my "female rocker bandwagon." They had a new plan. They had seen a "great vocalist" on that stage at Tramps, a technical singer who also knew how to work the crowd. They had determined that female singers were easier to market as solo artists, and marketing niches usually trump all else. They'd bring in the great producer Mike Chapman, who was working wonders with two other acts on their label, the Knack and Blondie. I'd be a pop star or a New Wave singer. See, all better.

But when I met with Chapman, the opposite thing happened. He got it. He knew exactly what I had been talking about. He started suggesting songs like "No You Don't" and "I Need a Lover." I was instantly drawn to "I Need a Lover," a song that John Mellencamp ("Johnny Cougar" back then) had first released as a single. While it didn't do much in the U.S., it went to number I in Australia. Mellencamp included it on his next record, and it charted in the U.S. It was exactly the kind of material I was looking for. The idea of singing that lyric from a female point of view was perfect. Chapman also thought "Heartbreaker" was the ideal vehicle for me lyrically and that the sentiment it exuded was spot-on. We both agreed that there wasn't any female out there shoving that kind of message in your face.

Now all we had to do was get those tracks to rock. Not someone's idea of how a "girl" would rock, but the real thing—only sung by a female. Chapman even thought he had an idea about where I could find that elusive guitar-playing partner I so desperately wanted.

I'M JUST GOING TO put this out there once and for all: without Neil Giraldo (or "Spyder," as I'd later dub him), my career would not have happened. I'm not saying that I wouldn't have had any success as the pop princess Chrysalis wanted. But I never would have succeeded to the degree I did, made strides for women, been part of the eighties rock movement, had my face on MTV, won four Grammys, sold millions of records, and still been around thirty years later without the genius and heart of that man.

Because *I* am not responsible for it; *we* are responsible for it, all of it. From the moment he stepped into the room at SIR, our lives changed—first musically, and later romantically and spiritually. We were each other's muse. It was like we had each been missing a part and when we met, we were finally whole, connected on a primal level. The sexual tension between us and the instant musical compatibility was intoxicating. The creativity that flowed was unstoppable. And even though I was crazy for him from the moment he walked into SIR's rehearsal hall, Spyder and I did not become a couple at first. We had music to make.

From the moment we first started collaborating, I knew Spyder was a visionary. His mind *never* stopped. He was constantly experimenting and trying new things, yet he knew precisely what needed to be pushed farther and what needed to be discarded. It was exactly what I'd been missing. That's not to say I had no vision, but I was such a grounded person. A lot of that had to do with my musical upbringing. There wasn't much room in classical music to go crazy or experiment. Your main job was to deliver what had been written in a precise and techni-cally perfect way. Artistry was valued over innovation. Spyder was the perfect counterpart to my organized, by-the-book self. He'd get these out-there ideas, and I'd make them palatable to human beings. To-gether we worked beautifully.

The fact that we meshed so well was surprising given how differ-ent our musical backgrounds were. His experience was the antithesis of mine. Unlike me, Spyder grew up in rock and roll and spent his entire musical life playing it. He came from a Sicilian-Czech family from Parma, Ohio, just outside Cleveland. In the beginning, he'd balked at playing music. His sister played accordion, which his mother (from the Czech side of the family) loved. But Mrs. Giraldo thought that for family gatherings on a Sunday afternoon, the accordion would sound better backed with an acoustic guitar. Spyder was natural musician and a great acoustic player, but he had no real interest in the whole thing until his uncle stepped in.

Uncle Timmy was much younger than Spyder's mom, and he was a rocker. Timmy was into the Stones, Zeppelin, and Hendrix, and being only four years older than Spyder, he helped bridge the generation gap. After listening to Spyder play acoustically and gripe about it, his father bought him an amp, but once his Uncle Timmy showed Spyder how to turn that amp all the way up, all hell broke loose. Nobody ever had to tell him to practice again. Music was his entire universe. While I was practicing arias, he was finding new ways to bend the strings on his guitar and turning his amps up to "eleven." At fourteen, he was sneak-ing in back doors to play in clubs, and this prolonged exposure to the fringe of rock had pushed his musical taste and creative sensibility far left of my own.

I'll say this about Cleveland: that city *is* rock and roll. Those people love music to the point of being insane. They're crazy. Spyder says it's because it gets so cold there, that Cleveland has the worst weather in America. People out scraping the ice off their cars in 4-degree weather don't complain like some of us do. They've got to get to the steel mills to get to work. Cleveland ain't Hollywood. It ain't foo-foo. They need something to distract them. So they play football and they rock. The music they make is gritty. You're not going to find that scene anywhere else.

Spyder's connection to Mike Chapman came through his work with Rick Derringer. In 1978, Rick was getting ready to go on the road to promote his new album, *If I Weren't So Romantic, I'd Shoot You.* Rick held auditions to replace his guitar player, who quit just before the tour. Out of the two hundred players who showed up, Spyder was chosen. The gig was perfect for him because Mike Chapman, the album's producer, had put keyboards on the project, and Spyder was a multi-instrumentalist.

When Chapman came out on the road and heard the band, he was sold on Spyder's fierce and innovative approach, as well as his understanding of the songs. Chapman also loved how aggressive Spyder was on the stage. After working out so well on the road, Spyder played on Rick's next record, *Guitars and Women.* Just about the time they finished up recording, Chapman was brought in on my project.

From the beginning, Chapman thought that what I needed was a guitar player who had a good feel for the structure of songs, who came at music from an organic place instead of just playing along on whatever someone handed him. That fit Spyder perfectly, and as I watched him play guitar on that first day, I knew he was the right one.

Buzzard watched my face while Spyder played, and as Spyder finished, Buzzard lifted me up, walked over to where Spyder was sitting, and plopped me right in his lap.

"He's our guy!" Buzzard announced.

Buzzard didn't know the half of it. I was embarrassed and furious; I was *never* that transparent with my feelings. More than Spyder's guitar playing had hit me in the gut. Spyder later told me that he too felt an instant attraction, but they had told him I was married and he was in a relationship himself, so he put those initial feelings aside (of course, he could just be saying that so I don't look like a lovesick dog). Regardless of the attraction, he'd felt a good vibe between us, good enough to know we could work together on a record. That was how I saw it, too. But my head was simultaneously in the clouds.

My relationship with Dennis was disintegrating, and I knew that this meeting was the motivation I needed to get serious about my divorce. I went straight back to my apartment and called my best friend, Cynthia Zimmer.

"I met the father of my children today," I announced.

She exploded. "Jesus Christ! Are you crazy? You're just now trying to get a divorce! Give me a break. Live alone for a little while! Don't be a dumbass!"

"No, you don't understand. This man is going to be the father of my children."

"It's 1979, you don't have to marry him to sleep with him!"

"That is not gonna happen. I won't be able to get this man out of my system."

"Dumbass."

With Spyder signed on, we started making plans to record the first record, *In the Heat of the Night,* in Los Angeles. In the beginning, Chrysalis was infatuated with Spyder. He was miles ahead of me in terms of recording experience. They were relieved that they didn't have to spoon-feed the novice every step of the way. He'd do that for them. He quickly became the guy who was getting it done. They stood by his decisions, especially when it came to the band. Roger "Zel" Capps had been playing with me since the Richmond days. He'd been the bassist for Coxon's Army, and he'd actually moved to New York when I did. We'd been playing together in the city ever since. I was comfortable working with him, and Spyder liked his playing. But Chrysalis wanted him gone.

"He's been playing in lounge bands with her," they protested.

"That doesn't matter, I'll get him rockin'," Spyder countered. "Pat's worked with him and she likes him. He's a nice guy who will be easy to have around on the road. And besides, she *should* have someone in the band who's been with her from the beginning. He also sings backup."

Chrysalis went along with him. And so we auditioned more players and got the band together. After we got Zel on board for bass and backing vocals, we hired a drummer, Glen Alexander Hamilton, and a rhythm guitarist, Scott St. Clair Sheets. Spyder would play lead and slide guitars and keyboards. Then we set off to California to make a record at MCA Whitney in Glendale.

As much as we were thrown together and I was incredibly attracted to him, I didn't look to make it anything more than just infatuation while we were making the record. For one thing, when I'd met him, he was dating the actress Linda Blair. I wouldn't have tried to split up a couple, whether they were married or merely dating. But it was hard to control myself. It was torture. I'd never had such a chemical reaction to anyone before. But it was more than that. We were connected on every level.

Some mornings he'd pick me up to drive me to the studio. When it came to his car, he was "relaxed" about neatness, which ordinarily would drive me crazy. Cleanliness and organization were always a big deal to me, and I was the kind of person who couldn't go to sleep if there was a spoon in the sink. Spyder would open the door and a mixture of burger wrappers and paper cups would come spilling out onto the pavement. He'd knock a bunch of papers off the passenger seat and onto the floor so that I could sit down. His ashtray was overflowing with cigarette butts. And yet somehow, I never saw any of that; I saw only him.

Sitting so close to him in the car was the most intense time of my days recording that album. I'd sneak looks at him while he was driving and think about how good he smelled. Whatever it was—cologne, shampoo—it drove me nuts. This was so unlike me. I was always in control of my emotions. I was never the pursuer, always pursued. He short-circuited all of that, and my mind went crazy.

I'm gonna die. I am so in love with this man. I'm gonna kill myself if this doesn't happen. I'm gonna kill him. And there's Linda Blair. I might kill her.

So while I was busy plotting to kill Linda Blair, Spyder was busy getting the sound of the record right.

Still, we kept it professional during the recording. We worked in the studio eighteen hours a day. I'd never been to L.A. before, but there was little time for socializing or hitting the L.A. scene. It was round-the-clock recording. One of the first things Spyder told me was that my instincts had been right all along—everything depended on me having the right sound, the right direction, and the right players. What I needed was a band where the bed of the music was aggressive and strong, a band that would push me to sing harder, tougher. As he says, I needed a Sicilian guitar player from Cleveland to dirty it up some.

And when Spyder made that sound a reality, I thought the very same thing I'd thought a few years back at the Liza Minnelli concert: *I can do that.*

I'd had it in me all the time, but it was Spyder who let it out.

Spyder understood that my classical training could be either a plus or a minus, and maybe both. I was always going to have that range and clear quality to my voice, because I'd spent years training for five and six hours a day. Whereas most rock musicians might see that vocal clarity as a detriment, he actually thought the contrast of pristine vocals with hard-edged playing would be unstoppable—the unique combination we needed to produce a powerful sound.

What we both heard was unmistakable: with the right music behind me, I could go head to head with any rocker and still have the years of classical training help me with both stretch and stamina. What I really had to put behind me was the time I'd spent singing covers of Ronstadt and Streisand. I literally stopped listening to all music while I was recording that first album, because I was still very impression-able musically. If I listened to Linda Ronstadt, I might put some of her vocal mannerisms into a song. The same thing went for Chrissie Hynde, whom I admired vocally and didn't dare listen to before I went in to record. I avoided listening to even the male singers I loved, just to make sure that what I was doing was me and not outside influences.

In the Heat of the Night was recorded in twenty-eight days for $82,000. Because of his hectic schedule, Mike Chapman was only hired to produce four of the songs. As Chapman was winding down his involvement, he sat down with Pete Coleman, the engineer/producer, and Spyder.

"Okay, Peter, why don't you continue to engineer and work on the rest of the album with Spyder."

Spyder turned to Peter questioningly. "Is that how you want to work?"

"Sure," Peter said. During the short time we'd been recording, Pete and Spyder had developed a good rapport. They were a great team, with Pete a patient and thorough teacher. He loved explaining every minute detail of the recording process to Spyder and seeing Spyder absorb every word of it. Soon Spyder was Pete's equal. And so the ma-jority of the material on *In the Heat of the Night* was produced by Peter Coleman with a great deal of help from Neil "Spyder" Giraldo, but Spyder neither asked for nor received credit for his extra work on the album.

As it turned out, I didn't get my name on the song "Heartbreaker," either, despite the fact that by the time we laid it down, I had rewritten so many of the lyrics and we wouldn't have used it otherwise. But the writers wouldn't go for giving me credit. I was an unknown, and Chrysalis did not stand with me. It was one of the first times that they put their interests before mine.

"Heartbreaker" was the first song that the new team of Coleman/Giraldo recorded. It was a blistering recording, setting the tone for the entire record. We included the John Mellencamp song, "I Need a Lover," and three by Mike Chapman and his frequent collaborator, British writer/producer Nicky Chinn: "If You Think You Know How to Love Me," "No You Don't," and the title cut, "In the Heat of the Night." Zel and I had two songs on the album, "So Sincere" and "My Clone Sleeps Alone." "Rated X" was a Nick Gilder/James McCulloch song, and "We Live for Love" was written by Spyder.

I noticed right away that Spyder was careful not to try to bring his own songs to the table, especially after he was tapped by Chapman to work with Peter Coleman. A very conscientious person, Spyder began to see that he was influencing much of what was happening with the record, and he didn't want it to look like he was taking over, even though he wasn't. He was the driving force, the catalyst making it all happen. He thought that by adding songs he'd written, his influence would be disproportionate.

But when we cut everything that we liked, we still needed one song. That's when he invited me to his house to hear "We Live for Love." (In the years since that album came out, Spyder has always said that he wrote that song for me, and I always call him on it, because he wrote the song before we had anything going. He says that's just part of my shtick, but I know better.)

As good as we all knew "Heartbreaker" was, it wasn't the first single release, because Chrysalis, in their continuing infinite wisdom, didn't think it was a hit. Disco was dying, but the label didn't see it.

Those guys were positive that disco-loving deejays would not play the song because there was too much guitar on it. The irony is that the resurgence of guitar-driven music was about to happen. The Clash was ushering it in, with punk becoming the antidote to disco. Thank God. We were going to bring guitars back into the mainstream and we were moving in the right direction, but at that moment, we were the only ones who thought that. I was in love with Spyder's guitar playing, and as far as I was concerned, there was never enough of it. I was the one pushing him to play more guitar. Our conversation usually went like this:

"I think that song needs more guitar."

"No."

"Come on, put another guitar part on it. I swear to you that it will work."

"No, it won't. Listen to the song structure."

Spyder had a theory about the way that guitars and vocals should work together. He wanted the guitar solos to be melodic—to lead into the vocals, not fight with them. It all had to do with keeping people musically interested in the song. When the vocal stopped, the guitar would take over. When the guitar stopped, the vocals would come back in. He saw a good song structure as being like a story with no lulls for someone to get bored. Every note would lead into the next, set the scene.

"Heartbreaker" was teeming with that kind of back-and-forth, but Chrysalis lived in fear of disco's popularity and wouldn't release it. So the first two singles were the safer choices "I Need a Lover" and "If You Think You Know How to Love Me." They were released respectively in August and October of 1979, and neither of them did what we needed them to commercially. However, the important thing they did do, especially "I Need a Lover," was introduce us to the world. "I Need a Lover" created a huge buzz. Including it was a brilliant suggestion by Chapman. It was a song that was relatively unknown in America but had proved itself in Australia. And of course lyrically, it was perfect. Radio stations loved it. They even began splicing our two versions together. In the end, "I Need a Lover" got us airplay, just not enough to break us out.

The thing about albums is that not all songs have to be hits. I subscribe to what I'm sure is a widely held belief that not all songs are meant to be number one records. All songs are pivotal, important stones in the path that you're walking, stones that you follow to your next destination. Each one leads to the next. They're not all meant to be commercial successes. But they need to be successful for the artist on some level.

I believe that everything is connected. When you ask someone to listen to an album, you want them to feel like they are listening to someone's heart and soul. You do not make records for the fans, for radio, or for sales. You make the record that needs to come out of you. Then, and only then, do you give it to the public. Then it becomes a personal gift from you. And the truth is, if you are honest about making music, it is irrelevant whether the public likes the album or not. What is important is that you made the record you wanted to make, one that says something about how you're feeling at the time. It's completely narcissistic and at the same time you hope it has relevance for someone else. And when it does, you've tapped into the "common thread." This can't be fabricated; it's not something you do by design (well, I guess some people do, but I never could). It determines hit records, it's elusive, it's coveted, and it's best left to the whim of the universe.

If all those songs happen to end up radio hits, that's great. As long as you don't compromise art for the sake of commerce, I'm all for it, but it's not always easy to do. There were many times throughout our career that we were forced to do just that. It always felt wrong and it always came back to bite us in the ass.

In the end, the recording process went better than any of us could have expected. Whatever "it" was, we'd captured it and we were all ecstatic. Strangely Chrysalis seemed lukewarm about the finished product. Terry even commented to me, "Don't expect too much." But there was no doubt in our minds that we'd made a great record. It was going to take a lot more than a music exec to bring me down.

When we finished, I went back to New York while Spyder stayed in Los Angeles for about a month, until we started rehearsals for our live show. In order to promote the album, we'd landed a gig opening for David Werner, who'd just released a glam rock album that was sometimes compared to David Bowie's *Ziggy Stardust*. Though we'd been refining our sound in the studio for the last month, we'd never played a live show as a full band. We had work to do.

CHAPTER THREE

AN IMAGE PROBLEM

I FILED FOR A divorce as soon as I got back to New York. I didn't know what was going on between Spyder and me, but I knew that those twenty-eight days we'd spent making *In the Heat of the Night* had been some of the best of my life. Dennis and I hadn't had a real marriage for so long it just felt like a detail that needed to be handled. And it was a way to get my side of things rolling, whether Spyder was still involved with someone or not.

The month before Spyder came back to New York to rehearse was agonizing. With the record release and our tour with David Werner coming, we talked on the phone almost every day. But when he arrived from California, I didn't know what to do with the emotions I felt. With each day I became more certain that this was a lot more than infatuation. This was not a man I was ever going to get over.

To hold it together, I kept having little talks with myself. *Stay businesslike. Concentrate on rehearsing, on this first tour. Don't be a dumb shit and throw all this away.*

Spyder didn't help matters. He teased me mercilessly in just the right way to make me think that he felt the same way I did, and I knew he was serious about the flirtation. It was that awful dance that people do when they are so attracted to each other yet, for one reason or another, can't be together. It was exquisite agony. At first, my responses to him were more of the "Yeah, sure" variety. Then one day at he started playing the familiar chords of "Somewhere over the Rainbow" on the piano, and when I asked him why he was playing it, he said, "It's 'Somewhere over Montana'—me and you." We were going on tour through Montana.

That did it.

"You know what? You're full of shit."

"Montana, you and me," he said with a little smile.

"You've got a girlfriend. Don't talk to me."

Over the next week, he kept it up, mentioning Montana every so often, like we were going to head off into the wild and start a new life together. I became very blunt. Every time he mentioned Montana I'd say, "Figure out your own situation. Then we'll talk about Montana." I was trying to protect myself. His relationship with Linda seemed intact, and I wasn't going to play the fool.

I couldn't imagine what it was going to be like with him out on the road. It had been hard enough being around him most of the day while we were recording, but at least he went home at night. On the road we'd be together twenty-four hours a day. How was I going to do *that*? There was *no way* I could travel on a bus with this man and not really be with him. On the other hand, I couldn't help thinking that something had changed, that whatever relationship we had was being taken to the next level, even if superficially nothing was different.

One evening toward the end of our rehearsals for the tour, Spyder asked me to have a drink with him at a little seafood restaurant named Pier 52 on the West Side of Manhattan. There wasn't anything odd about his invitation, and I didn't anticipate that anything out of the ordinary was happening. We sat beside a big aquarium, talking about the rehearsals, just making casual conversation. Finally he said he needed to have a serious talk with me.

Oh crap! He's gonna quit the band!

"I'm having some problems," he said.

God, no! What if he's on drugs?

"I think Linda is cheating on me."

I mentally raised my arms in triumph. I couldn't believe it. She had screwed up. She'd cheated. How could she want somebody else? Was she crazy? *Give him to me, I love him.* I wanted to throw my arms around him and tell him to forget about her, but I tried to control how happy I was. I could see he was hurt. "Oh, I'm so sorry, Neil," I said, barely managing to conceal my smile.

He had a solemn look on his face and just nodded.

I had my chin in my hands, and I leaned in toward him with my most sympathetic look and spoke very low. "What a bitch! I don't know how she could do that to you. You are the sweetest person in the world. You don't deserve this."

But right under the sympathy, I was thinking, *This is a done deal, Neil Giraldo. You. Are. Mine.*

He nodded. I commiserated with him, thinking how everything that I'd been saying really was true. He really *was* the sweetest person in the world, and he really didn't deserve to be treated like this. There was something grounded, moral, and *Midwestern* about him. Even though we were both rockers and we were both serious about our music, in his own way he was just as traditional as I was, which was no small feat.

It took a couple of weeks for us to take the next step. Like me, Spyder is a conventional person. So while the attraction between us was mutual, he wasn't the type to end a relationship and jump right into another one. His attraction to me was real, but so was his hurt over being cheated on.

We went out with some of the band members as a group a few

times, never addressing the fact that the sexual tension between us was building. He and I were together constantly. When we weren't playing, we were shopping, listening to music, or running errands. We ate with each other every day. We were never apart, and it was getting intense. Then finally we went to Little Italy for the San Gennaro Festival, New York's September tribute to its Italian immigrants—just the two of us. Every year they hold parades, dances, and cannoli-eating contests. It couldn't be missed if you were an Italian boy and a girl who always felt like she should have been Italian.

We walked around Little Italy, watching people in costumes dance down the street, sampling some of the foods, and listening to the ethnic bands play. We stood there listening to the music, and the next thing we knew we were kissing. Neither of us hesitated or questioned it. We knew it had been coming, so we just let it happen. I thought back to all those morning car rides in L.A., the rehearsal sessions, how closely we'd worked with each other. Standing there in the middle of a narrow street in Little Italy, I knew this wasn't just hormones—this was something else.

From that moment on, we were a couple.

In the Heat of the Night was officially released in October of '79, around the same time that we started touring with David Werner. The shows were primarily in big clubs with big stages that gave us the chance to get our act down. It was a great time. We had our first album out, the road show was well received, and Spyder and I were madly in love.

When Chrysalis decided to take a chance and put out "Heartbreaker" as the third single that December, all hell broke loose. We'd only played ten shows with David when "Heartbreaker" exploded, but after that, we were fired from the tour. The crowds turning out were there for us, and when we left the stage, they almost rioted. Finally

Werner's people said we had to get off the tour. We were causing chaos, and it was hurting David's show.

Though "Heartbreaker" gave us a ton of momentum coming off of David's tour, it didn't take long for us to be humbled. Shortly after leaving David's show we opened a show for Journey, and out of the thirty thousand people out there, I knew that maybe eight thousand had come to hear us. It was good exposure to be in front of a much larger crowd, and it gave us experience in front of a massive audience, but it wasn't always the warmest reception. The audience was mostly ponytailed hippies and they weren't all that interested in us, which was their loss because we were putting on a really good show. We won them over by the end when we did "Heartbreaker," but before that, they were all a bit too laid-back to get into it. We were way more aggressive and defiant than what they were used to. If the audience wasn't ready for that, they would just have to deal with it.

From then on we were scrambling. We moved quickly through a process that usually takes several years: playing the big clubs like the Agora in Cleveland, then arenas and amphitheaters like the Universal Amphitheatre or Denver's Red Rocks. Everything jumped so fast that we were always just trying to catch our breath. I never had a moment when I could pace myself or find the time to get a grip. Trying to keep up was stressful, because I was (and still am) such a perfectionist. I could not do things half-assed; every night, every show, was all-important to me. I needed to give the audience everything I had.

Long before I began playing arena shows, I knew what I wanted to do for an audience. Even when I was singing in cover bands, I wanted to give the people who came out to see me more than a performance. I wanted to take them out of their world. If they had bills to pay and pressures at work, I wanted them to put them on hold for a couple of hours. I understood that world and what those long nights at the kitchen table felt like. I knew how badly people needed some relief from the daily grind. I looked out into a sea of faces and wanted to grab hold of every one of them. I wanted to let the audience live out fantasies, go into some other time and place with me. I was living mine and I wanted them to come along.

But even though I wanted to take the audience on a journey, it was always on my terms. I became a completely different person onstage. I prowled around and played with the audience. I never thought of myself as sexy. I never thought about it period. Never. Growing up, I was skinny and flat chested, with big teeth and thin, straight hair; I left sexy to the Italian goddesses at my high school. Sexy didn't even occur to me. I was a product of the women's movement. I dressed the way I did because I liked it, not because I thought men liked it. I didn't care what they liked. *That* was the point. I was much more interested in showing how strong-minded I was. It was all about not taking crap from anyone for any reason. I wanted the stereotypes to disappear. I didn't want to be a female rocker, I just wanted to be a rocker. My look and persona were about freedom, strength, and power. The combination proved to be provocative.

I took to touring pretty naturally. Even though I was the only female around a bunch of guys all the time, nothing about it struck me as weird. Over the years, I've heard so many female singers say they had problems with it, but I never did. I loved it. I relished being female, but what I was after was respect as a musician. Despite the rampant sexism in the music business, remarkably the band never behaved that way. We were equals on every level, and those boys were close friends of mine. That made a big difference when we were touring; they always treated me with respect. The fact that Spyder and I were romantically involved was irrelevant. I wasn't a "pop tart." I was a serious, dedicated, formidably rockin' lead singer who happened to be a girl. And that's exactly how Spyder saw it, too.

Chrysalis was ecstatic when "Heartbreaker" hit big. But that excitement died when they found out that Spyder and I were involved. They were horrified. Each of us got a phone call.

"This is going to ruin your whole career. Don't you remember what happened with Stevie Nicks and Lindsey Buckingham? They almost broke up Fleetwood Mac!"

We both had the same reaction: "What? Who the hell are you?"

They tortured us about it, convinced that we were on the road to ruin. We explained that we were making music that they liked and doing our job. Our personal life was not their business. They looked at our situation and saw the worst-case scenario: a rocky relationship that ruins the band. While I understood that there were other bands that had fallen into that trap, the truth was, band tension was always a variable—not just in male/female circumstances. A lot of all-male bands split up because of friction between members. It was ridiculous and intrusive.

Awkwardness in the band was just their cover story. What they really cared about was my image. It's an old tale in the entertainment business that record labels—whether they're dealing with men or women—want solo stars unattached and seemingly available. I've always found that train of thought insulting and sexist. I wasn't a boy toy. My image was for my pleasure alone. I didn't think my fans cared about any of this, and I certainly didn't. This was 1979, not 1950. Women weren't objects anymore. I wanted to make music, but I wanted to do it on my terms. I wasn't in this to fit some male fantasy of what I was supposed to be. That meant living my life however the hell I wanted to live it.

This drama over our relationship was part of my introduction to fame that began following that first tour. It wasn't overwhelming at first—nothing like later on and definitely nothing like today's celebrities have to deal with—but I started noticing people looking at me or whispering to each other when I was in the market. I wasn't sure what was going on for a while. I thought maybe they were looking at someone else, or maybe I just looked weird. Finally someone came up and said my name as if they knew me personally. It's an unsettling feeling. You're thrilled that people know you, because that means you're being accepted. But I'm basically a private person, and it was difficult to comprehend.

We still didn't really understand the magnitude of our career—not surprising, considering we lived in a vacuum. Traveling around on a bus was especially isolating in the early eighties, without cell phones or laptops. *Billboard*'s charts were not calculated electronically through SoundScan. If an album was taking off, it took longer for everyone to get the message. We were among the last to understand the impact of both "Heartbreaker" and the album. The world was a different place: no Internet, no daily glut of information.

By the time our tour reached Virginia Beach, we finally saw the scope of what was happening around us. As we pulled up to the club, we saw that it was surrounded with a police barrier, and there appeared to be a massive riot going on. We didn't know what the hell had happened. An armed robbery? An explosion? Not quite. The club had oversold the show, and people who'd paid to see us couldn't get in. It's common practice for some clubs to oversell a show, counting on no-shows. But that night, the no-shows showed up en masse. They ended up cramming more inside than there probably should have been, and I'm sure the local fire marshal would have been pissed if he'd been there to see it. Still, I'm sure some ticket holders went home mad.

What made this sight all the more shocking was that back then there were few outlets for artist exposure. The television shows newer acts could get on were few and far between—*Don Kirshner's Rock Concert, The Midnight Special*. There was no video exposure, no cable entertainment shows. You had radio play and your live show. The only way we knew something was happening was that with each performance, the crowds got bigger and wilder. You could feel the excitement building, escalating even more after the release of the next single, Spyder's song "We Live for Love."

That night in Virginia Beach, our hotel room faced the ocean and had a small balcony. After the show, we were standing on the balcony, admiring the view and looking at the cluster of bars down on the beach. The beach was covered in the gauzy haze of the various marquees, and one of them said SPYDER'S in black and yellow lights. At that point, we were really into giving everyone nicknames, partially because Spyder had always been a nickname guy. I thought he should have one of his own, so because yellow and black were his favorite colors, I started calling him Spyder James. It just had a way of sticking.

A few weeks later we were playing a club in Florida, and again the place was oversold and teeming with people. We'd just begun our set when our tour manager rushed up to the stage yelling something inaudible. Because we were extremely loud, I could barely make out his words beneath all the noise, but he seemed to be saying, "You have to get off!"

I looked at him in disbelief. What the hell was he doing? We were in the middle of performing. Get out of my face. But he was panicked.

Finally I heard him say, "You've got to stop, get off . . ." which was followed by something unintelligible that sounded a lot like "you're *bombing.*" I shot him a look like he was a mental patient. The audience was going nuts. They were hanging on every note.

"What!? Are you nuts?" I shouted back. "These people are going crazy!"

And that was when he grabbed me by my jacket lapels and screamed, "There's a bomb!" There was no mistaking those words.

It turned out that someone had called in a bomb threat and everyone had to vacate. Needless to say everyone filed out of the theater and stood in the street until the bomb squad gave the all-clear. Then everybody went back inside and we continued our show like nothing had ever happened.

That tour was all about having fun and enjoying the fact that we were actually getting paid money to do this every night. We couldn't believe our good fortune that we were getting to live out our dream and we pretty much celebrated that every day. Zel sometimes celebrated more than he should have.

Zel was definitely the colorful member of the band. At over six

feet tall, he was a huge Southern boy who loved women and drinking. He was a sweet soul, but he liked to get crazy from time to time.
One night in particular, he partied a little too much, and as we were
all going our separate ways for the night, he said he was going to take a
shower and go to bed because we had a show the next day. The motel
we were staying in was nothing fancy, and we all retired to our rooms
ready to wake up and do it all over again.

In the morning, we were all going to have breakfast together before
we got on the bus to go to the venue for sound check. We went to Zel's
room and knocked on his door—no answer. We called out to him and
knocked again—still nothing. But we knew he was in there because we
heard the shower running. We called our tour manager, Chris Pollan,
and told him we couldn't get Zel to answer the door, so he sent someone to us with a spare room key.

The instant the door opened a blast of steamy air smacked us in the
face. The entire room looked and felt like a steam bath, and there was
Zel, in bed, snoring away. He'd passed out and left the shower running
the entire night. Everything was soaking wet, and because this wasn't
the classiest joint in the world, he'd even managed to steam all the wallpaper off the walls. It was lying in colored piles all over the room.

The longer we played on the road the tighter our show became.
By the time our tour made its way to New York, my family members
were beside themselves. Everyone showed up at the Bottom Line in
the Village for a big show in November of '79, and I can safely say that
they were among the most enthusiastic members of the audience—no
one more so than my mom. Both she and my father were ecstatic and
proud, though he was so shy, he didn't show it as much. I was the first
person in my family who had a job that didn't involve punching a time
clock. And my cousins? They were roughly my age, so they were right
there, screaming along with the other fans, jumping up and down, and
yelling, "That's my cousin Patti!" The aunts and uncles shook their
heads and said, "We knew she sang good, but . . ."

Of course having my mother at a show meant she'd get to see my act firsthand. Not surprisingly, she didn't really care about my outfit (after all, inside her conservative exterior beat the heart of the same wild woman who'd let my brother and me get a monkey). But she was horrified at my language onstage. She never swore, and saying the "F-word" was sacrilegious. For me it was like saying "the."

Georgia Ruel got a kick out of it all—the success, the image, everything. She was as proud as my parents. At one point, someone asked her, "I thought Patti was going to be a sex ed teacher?"

"She is," Georgia answered with a wry smile.

Truthfully, though it had only been a few weeks, I was already getting tired of the image. It was already becoming one-dimensional, a boring distraction and the focus of what we were doing. That was never my intention. The girl who'd hiked up her school skirt as high as possible and pissed off the Matron was long gone. In her place was a fiercely confident young woman who was only interested in making music on her terms. The image was mine; I made it up. Now I was done with it. It had served its purpose. I was ready to move on. The label was pushing the look so much that it was getting in the way of the music. The artist in me didn't like that at all. Neither did the woman who was in a loving relationship.

Phrases such as "seductive vamp" have legs, especially when they are included in press releases that get picked up by radio and by print journalists. But every time I talked to management or the record label and said I wanted the sex-kitten rhetoric toned down, my words fell on deaf ears. I was being sold as much for my image as for my music, and I was *not* happy about it.

WE TOURED ALMOST NONSTOP during that time and even took the show to Europe, where the crowds were just as big and just as passionate. I'd never traveled outside of America, and I was like a kid seeing Disneyland for the first time. We didn't have a moment to enjoy the success or rest on our laurels, though. The clock was ticking, and thanks to Chrysalis more recording sessions were just around the corner.

My contract had what's called a suspension clause in it, meaning that I had to do my next album in a certain time frame or they else could hold back royalties and delay payments. Any royalties or payments I was due would be frozen. That is a terrifying concept to a band just starting a big tour and dependant on any and all monies they can put together. Our recording schedule was at Chrysalis's discretion, and they wanted a record every nine months no matter what. It was unfathomable.

So while we were breaking our backs on tour promoting *In the Heat of the Night,* the label was already talking about a second album. Being the front woman for the band, I found this especially distressing. All the radio and print interviews fell to me. If we had two days off, it seemed like I was scheduled round the clock for publicity photo shoots and in-store events. I understood that press and publicity helped keep the buzz alive. But to even think about making another record in the middle of the craziness seemed impossible. No thought was given to my physical or mental well-being. I was treated like a machine built to serve the record company's whims.

Touring and promoting an album are counterproductive to creating new material, and I've never been able to write when I'm in performance mode. Complicating matters was the fact that Spyder and I were just starting to seriously write together. It worked fine when we were off the road and had our heads clear. But writing wasn't something we could do on the fly. Because I wasn't a seasoned writer at the time, I didn't care as much about having a lot of my own songs on the next album. However, that didn't mean I wanted to rush the writing process. From what I'd learned so far, I loved the process of writing, and I wanted more time to hone that skill. Meanwhile Spyder was already an accomplished songwriter, but what he needed was to have his work heard.

I wanted this second record to be better than *In the Heat of the Night*. I wanted it to be more personal, more representative of us as a band and as individuals. We were determined that our next work would not suffer from sophomore syndrome. We would not be a band with a smashing debut album that can't follow it up. Neither of us thought in terms of writing a *hit* song. We wanted to write songs that had relevance to where we were in our lives. If a hit emerged, that was great, but we wouldn't focus on that. Back then, we looked to outside writers to provide the hits. It was my job to sift through the box-loads of song demos submitted by songwriters, since that wasn't something that Spyder enjoyed doing. He always insisted that we were capable of writing commercial songs without compromising our integrity as songwriters. He was right, of course.

While we were on a short break from touring and getting ready to record in Los Angeles again, Spyder and I decided to move to California. I'd dreamed of beautiful beaches and tropical climates ever since the days I was on the grade school slide, making up stories about what my life would be like. So in February of 1980 we rented a small house in Tarzana. Our next album would be recorded at Sound City, which is located in Van Nuys. (It was not exactly a tropical paradise, but it was California!)

As far as Chrysalis was concerned, Mike Chapman was the obvious choice for producer. It didn't matter to them that he hadn't actually produced much of the first album. Because his name had been on it, he was tied to its success. But although Chapman had a huge impact on the first record, I didn't think he would be the right choice for the next one. I hoped we'd record with Peter Coleman. After all, Chapman had turned the first record over to him when he'd left. Peter was never heavy-handed with us, providing the freedom we needed. Chrysalis didn't want Peter to produce the new album, and instead they hired

Keith Olsen. It seemed like a smart choice, because Olsen had an impressive background. He was an award-winning, platinum-record-selling, big-name producer who'd worked with bands like Fleetwood Mac and the Grateful Dead.

Despite the tight schedule, I was excited to get started and looking forward to working with Olsen. I was starting to write more, collaborating with Spyder and Zel, our bassist. Together, the three of us wrote one song I felt strongly about: "Hell Is for Children." The idea came from an article in the *New York Times*. Until I read that article, I knew very little about violence against children. My childhood might have been a little crazy once in a while, but my parents were nonviolent. They barely raised their voices at us. Growing up, Andy and I seldom got spanked, and if we did it was just a little swat on the butt. I didn't know any kids who got knocked around either. I'd never known anyone who had to hide bruises or slap marks. Kids at school would have suspected if something bad was going on with one of our friends. At least I hope we would have, even as sheltered as we were. Reading that story, however, opened my eyes.

That morning, sitting at the kitchen table, it suddenly dawned on me that I'd been asleep for too long about this. Where had I been? How could I have been totally unaware that all this ugliness had been going on? I was crushed that anyone could harm children like that. Writing had become cathartic to me, so I started working on some thoughts, putting them down free-form. I wrote and wrote. When I started turning the thoughts into lyrics, Spyder was busy preparing the recording schedule, so I went to Zel, who by that point was the only person left who had been with me from the beginning. We'd written songs before, and I felt comfortable sharing these thoughts with him.

Zel started to write lyrics as well. Together the two of us refined it. I kept thinking that if we could put a message out there in song, maybe it would help raise awareness. Maybe it would inspire people to get involved. I didn't set out to be a crusader, but I did hope that people would listen. I just wanted to reach people and using my voice seemed like the best way to do that. When we'd written most of the lyrics, I talked to Spyder.

"Take a look at what Zel and I have been working on. I don't know what to do with it, because it's got nothing to do with the music we've been making. But I feel strongly about it and want to do *something*. Can you make it into a song?"

Spyder agreed and wrote all of the music, taking our words and creating a chilling, wailing melody that turned all the pain and suffering in the lyrics into a searing rock anthem. In its original form, the song was about ten minutes long. We cut it back to five to fit it on the album. Of all the songs I've recorded, it's the song I'm most proud of. Over the years, we've received thousands of letters from people who were abused as children, saying how much it helped them and how happy they were that someone cared enough to write a song about them, a song that reminded them they were not forgotten. Even today, we play it at every concert we do, in a show of solidarity.

"Hell Is for Children" was the first song we cut when we got to Los Angeles. I went into the session hoping for the best, and coming off such an amazingly successful year, we could see we were on the ascent. We had a hit record, but we didn't want this just to be a remake of the first album. This needed to have a new approach, a fresh sound. We had spent over a year performing live, and the sound that had evolved was grittier, heavier. My voice began to settle and work together with the band, which had become a thunderous and raw wrecking machine. We wanted to capture that intensity on the new record. In terms of both sound and subject matter, "Hell Is for Children" would set the tone.

Problems with the recording began almost immediately. While we'd entered poised and confident to make this record, the fact that we had to contend with a totally new producer complicated things. The rhythm that we had established with Peter Coleman and Mike Chapman was gone. We had to start all over again with Keith Olsen. This was unnerving. Even though we felt we'd made tremendous strides in our playing, we were still neophytes with a lot to learn. We weren't ready to take on another record alone, and unfortunately that was what we ended up having to do.

At first Keith Olsen seemed like a great guy. His success was well documented, and it made us optimistic that he would bring us closer to our goals musically. We were eager to learn what this new "mentor" had to offer. But as I watched him put down tracks for the songs, something appeared off. For one thing, he didn't seem to be paying attention to much of what we were doing. He was distracted and distant. I couldn't figure out what was wrong. If this was just his style of producing, I didn't like it. It was uncomfortable, as if there was no one at the helm. There always seemed to be something else going on that was commanding his attention, and that feeling of no one being in charge made me incredibly anxious.

One day Spyder was working on some songs, and he mentioned that he liked to write in his head while he's driving. Olsen threw him a set of car keys.

"No problem. Take my Porsche. I'll get Pat's vocals down, then when you get back we'll work on some overdubs."

Spyder was only too happy to drive around in that Porsche and write songs. Of course, the instant he left, the session turned bad. Olsen kept getting up and leaving—disappearing right in the middle of my singing. Peter Coleman and Spyder had done such an excellent job of recording my vocals on the first record. They knew how fragile the atmosphere was when you were trying to coax a performance out of someone. Singing is such an organic process: no amps, no instruments, just flesh and muscle and psyche. I was panic-stricken. I couldn't stand his half-assed attitude, and the longer I sang, the more I felt that the session was going south. The vocals sounded horrible. By the time

Spyder got back from his songwriting trip, I was in tears and Olsen was nowhere to be found. Spyder took one look at me and freaked.

"What's the matter?"

"I can't work with this guy. He doesn't understand my voice and he doesn't stick around long enough to find out," I said. "This album is not going to work like this."

Spyder immediately took charge and calmed me down, setting up a vocal mix with Chris Minto, the engineer. Keith came back at that point. I went back into the booth and cut the vocal. Whether or not he was completely ready to take on the task, Spyder stepped up. Whatever anxiety he had about his producing talents was put aside for the good of that record. He knew it was going to be up to him. He continued his technical education on running the board with Chris Minto, taking everything that he'd learned from Pete Coleman and Mike Chapman and becoming a producer. Spyder never left the studio again.

As things progressed, Olsen showed up less and less, and when he was there, he was often asleep on the couch. Eventually we came to learn that his apparent disinterest stemmed from problems in his personal life that kept him perpetually distracted. It was unfortunate for all of us that it had to happen during our record. It wasn't that he was a bad person; he'd simply gotten himself into a situation in which it was hard for him to maintain his professional duties and sort through the problems he was facing elsewhere. When he saw that Spyder could handle things and that we were capable of doing what needed to be done, he left us to it. Still, Spyder's presence was no excuse for his detachment. We were all professionals, and we were supposed to be able to put personal things aside to get the job done. As the artists, it was certainly expected from us on a daily basis. He'd been hired to produce an album, not deal with his shit. Maybe the absentee-landlord technique works with some artists, but I loathed it.

It wasn't a good way to make a record—in fact it was downright awful. But as maddening as his disconnection was, there was a silver lining. It forced us to mature musically and vocally, while also thrusting Spyder into a job he was born to do. More than anything else, though, it cemented my relationship with Spyder in ways that neither of us could have predicted. Things had been intense between us since the beginning, but dealing with the emotional drain of recording that second album deepened our connection in ways that Chrysalis would come to regret. Now more than ever before, we were partners in this. Everything I did belonged to him as well. Peter Coleman commented that he had never seen two people who connected musically like we did. It seemed like we were one person split into two.

Despite the drama with Olsen, those sessions led to some incredible material. Spyder might have just been starting out as a producer, but as musicians everything we were doing seemed to fall into place. "Hit Me with Your Best Shot" was a song that had been originally pitched to Rick Derringer. Spyder had liked it and kept a copy. It was written by Canadian writer/artist/producer Eddie Schwartz, and it would become his first big songwriting chart success. Chrysalis also had a copy of the song, and they pitched it to us. Spyder thought the song was catchy, but the demo didn't really show its potential. He started working with the band while we were still in New York and had his own demo version by the time we got to Los Angeles. So this session came together quickly. Even though it was pivotal in propelling the album, I always joke about how much I hate this song. It comes from its being played incessantly when it was released.

Given our schedule, it's surprising that any of us in the band were able to write anything for *Crimes of Passion*. In addition to the group effort that produced "Hell Is for Children," Spyder wrote "Little Paradise," and the two of us wrote "Never Wanna Leave You" and collaborated on "Out-A-Touch" with our drummer Myron Grombacher, who had come with us from the first tour. He was Spyder's closest friend; they were like brothers. Myron was the perfect complement to Spyder's guitar style, bringing the forceful drum sound that Spyder wanted for the band. Together the three of us made up the sound that became our signature. Rhythm guitarist Scott St. Clair Sheets wrote "Prisoner of Love," and at Spyder's suggestion, we did Kate Bush's "Wuthering Heights" and Billy Steinberg's "I'm Gonna Follow You." We also did "You Better Run," written by Eddie Brigati and Felix Cavaliere of Young Rascals fame, which had been one of the songs I used to sing when I was on my own.

Listening to the playbacks was enough to give you chills. After all the stress and horrible shit we went through recording this record, we'd done it. We'd made the record we needed to make despite all the obstacles. *Crimes of Passion* reflected more of what we were about than *In the Heat of the Night*. Between Spyder stepping in on the production end and our live band hitting its stride, it had turned out to be a *great* recording. The band was solid and intense. Every one of them understood the sound that we wanted and delivered it.

When we were finishing the album, I told Chrysalis that I thought Spyder should be listed as co-producer on the record. After all, he'd done a lot of the work. I kept telling them that it wasn't fair to have him step in and save the record, then act like he'd done nothing. Not only did the label say no, but surprisingly Rick Newman agreed with them. When I asked Rick why, he was blunt:

"Keith Olsen won't hear of it. Keith never shares producing credit with anyone." And just like that it was an across-the-board decision. I was dumbfounded. After the way he'd abdicated his role during recording, the arrogance of this was intolerable. Olsen knew what had gone on, how he'd stepped aside and let Spyder do his job. Olsen knew that everyone in the band had witnessed his abandonment of this project, but he didn't care. He was shameless. There would be no production credit for Spyder. Olsen had said no, and my manager and my label refused to back me up. I was livid.

While Chrysalis's lack of support was nothing new, seeing Newman's lack of support left me disappointed and confused. Suddenly my eyes were opened to how allied Newman was with the record company. In his mind, he was making necessary compromises, but I felt betrayed and angry.

When I started out in New York, I might have been young and somewhat naïve, but I was never ignorant enough to trust just anyone. I knew enough to be skeptical of people and keep my guard up. But once I let you in, that was it: I trusted you. And that was the case with Newman. For years he'd shown himself to be someone I could rely on. He was a guy I expected to have my back. Now it was like I'd fallen off a turnip truck, a girl from Long Island with no concept of how the world worked or that your own people see you as simply a cash cow.

I never saw this one coming. All at once, the harsh reality of the music business began to rear its ugly head. Of course, I'd seen it at a distance since the beginning through my run-ins with Chrysalis, but this was different—more personal. Sadness and disappointment turned into defiance and contempt. I don't like confrontation and neither does Spyder. I'm normally an easygoing person. Just don't cross me. And absolutely don't try to hurt someone I love, because then I will jump right in the ring. I'd had balls ever since I was growing up with all those neighborhood boys, but this was different; this new level of vileness would have taken more than anatomical correctness. They were officially the enemy, and this was going to take unrelenting retaliation.

I said fine, if not production credit, then production payment. If not, then they could put the album on the shelf. Chrysalis didn't like paying money, but they also didn't like losing money. Shelving that album would have cost them, because after the success we'd had with *In the Heat of the Night*, they knew this album could be even bigger. So that was how the battle was won. Spyder got no credit publically, but he did get paid for producing. Of course, neither Chrysalis nor Olsen would foot the bill to pay Spyder. In the end, his payment came out of *my* royalties. Olsen wouldn't even split the cost with me, and unbelievably, Newman went along with it.

It felt good for Spyder to be compensated, but it frayed relationships at all ends. I stayed mad and Spyder remained hurt. He didn't say much about it, but I knew he was. He's not the kind of person who demands praise or public recognition. He was never into self-promotion. It wasn't the credit that was so important to him; it was the principle of why they would treat him like that. To be denied that production credit was a slap in the face. It was an insult because it was coming from our own people. Furthermore, it's just not how either of us would have handled things. If the situation were reversed, we would have insisted the person be recognized for his work. No questions asked. Good work should be rewarded. That's how we were both raised, and that's how we wanted to do business.

This was the first time I started to understand just how different Spyder and I were from some of the suits in the music business. We were working-class people, with working-class standards. Treat us fairly and with some respect, and we'll work our butts off for you. In their world, we were just another revenue source. And to think my family was proud I wasn't punching a time clock. Working for this group of mercenaries was obviously nothing to write home about. I couldn't trust the label. When they had been haranguing us about our personal life, I'd hoped things might change. Clearly I was wrong.

THAT WAS JUST THE beginning of the shit storm.

For weeks, I'd been asking Chrysalis when they were going to set up a photo shoot for the cover. I couldn't figure out why they kept giving me the runaround and refusing to put something on the calendar. That started pissing me off, because I had some definite ideas about the cover. The label knew this. I'd told them that I wanted to capture the energy of the live show on the album cover. Remember, this was when we had large album covers, not CDs, and certainly not MP3s. You could really make an artistic impact with an album cover. Either a performance shot, or one of me and the boys. Either way, I wanted to establish what we were: a band. That's what I believed this album proved.

"Wait and see," label head Terry Ellis said.

Wait for what? I thought.

One day, while we were in the final stages of recording the album, Billy Bass, the head of marketing for Chrysalis, asked if he could come to our house to talk over ideas for the new album cover. It was a strange request, given that we still hadn't finished the record, we hadn't chosen a title, and I hadn't formally even told them what the album was about. Normally, you choose a title based on the content of the record, which in turn dictates what direction the artwork will take. You don't choose a cover in a vacuum. But that's precisely what they had in mind.

Billy came to our house that day with a stack of photos from a recent publicity session. Spyder was sitting with us and together we pored over the photos, all of which were of me in a tight tank-type top with skinny little shoulder straps. I didn't particularly like the pictures, but if they were just sending them out with a bunch of other press photos, I could live with that. He kept coming back to one in particular. Then he showed me a mock-up of the cover. It was the same photo.

While it was nice enough for what it was, it had absolutely nothing to do with anything. There was no link to the material on the record, and more important, there was no link to the collaborative process that had gone into making the record. My intention had been to elevate the band's position on the cover because they were such an integral part of what we were doing on the record. The cover art he brought that day only had photos of me—good photos, sure, but totally irrelevant to the content of the record.

Saying nothing about it to me, the label had picked a cover shot from these supposed publicity photos. I was stunned. How could you make an album cover with no relevance to what had been recorded?

"We haven't done a cover shoot," I reminded him.

"You're going to love it when it's finished," he said. The back of the cover mock-up was another shot of me. No mention of the band. No names. Nothing. Seated next to me, Spyder didn't say anything, but we could both feel the tension building. I took a minute to keep myself in check before I really lost it.

"This isn't going to work," I said after a long pause. "At the very least, there has to be a photo of the band on this cover." That was not what he wanted to hear.

"Do you have any idea how stupid and naïve you are?" he asked in his most patronizing tone. "No one wants to see the band. This is about you. No one cares about the band."

For a split second, I was speechless. *Did he really just say that out loud? With Spyder, a band member, sitting right here next to me?* It wasn't just the sentiment that surprised me. After all, everything the label had done told me they felt this way. It was the fact that he'd come here, to the living room that I shared with Spyder, and said those words to my face. In addition to being blatantly insensitive, it was disrespectful to both of us. There was absolutely no concern for Spyder and no concern for discretion. They were just dissing him to his face without an ounce of remorse. My anger, which had been building for weeks and months, boiled over. I threw him and his cover out of my house. We were done talking.

This was an issue for my manager to handle. It was his job to represent my interests in disputes with the label. Frustratingly, I got the same amount of cooperation on the cover issue as I had on the question of Spyder's production credit. None. Newman would not support me. Coming so soon on the heels of the producing debacle, I could see that he was caught up in record label politics. Something had changed. Newman was making the huge mistake of trying to stay neutral. He'd protect me only so far and stop short of offending them. While he did his best not to hurt me, he thought that he could straddle the middle ground without jeopardizing his relationship with either side.

As usual the only person forced to compromise was me. The front cover would remain of me alone, and the back would be a photo of the band. Contractually they had the advantage. Normally, after a success like we'd seen for our first record, the manager would have gone back in to renegotiate the artist's contract for the next album, giving the artist more control over things like artwork and song choice. For some reason, that never happened with us. Chrysalis had total control over this album cover, just as they did with the last one. I had no option but to keep the front cover they'd chosen, of me alone, and shoot the back cover with the band.

On the day of the photo shoot, the boys arrived dressed in the clothes they wore onstage, only to be told they were to change into the wardrobe some stylist had brought along. It was a bad day. The glammed-up outfits could only be described as lame. Rock and roll band? *Please.* The guys looked like they'd stepped out of the pages of GQ magazine. The expressions on their faces in that picture are priceless. They were all thoroughly disgusted. From then on, the band and I referred to what would become my biggest album as *Crimes of Fashion*.

It was too late to do anything about it, though. I didn't have one bit of control over what was done with regard to cover art, or much of anything beyond the music, at that point. I was the resident star, but that status got me nothing.

I like to think that I have a pretty good asshole detector. But I realized then that I had been dead wrong about Terry Ellis. I liked him very much when we first met at Tramps. He seemed like a stand-up guy, interested in me as a person and in my music. Instead, he was turning out to be one of the most arrogant and overblown men I'd ever met. And with the exception of our one ally, Buzzard, Terry surrounded himself with people who were just like him.

The label wasn't finished pissing me off. The biggest insult came as the new tour to promote the release of *Crimes of Passion* got started. I picked up a copy of *Billboard* in the Denver airport, knowing that Chrysalis had taken out a full-page ad to promote the album. With no advance warning, no hint of what was going on, I saw myself practically nude on the pages of the most important music trade magazine in the nation. I slammed the magazine shut and tucked it under my arm. I felt like I'd been raped.

They had taken the cover photo to the album and airbrushed off the tank top I was wearing. In its place, they'd put a sign over my seemingly nude chest that announced the release date of the new record. As if that weren't enough, they'd also given me a boob job. So I was not only naked, but naked with cleavage. I am a very small woman. I do not have large breasts (I only weighed ninety pounds back then). In fact, I'm damn near flat chested and that's just how I like it. But they'd drawn on breasts and cleavage, which was insulting and humiliating.

I kept thinking, *Who approved this? Not me.*

Aside from being embarrassing, the photo was stupid. Didn't they understand that people already knew how I was built? All people had to do was take one look at me and they'd know I didn't look like that. Were *Billboard* readers suddenly going to flock to my album because I'd miraculously grown new breasts? It was sexism at its worst, and I immediately broke down. Months of stress, exhaustion, and frustration came pouring out of me. I'd been going nonstop for so long. I'd toured relentlessly and promoted as hard as anyone could. In the face of numerous obstacles, I'd recorded an album that I knew had enormous potential. I was on the cusp of something great, but in that moment, all I felt was shame.

I called my parents. I had to prepare them.

"I don't know if you've seen it," I began, "but I promise you that I am not naked in *Billboard*!"

I was a long way from short skirts and matrons now.

CHAPTER FOUR

ROCK AND ROLL'S DIRTY LITTLE SECRET

CHRYSALIS'S PROMOTIONAL TACTICS FOR *Crimes of Passion* may have been questionable, but the music was a stratospheric success.

Crimes of Passion was both a critical and a commercial smash, with a lot of journalists picking up on what we'd been trying to do, pointing to the hard-rocking grit and interplay between vocals and guitars. It sold over a million records just on the strength of the debut single, "Hit Me with Your Best Shot," on its way to sales of over five million. *Billboard* pronounced me dominant among female rockers. The album was nominated for a Grammy award for Best Rock Performance, Female.

On the heels of "Hit Me with Your Best Shot," "Treat Me Right" became the album's second hit single. Meanwhile AOR (album-oriented radio) started playing "Hell Is for Children," and the song got great reviews, including one from *Billboard* calling it "a stunning rocker." Given this initially warm reception, I couldn't have been more surprised when the song became controversial.

To support the album, we went out on tour that fall, and my first hint that anything was going on was when someone came backstage at a show and told me that there were some people picketing the venue.

The protest was over the use of the word "hell" in a song involving children. I was stunned. What was child abuse if not hellish? And with all of the things going on in the world, was a song exposing child abuse really something to protest? I had written the song believing that I was helping to raise awareness of a major social problem.

Thankfully, the negative reaction from this one group wasn't shared by many. By the time we came off the first leg of the tour, the management office was receiving mailbags full of thank-you letters from people who had been abused as children. I sat there on the floor and read every one of them. Most were from adults who said that it had meant so much for them to hear the lines "You shouldn't have to pay for your love with your bones and your flesh."

But despite the critical raves and the instant sales, the year after the release of *Crimes of Passion* turned out to be the worst of my life. It should have been a year of celebration, enjoying our success, and relishing that we were making music that people everywhere were embracing. Even though they loved what we'd done in the studio, the record label continued to mess with Spyder and me. Strange things started happening to Spyder when it came to things that Chrysalis handled. Spyder wouldn't get paid on time and would have to ask about his check. If the band members' names were listed on a marquee, Spyder's name might be left off. Often, he wasn't invited to meetings.

They treated him like dirt, and it was shameful. I could tell it was starting to wear him down, because it was also starting to wear me down. My desire for us to be seen as a band hardened even more. Over and over I was given the credit for what we were doing. And over and over I tried to counter that idea. I kept reminding everyone—the label, journalists, radio—that the success we were having was due to everyone, not just me. But people saw the name "Pat Benatar" and assumed I was the sole reason for the sound. This misconception was the gorilla in the room in our relationship, and I spent the next twenty years trying to undo this perception. (Today, after almost three decades, I finally feel that people know the real story of Spyder's contribution, but it's been a long, frustrating road.)

I wasn't the only one who believed Spyder was being treated shabbily.

In October 1980, the same month that "Hit Me with Your Best Shot" entered the Top 40 chart, *Rolling Stone's* Steve Pond noted that Spyder's position in the band appeared to be "tricky." Pond pointed out Spyder's significant involvement in the recording process, adding, "Not everyone wants his contributions publicized. On the back of her new album [*Crimes of Passion*], Benatar thanks him 'for all the heart and hard work in the Production of this Record. I love you.' But the current Chrysalis bio doesn't even mention that he writes songs."

The record label's attitude started to fray the relationship between Spyder and me. He began to believe that mixing personal relationships and a band *would* cause problems, just like Chrysalis had predicted. The frustrating part of it was that the label's treatment of us was causing trouble for the relationship; our relationship wasn't causing problems for the music. The real problem for them was that the difficulties with Olsen and *Crimes of Passion* had made us even closer than we were before. They couldn't get between us or around us. They lost whatever control they thought they had over me, and treating Spyder poorly was the closest they could come to payback.

This tension was fueled by the label's continued inability to back me up when I needed their support. I had interviews and visits to the local rock and roll station in every city we played. I could just about count on half of the deejays or program directors hitting on me, and not in a subtle way. I'd walk in and some jerk would pat his lap.

"You come right over here and sit down, honey. We'll see if we can't get that record played."

"Fuck you," I'd fire back. Suddenly I was back in the Roaring Twenties Café with the men chomping their cigars. Only this time, when I said, "Fuck you," nobody was laughing.

The label and Newman were in hysterics.

"You can't say 'fuck you' to radio people!"

"The hell I can't. I just did." I never had to put up with that shit from my band. I never had to put up with that shit from guys at Catch a Rising Star or other places I'd played early on. Why would I put up with that trash from some radio guy?

But Chrysalis didn't see it that way. There was a double standard for women in this business and they were all too willing to remind me of that. If a guy said "fuck you" to someone it was rock and roll; for a woman to do it was disrespectful. This was rock and roll's dirty little secret: it was 1980, the women's movement had been around for almost twenty years, and yet overt sexism and misogyny were alive and well. With all its posturing as a crusader for liberal beliefs, the music business was overrun with chauvinism.

There were so many different ways that the issue would rear its ugly head. While there were the blatant things, like my image and being harassed by radio DJs, it was also more subtle. We'd be pushing to get airtime for our songs, and radio programmers would say things like, "We'll definitely put the single in heavy rotation at the end of the week, but we can't right now. We're already playing a single by a girl." When the guys at radio stations weren't hitting on me, they were bringing out some sexy poster and wanting me to sign it to them, to write some personal note. I knew they didn't do that with the male rockers who visited their stations, and I was livid.

I've sometimes heard people say that I was exaggerating about this. Maybe it wasn't happening to them. Maybe their people did a good job of insulating them from what was going on. I can only speak for myself and my experience, but it was happening to me on a daily basis and I was out there alone. No matter what I was doing, the sexual implication was always there. I wondered what would happen if I uglied myself up—quit wearing the tight pants, put a jacket on. The whole idea of being a pretty girl who could sing wore on me.

While I was well aware that the sexy image was something I'd created, I never meant for it to be the focal point. What I wanted was the image of the attractive-yet-capable woman that I had made up. My problem was not that people thought I was sexy, it was that Chrysalis *only* wanted the sexy part. It was offensive but also boring—typical of most men's thinking in postfeminist America.

I started to question whether I was cut out to be a star. Celebrity can be a terrible thing. Your life is no longer your own. Boundaries that were once respected are torn down. And if that happens quickly, it is overwhelming. Now before you start that "poor little rock star, five million records sold and she has to sign a few autographs" shit, understand this: sudden stardom really is difficult. Anyone who says different is lying. That doesn't mean it's not fun or totally worth it, but no matter how much you want to be in the public eye, no matter how grateful you are to have been given the opportunity, nothing, and I mean nothing, can prepare you for celebrity. It changes your life in ways you can't predict. It happens so quickly that you spend all of your time trying to adjust and all of your energy goes into finding a graceful way to navigate this new addition to your life.

I was clueless that we'd become celebrities until it was so blatant it was unavoidable. It was all happening so fast, and I was too busy rehearsing, doing press, and performing to really take notice. But we were playing a show in Gainesville, Florida, that fall when I learned just how strange this whole fame thing could make people act.

It was right at the beginning of the *Crimes of Passion* tour, and with only one other tour under our belt, we were relatively new at this. Gainesville is where the University of Florida is located, and we were staying in a hotel not far from the school. We hadn't yet graduated to the Four Seasons or the Ritz Carlton, so the hotel was a pretty cheap setup. The morning of the gig, we woke up, took showers, and went off to the venue, where we spent most of the afternoon tucked away in our dressing rooms. Eventually one of our crew members went outside for a smoke and noticed a tent that was set up in the parking lot with a sign that read, "Pat Benatar Souvenirs." Curious, he walked over to see what it was about.

Lying out on a table were little pieces of fabric and other odds and ends—not much to look at, let alone buy, but then he found out where they came from. It turned out that some college kids bribed the front desk at our cheap hotel to find out what room we'd stayed in. They unscrewed the windows, snuck in, and stole our bedding and our trash. They had cut up the sheets and pillowcases we'd slept on into little squares and they were selling them. They were also selling our garbage—old Kleenex, used Q-tips, and razors. Of course, management went out and confiscated everything, but they'd already made a good amount of cash.

Needless to say, the change of public awareness that we'd felt during the tour for *In the Heat of the Night* was nothing compared to what happened after "Hit Me with Your Best Shot" was released. Photographers hid out everywhere. You start to feel like you are being chased every time you leave the house. It was especially hard for me, because I never wanted to be rude to *anyone*.

And that was the trouble: I remained the same person I had always been. Private. Polite. Generally accommodating. This wasn't just because of the speed with which fame had hit. It was just who I was. It was almost impossible for me to be a jerk to total strangers, to act rude or brush off people. Especially when I knew they were following me around because they were fans. I never wanted to act like an asshole. Still, the attention had driven me almost over the edge, and the breaking point drove up in the form of a VW bus.

We were at home in Tarzana between touring and promotional appearances. I got up one morning, threw on a robe, and walked outside to get the newspaper. A bunch of kids in a VW van jumped out and started taking pictures of me with flashes flaring. I was startled and felt invaded. This was my own house. I was in a fucking bathrobe.

I knew then that I couldn't live there any longer. I was going to have to find a secluded house, maybe in a gated community, a place where I could have some kind of privacy. Up until then I would have laughed at the idea of my having to live behind fences. But that's how quickly things were changing.

BETWEEN SPYDER BEING INSULTED, the sexed-up image problem, and the reality of fame, Spyder and I found ourselves increasingly on edge. For the first time since we'd come together as a couple, I felt a space opening up between us. We hadn't put it there, but that didn't matter—it was there nonetheless. I was going crazy trying to tour and fulfill the publicity demands. Every city meant more interviews, more radio visits, and more anger from me about being treated like a sex object. Chrysalis's only response was to tell me to keep quiet about it.

In many ways it was much worse for Spyder. For one thing, *Crimes of Passion* was being heralded as brilliant, and he was getting no credit for it. Continual slights from the label not only insulted him but hurt him. He is such a good-hearted, *nice* person. I'm very quick to say that he is *much* nicer than I am. Nice people feel things, whether they bitch about it or not. It's there. In addition, the celebrity angle was as hard for him as it was for me. When we were together, it was a circus. Spyder could still walk down the street, go to a store. But when I was along, it was a different story.

The tension between us began to mount more and more, eventually building to the point that when I was nominated for a Grammy Award, Spyder didn't attend the ceremony with me. The show, which honored work done in 1980, was held on February 25, 1981, at Radio City Music Hall in New York. Spyder didn't come with me, so Rick Newman escorted me instead.

I wasn't sure whether winning would be a good thing. The Grammy is a mainstream award, and back then some in the rock and roll world believed winning—or even being nominated—damaged your credibility. If you did happen to win, it was understood that you should not act too thrilled, or gush, or bounce up to accept the prize. At that time I was concerned about giving the appearance of selling out. I'd heard a few rumblings that some people thought we were a "corporate entity." Ridiculous as that was, getting that label would have been the kiss of death in rock and roll.

Establishment event or not, I was giddy that night. I "dressed up," wearing the outfit I would later wear on the cover of *Precious Time*—a purple coat with tight black pants. Although it was televised, the Grammys didn't have the red-carpet fashion show in those days, and no self-respecting musician would have participated if they had. That was just fine by me. My excitement dimmed somewhat when I got there and learned that the category I'd been nominated in, Best Rock Performance, Female, wouldn't be seen on the regular telecast. My whole family was watching.

Even though the rules of rock dictated that I wasn't supposed to act thrilled to be there, I was incredibly proud. More than anything else it showed how far I'd come in such a short time. A little more than two years ago, I'd been singing other people's music at Catch a Rising Star. Now I was there with the giants of the business, in an audience filled with many of the most talented and respected people in the industry. I wasn't starstruck (it's not my way), and while I was awed to be in that seat, I wasn't surprised. This was something I'd been working toward, something I'd planned all along. It was vindication, compensation for all the shit that the label had put us through.

Christopher Cross had historic wins. It was the first time any artist had ever won all four of the general categories: Record and Song of the Year for "Sailing," Album of the Year, and Best New Artist. Bette Midler won Best Pop Performance, Female, for *The Rose*. There was a pall over the night, though. The music community was still reeling from John Lennon's death on December 8, 1980.

That had been a horrible day. I had been at home in Tarzana when Myron called and told me the news. I immediately called Spyder, who was mixing a live performance at a studio in Hollywood. We were devastated. I turned on the TV and sat transfixed as the details emerged. This was happening in our peer group, our music community; unlike Elvis, who had died a few years earlier, Lennon was our contemporary. Making things harder was the fact that I adored Lennon. My earliest memories of music were tied to him. He'd been a regular part of my musical life ever since I got that red transistor radio for Christmas. I loved his voice. All throughout high school, as I'd been learning to sing, I'd always felt the impact of how he performed. I don't think there was anyone making music then who wasn't influenced by him (and there probably isn't now). It was an emotional night for everyone who cared about what he'd done for music.

I had a terrible migraine on Grammy night. Flying often gave me awful headaches, and this was no exception. The medication that I took for these headaches was administered with a shot, which had made me sick to my stomach on top of the headache. Before the awards started, I went into the bathroom and threw up. As I crouched there over the toilet, I heard someone else in the bathroom, and it jarred me.

Oh no, what if they think I'm doing drugs? I can hear it now: "Pat Benatar must be an addict—she's throwing up in the bathroom."

I came out of the stall to find the previous year's female rock winner, Donna Summer, washing her hands. Donna cast a hard look in my direction.

"Ugh! You're just the person I wanted to see!" she said to me in an exasperated tone.

Oh crap. I didn't know Donna, had never even met her. What had I done?

"Why?" I asked.

"My kid plays that record of yours every minute of the day! I know every word of it, and to tell you the truth, I'm sick of it!" She said it with a smile.

I had to laugh, thinking of when I was a kid playing the Beatles and my mother had said almost the exact same thing. And it made me feel good knowing that I was pleasing kids and driving parents just a little bit crazy. It was the first time I'd heard someone complain that my music was being played too much.

By the time they announced the nominees for Best Rock Performance, Female, my headache was gone. I think it was the kid in me, the excitement, the anticipation. I was completely caught up in the whole thing. There was something incredibly satisfying about knowing that even after all the crap Chrysalis had done to make life hell, they couldn't spoil this moment. I'd found a way to keep the joy of it all locked away in a safe place, somewhere they couldn't touch. They read the names of the nominees: Grace Slick for *Dreams,* Marianne Faithfull for *Broken English,* Joan Armatrading for *How Cruel,* Linda Ronstadt for "How Do I Make You," and Pat Benatar for *Crimes of Passion.* They took the winner's envelope and opened it. "And the—"

"Don't be mad if I don't win," I whispered to Rick.

"—winner is Pat Benatar, *Crimes of Passion!*"

I bolted out of that chair like there was a spring up my butt. I went flying up to the podium, all worries about being seen as a sellout gone. I was so thrilled.

I was hyperventilating. All plans of being übercool and nonchalant vanished as soon as I heard my name. Looking back on it now, I can't remember exactly what I said, but I'm pretty sure I gushed—not exactly Sally Field's "You like me" speech, but probably close. Then, when I walked offstage, I took a real look at the award. It was set on a wooden block, but the little Victrola was plastic. I remember thinking, *Wow, plastic! That's kind of chintzy!*

Chintzy, maybe. But thrilling nonetheless.

⸎

CRIMES OF PASSION WAS still a top ten album in the spring of 1981 when Chrysalis started pushing us to get back into the studio for a new record. It was insane to think that we had to make a third album while the second one was still being promoted. We should have used the leverage we'd gained from *Crimes of Passion,* taken control, and avoided jumping right back into the studio. But once again Chrysalis invoked the suspension clause of our contract. They had the right to request a new record even though we were still promoting the last one. At least we were starting from a small base of material. We had a few songs that had been recorded but not used on the second record that we planned on carrying over to the new project. Unbelievably Chrysalis brought Keith Olsen back in to produce; however, this time they offered Spyder co-production, with producer credit and full pay. While Chrysalis had fought us every step of the way about giving Spyder credit, the irony was that they saw the talent that he had for producing. They loved his actual input, which was why it was so mystifying that they didn't want to acknowledge his contribution. Depending on how you looked at it, this was either a peace offering or a consolation prize, but it didn't hurt that he got his own attorney.

Even still, there was a lot of tension. Keith clearly had been forced to give Spyder the production credit and he was not happy about it. As a result, he did even less than he had on *Crimes of Passion.* On that record he at least had a façade of involvement. This time he was much more blatant about checking out. His attitude toward Spyder was basically, "You want to co-produce? Have fun, I'm outta here." In all honesty, we were glad. At least this time it was more up-front, and we knew how to react. Things ran much smoother in his absence.

The strange thing about recording this third album, *Precious Time,* was that I felt little of the pressure I'd experienced during the making of *Crimes of Passion*. With *Crimes of Passion*, I felt like I had to do something to top *In the Heat of the Night* and "Heartbreaker." Now, even with the strength of *Crimes of Passion,* I felt easier about the whole process. I had a lot of faith in the routine and collaboration we'd established on the first two albums, and now that Spyder's role in the process was clearly defined, things would move even more smoothly. Not to mention that the confidence that came from multiple successes was immeasurable. It wasn't that we were arrogant, but we finally trusted ourselves—no small thing in a business where instincts are usually the difference between a good record and a great one.

From day one, it was evident that Spyder appreciated going into the process on equal footing instead of simply being the lifesaver. As usual, he busted his ass in the studio. He was a perfectionist, sometimes recutting a song time and again before he was satisfied. The one time that Spyder's state of mind showed up on the album was on the reggae-flavored song "It's a Tuff Life." Here's how he explained it: "I really didn't like the things that were going on in Southern California at the time. More of the same hollow excess that seemed to permeate every aspect of the record business. Reggae seemed to fit the lyric—*You thought you'd move to Jamaica, so you packed your bags and headed south to get an even tan, But you didn't count on the rain.*"

I wrote more melodies on this album. I was sometimes reluctant to go for the melody because Spyder was so good at it. However, with "Promises in the Dark," I put together the whole melody with the exception of the bridge, though I was so new to songwriting that I wasn't at all confident about my skills. I was also embarrassed to write about anything personal; most of what I'd previously written was more observational. But this song was about our relationship. When I'd first written the lyrics, Spyder was working in the music room in our house, and I was so nervous to share them that I literally slipped them under the door and walked away. When I came back he told me how much he liked what I'd done, and we immediately began constructing the song.

This became our writing process, with one of us beginning an idea and giving it to the other one, then stepping away so that the other could put all the ideas together to complete the song.

The end result was a record that was more contemplative, more reflective, than either of the first two. Some of the songs are very long—but it's been called a masterpiece of layered, explosive rock and roll. And while the label worried about the length of some songs, they primarily cared that they had a couple of strong radio songs. They found them in "Fire and Ice" and "Promises in the Dark."

The recording, though, had taken its toll. By the time we'd finished the record, we were ready to move from the house in Tarzana, but both of us were unhappy—not as much with each other as with the situation. For such a long time, I would have laughed at the idea of anything coming between Spyder and me. Then one day, in the middle of our tour, Spyder sat me down and when he started talking, his words froze me.

"I love you so much, and I thought I was going to spend the rest of my life with you. I thought we were going to make a family together." He paused just long enough for me to fear the words that would follow. "But you know what? It's just too hard. It's killing me."

"What are you saying?" I asked.

"I don't know what I'm going to do. But I can't do this anymore."

I tried to talk to him, but he was adamant. He was getting killed emotionally. He said that he wasn't coming with me when I moved, that we'd still stay close and we'd keep the band together. But he just had to separate himself from the relationship.

I couldn't believe that this was actually happening, and I had no idea how it had gotten to that point. I felt I had no choice but to go ahead and move. I bought a house in a gated community there in Tarzana, and in February of 1981 I moved in alone. I knew that we were meant to be together, but the situation had driven a wedge between us—a wedge that it didn't seem we could move past.

In a little over six months I'd hit just about every high and low imaginable. The euphoria of having a bestselling record was now tainted by my crumbling relationship. I was devastated—pushed to the brink of a nervous breakdown. This was the man I planned to spend the rest of my life with, to have my children with. We had it all planned. Now there was no plan. Except that we would make this band work.

When we were in Los Angeles, Spyder came over every night for dinner. We talked about music, about what the album was doing. We talked about upcoming shows. We made small talk. But there was no outward display of emotion. It was like we were back to the beginning again, with every moment spent close to him my own private agony. The worst part was that instead of feeling like we were moving toward something, we were moving farther away, and I was unable to set things right. He was the person I knew I was supposed to be with. There was no doubt in my mind that without the drama of the music and the label, we would have been together. If we were both just punching clocks somewhere in the Midwest, everything would have been fine, but we weren't. As a result we couldn't be together, and we had no physical relationship. Neither of us wanted to be with anyone else, but we just couldn't be with each other.

Sitting alone at my kitchen table in Tarzana, I had no illusions about what had gone on here. They'd won this round. There had been many slights and signs of disrespect since I'd had that showcase three years earlier and signed on the dotted line, but I felt this one more acutely than anything that had come before. They'd hoped for a breakup all along, and now they finally had it.

PRECIOUS TIME WAS SET to release in late July 1981, right before we debuted on a new television concept, a game changer in the music industry. The first I heard about it was when Chrysalis approached us about shooting a live performance to be aired on a television channel that was to launch in August. It was called MTV.

"It's cutting-edge," they said. "You'll be one of the first bands on the air."

Be a guinea pig? Sure. I loved the idea.

It would be a performance video of the Rascals song we'd covered, called "You Better Run." It had been a hit when I was in junior high, and when I moved to New York, my friend Cynthia Zimmer, who had an extensive record collection, pulled it out one day when I was looking for cover songs to sing at Catch. I ended up working the song into my live show when I was trying to land a record deal. "You Better Run" was one of the tracks on *Crimes of Passion,* even though we'd recorded it previously for the soundtrack to the movie *Roadie.* Keith Olsen had actually produced "You Better Run" as his trial run for the fiasco that would become the *Crimes of Passion* sessions. Because everything had gone smoothly during that recording we'd agreed to have him on *Crimes of Passion.*

Because *Crimes of Passion* was still going strong on the charts, we decided "You Better Run" would be a good cut to use for our debut video. Everyone in the band was incredibly excited to be a part of this new method of bringing music to the fans—everyone, that is, except for Spyder. This was uncharted territory, and he wasn't exactly on board. His skepticism came from his concern that having a visual rendition of a song would interfere with the listener's personal interpretation. His reservations were partly responsible for the look and content of the video. There was no artsy story line, no imagery that might take you away from the music. This was going to be just like a live performance—nothing more.

We weren't told what to expect from the video shoot, just that it would be shot near the docks in the warehouses of Manhattan's far West Side. There was no stylist, no wardrobe direction. So I just wore my own clothes: black pants and a striped shirt. All we really knew going in was that it hadn't been tried before and that it was supposed to be cool.

When we got to the docks, I was immediately impressed by how well they had it lit at night. The set itself wasn't really a set—just the barren, stripped-down corrugated metal of the warehouse with a corner where we were supposed to perform—but it was exactly what we were looking for, especially in light of Spyder's desire for this to be as true to our performance as possible. With no set dressing, no costumes, and no elaborate distractions, it was all about us and the music.

As we were getting ready, the director walked over to us. "We're going to turn a fan on you, and I want you to just do what you do. Just *go*!"

That told me he didn't get what we did. I wasn't a freakin' runway model.

"What do you mean 'just go'?" I said. *Just go? I don't just go.*

"Well, you know, start posing and stuff."

I was horrified. This was new territory, and it was going to be on television. If this MTV thing was going to make us look foolish, then we'd have to take a walk. This guy didn't know us, didn't know our music, and almost certainly had never even seen us play. He didn't know that I was not someone who walked the catwalk and posed on command.

"No! No! No!" I shot back at him. "Here's the deal. We're gonna play and you are gonna film it. There's not going to be any blowing hair, and there's not going to be any *posing*."

The director agreed that we'd just play the song, which we did *several* times. Even though the director let us do our own thing, I still had a bad attitude. In the end, that attitude ended up helping me with my performance for the camera. It was the perfect visual for that song. I was pissed and it showed in everything I did that night. My sneers were real. It was a complete accident, of course. I was so young and raw then, and I felt like we were on the verge of a big crash and burn. But I definitely had a *fuck you* look on my face.

When MTV launched that August, we were the second video played on the inaugural day, right after the Buggles' "Video Killed the Radio Star." The Buggles were an all-male guitarless band, which made me the first woman and Spyder the first guitar player to appear on the network. That day, we were sitting in a hotel room in Oklahoma, where we were staying to play a festival called Rock-lahoma (I know . . .). Miraculously the hotel we were in had MTV. Someone joked that it was one of the five places in America that had actually signed up. We were lounging around when Newman called and told us to turn on the TV, and the entire band sat there and watched slack jawed as history was made.

Coming on the heels of the Buggles' video, ours made for quite the contrast. Whereas theirs was produced with effects and imagery that displayed the fantastical side of what a music video could be, ours was simple and straightforward. The grit and grime of the location where it was shot covered the TV screen, as did the fact that I was so pissed off when we'd shot it. I gestured at the camera, pointing aggressively as I moved around the frame. It was high energy but it was a different energy from a live show. The dissolves between shots and elements showcased every aspect of the band. It was aggressive but contained. It was our performance but also something else entirely. I'd never seen anything like it.

I don't remember how many videos of other artists they played that day or that first week, but it seemed like they played us round the clock, every hour, twenty-four hours a day. They didn't have a full rotation of videos, and back then there were no game shows, no reality shows on the channel—only music videos. After a certain point, they ran out of options and would cycle back to us. "You Better Run" was inescapable.

In one week, our world changed. After *Crimes of Passion,* I'd become much more recognizable, but it was nothing like what happened after MTV. To have a hit song on the radio was to have someone know your voice, your sound. To have a hit video was to have someone know your face. The semi-anonymity that we enjoyed was gone. We had officially arrived, and America had seen our faces—a lot. In the week that followed MTV's launch, I could no longer go to the grocery store or the movies, because I was swamped. People didn't simply look at me and think I looked familiar. They thought they knew me. It was great and awful, a blessing and a curse. There was no handbook on how to deal with that kind of stardom. Even musicians who'd hit it big on the radio never had to contend with their faces being everywhere literally overnight.

It was obvious that there had never been a promotional opportunity like this before in music. Even if you had great success, you could live a relatively quiet life because aside from touring and recording, the marketing options were so limited. MTV changed all that. Today, we take it for granted that video content is available anywhere you look—on the Web, on TV, on DVD. If you're an artist today, the ways that you can reach your fans without actually playing live for them are seemingly endless. But back then, communications were so archaic that this really was a revolution in how music was brought to the masses. The timescale on music success was suddenly more immediate than it ever had been. I was living proof.

CHAPTER FIVE

GETTING MARRIED—GETTING NERVOUS

THE TIMING OF MTV's debut could not have been better. The "You Better Run" video brought interest in us to a fever pitch and fueled the launch for *Precious Time*. It also kept the focus on *Crimes of Passion*, which had been going strong for almost a year and continued to sell about two hundred thousand copies a week. In all, *Crimes* was on the Billboard chart for ninety-three consecutive weeks, eventually selling over five million copies in the U.S. alone. Despite this massive success, it never got to number one, instead getting stuck in the number two spot on the *Billboard* charts, right behind John Lennon and Yoko Ono's *Double Fantasy*.

Although *Crimes* didn't reach the top spot, I'd made Chrysalis about $75 million and in the run-up to *Precious Time*, it was clear that I'd garnered more than enough clout to renegotiate my contract. After all the issues surrounding the marketing of *Crimes of Passion*, I knew that I had to get more control over my name and my image. I wanted the label to understand that I didn't like the confining role I was being given. Women had been rocking big since Janis Joplin—maybe there had been a lull in that of late, but we were still there doing our music.

And we didn't need airbrushed posters and ads selling someone who didn't exist.

There was definitely an old boys' club at work, and it was time to take a stand against the unlimited power the record company seemed to have over me. I wasn't becoming a crusader, though. I didn't think of it in political terms. Like any worker who's been pushed around by their boss, I felt that the label was holding too many cards. I was just like every other girl next door who wasn't getting the recognition she deserves. What was happening to me was happening to every other female in America. The only difference was that I was in a unique position to do something about it.

Before *Precious Time* came out, Newman tackled the long-overdue renegotiation of my contract, but unfortunately my moment to take a stand ended up as more symbolic gesture than actual power shift. For his part, Newman worked tirelessly on our behalf, but he was still trying to walk the fine line between doing his best for us and not ruining his relationship with the label. This impossible task overwhelmed him. While he'd learned a lot in his first couple of years on the job, he was still playing catch-up, and being in slightly over his head only made those tough negotiations even harder.

Sometimes his efforts were aided by the handful of good apples at Chrysalis who wanted to help us. One executive named Linda Carhart knew that Newman hadn't managed a music act before and she put her job on the line many times by giving him advice on how to navigate the negotiations. Likewise, the president of the company, Sal Licata, was always trying to help us find compromises. Sal was in the difficult position of having to run the company and be a "Chrysalis guy" while also being fair and nonconfrontational. Sal adored Spyder and was often one of the few advocates for him at the label. As someone who loved the music business, Sal hated all the bullshit that went on as much as we did. He did his best to referee, but he had to answer to Terry Ellis and Chris, so there was only so much he could do.

In the end, my advance, payment schedule, and royalty percentages were increased, though not as much as they could have or should have been. While I got more control over song choice and artwork, I would have to "mutually" agree with the label on both of those points. In other words, I was still bound to their opinions. They couldn't make unilateral decisions, but then again, neither could I. The one thing we didn't gain any ground on was the suspension clause. They still retained the right to ask for a new album every nine months—whether we were ready or not. Given our success, it felt like they were just throwing us a bone with these "more favorable" terms. I was confident that we could have demanded just about anything we wanted and gotten it. We were in the perfect position to put them to work for us, but for some reason, we didn't.

This relaxed attitude toward the negotiations was frustrating. We didn't push for as much creative control as we could have, and I couldn't understand why we were taking such an accommodating approach. When I would press Newman and my attorney, Owen Epstein, they always had some elaborate explanation as to why we couldn't ask for more. I should have held my ground with my team and pressed the case, but I didn't. Back then, I could only see the situation as a confusing problem that I'd grown sick of. I was tired of fighting. Terry played hardball, and though Newman did the best he could, in retrospect I never should have acquiesced.

Still, heading into the release of *Precious Time,* there was no doubt that we'd made strides. The cushion of success that we'd earned was enough to make everyone relax a bit. Spyder was getting a production credit, and because of our negotiations, the *Precious Time* cover did not elicit the same knock-down, drag-out fight. We weren't novices anymore; we had proven ourselves completely. I was being called the "reigning Queen of Rock and Roll." For the first time since *In the Heat of the Night,* we were all actually getting along.

Of course, there were moments when the worst would come out

and the blatant sexism in the company would be readily apparent. Every few months, they held meetings with all of the execs to discuss strategy, marketing, and future album plans with us. Not long before *Precious Time* was released, we were at one of those meetings discussing ideas for a video—which song, who should direct, what the budget would be. It was a business discussion between eleven other people and me. Linda Carhart and I were the only females in the room, so I wasn't surprised when one of the marketing guys leaned across the table lasciviously and said, "What are you gonna *wear*?" his voice lingering on the word "wear" as he licked his lips like a predatory animal. *What was I going to* wear? We're in a business meeting talking about spending $350,000 on a promotional video and he wanted to know what I was gonna wear?

It was the same shit I'd had to deal with from the beginning; the only thing that was different was me. Instead of reacting with a crazed, militant response, I gave them reserved indignation. For a few seconds, I sat there silently, quietly looking at all of them with disgust at their behavior. Collectively they all shrank and became sheepish and apologetic. I stood up, accepted their apology, said, "Thank you, gentlemen," and walked out. Meeting over.

It didn't just feel good, it felt amazing. Finally, after almost four years of putting up with that crap, I was starting to take charge of my musical life. Not Newman, not my attorneys, not even Spyder—just me.

WHEN *PRECIOUS TIME* WAS finally released, it caught on quickly, becoming number one in the U.S. *Billboard* Top 200 chart and a Top 40 release in the UK. The first hit, "Fire and Ice," landed on the singles charts about the same time as the album release. "Promises in the Dark" came out a couple of months later in October. That single, too, was a Top 40 hit. The reviews were great. The *Los Angeles Times* called it "layered, fiery rock," even saying that one of our longest cuts, "Evil Genius," with its four-saxophone horn section, was an "epic" recording. It was clear to reviewers and fans that with our highly charged arrangements we were finally coming into our own.

Though only a few months had elapsed since our video for "You Better Run," we were all too aware that MTV's power and influence had grown exponentially. In that time, making videos had gone from a quirky, optional experiment to an essential part of a record release. Once the label knew what they wanted your first single to be, you had to plan and shoot the video that would accompany it. MTV was a force to be reckoned with and it could not be ignored.

We decided to do "Fire and Ice" and "Promises in the Dark" as performance videos. We rented a soundstage in North Hollywood and invited the members of the fan club, radio contest winners, and family and friends. With that crowd of people, we filmed a miniconcert. For the title cut, we did a concept video that was a story about a rich girl who was a prisoner in her own life. (Sound familiar?)

With our faces all over MTV and two hit records on the charts, we once again embarked on a tour, only this time, with me and Spyder broken up, things were much more complicated. Chrysalis's prediction came true: we made the tour a nightmare for the rest of the band. We argued, fought, and acted nothing like our old selves. It was like we were two different people. Even today Myron refers to that tour in support of *Precious Time* as the "Hell Is for Us" tour, "Us" being pretty much everyone who wasn't Spyder or me. As everyone came to learn, it is not that much fun touring with a warring couple. We fought constantly, and the band and crew were ready to commit a felony just to get us to stop. If it wasn't about the latest Chrysalis offense or insult, it was about an amorous fan thinking it was open season now that we had broken up.

As it became common knowledge that we'd split up, people's lecherous qualities came out. When Spyder and I had been dating, the girls in the audience who were crazy for him had always kept a respectful distance. Now they were exposing their breasts during our show. At one concert in particular, some obviously drunk girl in the front row opened her blouse during our first set and proceeded to bleat, "Neil, Neil," for the entire show. Occasionally she'd put her hands onstage, and when we got to the show's closer, "Heartbreaker," I stepped on them and stood there until the song was over just to shut her up.

Spyder didn't have it much easier. I was constantly being approached by men in one way or another, and it took massive amounts of restraint on his part not to react. There were many nights onstage that Zel had to hold Spyder back from using his guitar as a baseball bat on some overzealous male fan. Guys came out of the woodwork with no rhyme or reason, thinking that I was fair game because I was single. Even my attorney, Owen Epstein, hit on me, which was just creepy.

Everything was torture. That tour was the only time I ever trashed a hotel room. Spyder and I were arguing, and I was screaming at him about one thing or another. We were both raging mad, and I went into the bathroom and slammed the toilet seat down, breaking it in two. I was horrified! It stopped the argument cold. It was such an out-of-character moment, but in an instant we both could see just how bad things had gotten. I'd like to think that all that tension made us rock harder, but we all could have done with a little less rock and a little more peace.

What made it harder was that I loved the road. Live performance was the reason I started singing and will always be my first love. I was never one of those musicians who dreaded the rigors of tours. People would ask me all the time if touring was difficult, and I'd tell them, "Life is hard, the road is easy." Under most circumstances that's true. Being on tour allows you to step away from everything in life and just focus on performing. On tour I'd sleep until noon, have room service, wear black leather, put on lots of makeup, perform, hear people cheer for me, get on the bus, travel to the next city, and do it all again. I'd show up to packed arenas and sing my heart out for people screaming my name. I'd see the enthusiasm in the faces of the fans in the swirling mass of the crowd, and I'd work as hard as I could to give them everything I had each night. There was no reality involved and that was the whole point. For twelve weeks, you could step away from your problems and return to the life that began it all.

That is, unless your problems happened to be on the bus beside you looking incredibly hot and emotionally distant, while reminding you that you never should have broken up in the first place. The fact that we'd had no downtime and no break from each other only exacerbated things.

There were funny moments on that tour, though. One night, we were playing a huge indoor venue when we had something of a Three Stooges moment with Myron. His drum setup that year included a cage and a large gong on a stand. Myron was a little guy, wiry and compact, probably 124 pounds soaking wet. We were playing the encore, and "Promises in the Dark" had a lot of breaks and rhythmic stops. The ending of the song had us playing a crescendo and Myron was supposed to blast the gong just before the last note.

Myron was a brilliant drummer and an amazing showman—well known for his acrobatics on stage. He'd routinely climb all over his drum set like a deranged red-haired monkey. As the end of the song drew near, he positioned himself on the gong stand in anticipation of delivering the final downbeat. The gong was *much* bigger than he was, and it certainly weighed more. He swung the mallet as hard as he could and hit the gong, and when it swung backwards, he turned to face the audience, raising the mallet triumphantly in the air.

While he was facing the audience, the gong swung back, knocking him off the drum riser and onto the stage. He was out cold. We too were facing the audience with our backs to him, so we didn't even know anything had happened until we heard scuffling. Zel, Spyder, and I turned around to see Myron lying on the ground, unconscious, with his drum tech and assorted crew members waving towels and throwing water on him. Like a badass, he woke up and immediately staggered to the drums to play the final beat and end the song. In spite of what had happened, the whole scene was pretty comical, not worrisome at all. Not to mention it displayed exactly the kind of dedication we'd come to expect from Myron.

But that laughter and camaraderie came sparingly. By and large, the only time that we put the fighting with each other on hold was when we were dealing with the label. We would make this band work even if that meant that we couldn't be together. Even if we fought on the road, we'd do the right thing when it came to dealing with the label: put personal problems aside for the good of the whole. We argued our case together, stood up to them when we felt they were being unfair. Spyder and I are both Capricorns, confident, driven, and goal-oriented. When we are working toward something we can get tunnel vision. And we are very loyal people. Chrysalis made us dig our heels in. When we did have to meet with any label executives, we didn't walk in with Pollyanna attitudes, thinking everything was going to be sweetness and light. We knew better and we went into warrior mode, together.

Still, we were all too aware that the status quo was not sustainable. Neither one of us said anything about it but we both knew that something had to change. We just didn't know what.

AT THE END OF 1981 and early 1982, following the tour for *Precious Time,* we were finally able to take a few months off. For the first time since we started making music, we were on break. It turned out to be the best thing we could have done. Spyder produced the first solo album of British rock singer John Waite, who had made a name for himself with the Babys. For all the fights that we'd gotten into with Terry Ellis about Spyder's contribution and credit, Terry was incredibly pleased with Spyder's output and he recommended that Spyder produce John's solo debut for Chrysalis, called *Ignition,* which had the hit single "Change." Spyder had also started working on some songs with Billy Steinberg, whom we'd collaborated with on *Crimes of Passion* and *Precious Time.* Our friend and drummer, Myron, was featured on *Cat Dance,* an album from Outlaw's guitarist Freddie Salem.

While Spyder continued to work, I was ready to relax. After three records and three tours in two and half years, I was just fine being a domestic goddess for a while. I stayed home and remodeled the house I'd bought after Spyder and I broke up. I went back east to visit family and friends and, of course, Spyder. Spyder spent December in New York working on *Ignition,* while I stayed in California. We were miserable apart, so for my birthday on January 10, I went to New York to see him. We had dinner and talked but didn't get back together. When I flew back to Los Angeles we were still in exactly the same position, with both of us thinking, *Enough is enough.*

We were tired of being confused. I remember telling one journalist that it had come down to the career or our relationship, that to save the band we had to make a choice. If we kept on trying to be a couple, the band could have been doomed. We had spent the last year fighting and struggling with our relationship. We both thought that we simply *had* to go back to being friends instead of former lovers, and the only way to do that was to move on with our lives.

About the same time, we both decided to see if we could have a relationship with someone else. It wasn't something that we discussed with each other—we just did it. I went on one date, as did Spyder. I had a nice enough time on my date and Spyder enjoyed his. But throughout the night, I couldn't escape just how wrong it felt. I didn't want to be having dinner with someone else, I wanted to be having dinner with Spyder. As it turned out, he'd experienced the same thing. He called me the next day, and when I told him I'd been out with someone else, his frustration bubbled over.

"What are you doing?" Spyder asked.

"What do you care? And what have you been doing?" I answered accusingly.

"Nothing that matters. I care about you," he said.

"Really? You could've fooled me." I didn't want to hear this. I'd finally made up my mind that I was going to forget him, try to start over.

"I'm sorry," he said quietly. "I love you. I want you to come home."

I couldn't believe what I was hearing. It had been an entire year of pretending we didn't care about each other, an entire year of fighting every day, an entire year of hoping he'd change his mind and come back to me. It seemed too sudden, too perfect to be true. But that didn't stop me from jumping on the first available flight to New York.

The whole flight, I kept telling myself how crazy this was. My rational levelheadedness had once again abandoned me, thanks to Spyder. It didn't make any sense. After all, how could we heal the year of pain and hurt that we'd caused each other with a phone call and a visit? The yelling and the screaming, the hurt feelings and nights spent sulking alone in our hotel rooms? I wanted to believe it was true, that we really could do it, that we were strong enough and important enough to each other spiritually and creatively to make that happen. But I didn't know for sure—that is, until I saw him at the gate, holding a bouquet of flowers. That was when I threw caution to the wind.

At first, we just held each other, spending the day like awkward teenagers reunited after a prolonged stay at summer camp, talking and laughing—just enjoying each other for the first time in months. Ironically, it happened to be Valentine's Day, a holiday that both of us abhor, yet there was no doubt it would be a Valentine's Day to remember: after many hours of conversation, we decided to get married.

We didn't waste much time. The next day we went shopping for rings. Once our minds were made up we threw ourselves completely into it and never looked back. Just like that, the last year, all the tension, all the fighting, had been erased. Myron and his wife, Monica, were the first people we told.

"Good," Myron said. "No, wait, this isn't just good, this is great. We're so happy for you." Listening to his voice, I knew that his enthusiasm was real. He knew that this was not the latest saga in the drama between Spyder and me. This was the end, and he could hear it in my voice. He and Monica were our best friends. They knew Spyder and I belonged together, and many times over the last year, they'd been forced to sit idly by as we'd struggled. It had been painful for them to watch us go through all that—not to mention stressful to see the ways that we'd jeopardized the band. For everyone, it was a huge relief that we'd finally come to our senses.

We felt defiant when we informed Chrysalis we were getting married. I was ready to tell them to fuck off if they started their negative talk again. This time, though, they realized that there was absolutely nothing they could say or do to change our minds, so all of a sudden they did an about-face and started offering to help foot the bill—ordering Dom Pérignon and toasting us like they'd been behind us the whole time.

Neither of us wanted to get married in Los Angeles or New York. Spyder wanted a small ceremony in a remote place, and I'd already done that twelve-bridesmaid, two-hundred-and-fifty-guest wedding. We wanted this to be altogether different and decided to be married right away in Tahiti. However, as soon as I spoke with our travel agent, Diane Nardizzi, I knew we had a time problem. The Grammys were coming up on February 24 at the Shrine Auditorium in Los Angeles, and I was nominated for a second Grammy, this time for "Fire and Ice." Traveling to Tahiti, getting married, and having time even for a short honeymoon would be tight if we were going to be back in time for the ceremony. I explained that, primarily, we wanted the wedding to be private and in some beautiful spot—it didn't have to be Tahiti. We just had to be back in L.A. by the twenty-fourth.

Diane had a solution:

"There's a town on Maui, a little tiny place called Hana. You can't get much more private than that. It's way off the beaten path. My client Kris Kristofferson owns some property there, and according to him it is one of the most beautiful places on earth."

Diane made the arrangements. I flew back to L.A., and Spyder followed me the next day. We'd only been to Hawaii once before, and that was to Oahu to play the Blaisdell Arena. Having no idea how small and remote Hana was, I just assumed I could buy a dress when I got there, but at the last minute, five P.M. the night before we were leaving, it occurred to me to pick up something to wear, just in case. I went to Robinsons-May and bought a little white lace dress off the rack for $82. That's the OCD in me—*just in case*.

I had never been anywhere in Hawaii but Honolulu, so I didn't know what to expect as far as our travel accommodations were concerned. Not only did we have to charter a small plane to fly us there, but there were only a few hours that it was available. We flew from Honolulu to Kahului on Maui at night, and as we got closer, I could see the water lit by the moon and felt us getting lower and lower, to the point that I thought, *Oh my God, we're gonna crash*. Then all of a sudden, just as it felt like the bottom of the plane was going to touch the tips of the trees, the pilot clicked a remote and this little runway lit up, a stunning strip of white light beaming out of the darkness of the jungle.

There was a warm breeze, and the trees smelled fresh from a rain. The moon came out from behind a cloud, and we could see that the airport was really just a little kiosk in the cane grass. Barreling toward us was a small, old-model red bus that kicked dust into the air as it wound its way down a little road. Clearly this was our transportation to the hotel. We were hooked.

The Hotel Hana-Maui, originally named the Ka'uiki Inn, was built in 1946 by a cattleman named Paul Fagan. It literally saved the town of Hana. When the last of the sugar plantations closed, the entire area suffered. That's when Fagan got the idea to build a small but luxurious hotel to try to attract tourists. When he got a baseball team to hold their practices in the area, it created jobs not just at the hotel, but throughout the village. The Hotel Hana-Maui was a luxurious 1950s-style hotel, not Beverly Hills luxury, but better. There was a definite *Kon-Tiki* Pacific Rim atmosphere, old Hawaii. Spyder and I stayed in the Manager's House, a small addition that was even more private than the hotel and had a private pool. Our room had this wild and colorful Hawaiian-print wallpaper, woven mats hanging on the wall, and beautiful fresh flowers and linens. Every detail felt like paradise.

The woman we talked to about wedding arrangements was named Mary Estrella. From the moment we introduced ourselves, we knew this had been the right decision. Our names meant nothing to her. *Nothing.* After dealing with fame for the last three years, we were only too ready to be anonymous. The best thing of all was that even if the people in Hana *had* heard of you, they didn't care about it. All Mary Estrella really knew about us was that we were there to get married. She handed us a huge ring of keys and told us we'd need to look around to find the place where we wanted our ceremony.

"Why do we need keys?" I asked.

"'Cause you gotta go through the pastures, and we don't want to let the cattle out. Just lock the gates as you go around."

Oh yeah. We were in the right place.

"We've got three churches," she continued. "But people like to get married on the land. You can just look around."

So the next day we went looking. There are about seven hundred people in Hana, mostly local Hawaiians. For tourists visiting Maui, the road to Hana is a popular trip and people are welcomed to the town Hana-style. But because most people only stay for an hour or so and drive back the same day, it's still very quiet and peaceful there. Things are done in the old ways. There are no car washes, no dry cleaners, no movie theaters. The people grow their own vegetables and hang their clothes on a line outside. There are no streetlights. Cattle wander around in the streets, and if they are in your way, you just stop the car and let them take their time. People are never late because of traffic (if they are on a time schedule, which they rarely are); if someone is late, it's because of cattle standing in the road.

Just being around the town on that first day, we could tell that this was a truly special place. In the last three years, we'd been around the world, stayed in countless hotels, flown on planes, driven around on buses, but we'd never been to a place like this. It was a place without complications, without egos. A sacred place where we could finally catch our breath—even if only for a few days.

Spyder and I spent the next two days driving around in a little Jeep, looking for a place to get married. We looked everywhere, not because we couldn't find the perfect place, but because it was so beautiful we wanted to search out every pasture, unlock every gate. We saw several mountains—every cliff, waterfall, stream, pond, and hallowed spot. Finally we decided on a site by the Leho'ula cliffs.

Next, we needed to meet with Reverend Henry Kahula, the minister of the nondenominational Wainanalua Church. Spyder and I are both Catholic, but since I had gotten a divorce, we knew that no priest would marry us. Henry Kahula had two jobs. He was both a minister and a mechanic at the only gas station in Hana. Mary Estrella told us how to find him.

"You go on down to the Chevron station and look around. He'll be there."

So we walked in and called his name. He rolled out on a dolly from underneath a truck. Henry Kahula was a big man with huge hands and a big smile. Still stretched out on the dolly, he told us he was only too happy to officiate, just needed a few details, like what time, if we had witnesses, and whether we wanted a Hawaiian ceremony. We explained that we'd already asked a couple of people who worked at the hotel, Louisa Pu and Les Mederios, to be matron of honor and best man, and that yes, we'd love to have a Hawaiian ceremony. The best part was, Reverend Kahula never got off the dolly during the entire conversation.

There were no stores in Hana to shop at for wedding-appropriate dresses, so I wore the white lace dress I'd brought with me. I married the love of my life wearing an $82 dress, and it couldn't have been more perfect. Spyder and I both had leis around our necks and *po'o* garlands of flowers on our heads. We had flower petals from the local gardens strewn around on the cliff. It was a spectacular day for a wedding. The sun was shining over Maui. The birds were flying and waves were crashing against the cliff. It was February 20, 1982, and we both knew that we would forever be tied to that island paradise.

We stayed at the Hotel Hana-Maui for a couple of days of honeymooning, loving the isolation and each other. It was amazing to realize that we were married at long last and that we'd moved so quickly to put the past year of separation behind us.

Flying back to Los Angeles for the Grammy awards, a jolt of reality began to set in. Of course it was thrilling to be there, but for the last week we'd been as close to paradise as either of us ever had been—both literally and spiritually. Returning home to an awards show would be a cruel awakening. At least this time, Spyder would be there to kiss me if I won.

I wish I could say that the Grammys were great that night or that it was fun for Spyder to attend, but we were so distracted by the euphoria of the last six days that the mad dash largely overshadowed the Grammys. It had nothing to do with the awards; with the exception of each other, *everything* in our lives was trivialized by the fact that we were back together. All we wanted was to insulate ourselves for a few days. Having to participate in an awards show was surreal—a strange juxtaposition of the conflicting agendas of our public responsibilities and our private lives.

Even though I won that night, I don't remember much that happened. We were both jet-lagged and dressed up, and Spyder was miserable in his monkey suit. He was still smoking back then and was fidgeting because he couldn't grab a cigarette. He wasn't the only fidgety one. Best Rock Performance, Female, still wasn't televised, and there was something unsettling to me about receiving an award that seemed tainted by that sexism. I was up against Stevie Nicks for "Edge of Seventeen," Yoko Ono for "Walking on Thin Ice," Lulu for "Who's Foolin' Who," and Donna Summer for "Cold Love." I was up against a bunch of talented, terrific women who knew how to rock. Why wouldn't they just put us on television? What was the problem? In the end I walked up to the podium, accepted the award with a smile, and thanked everyone I could think of—especially my band and my new wonderful husband.

John and Yoko won Best Album in the general category, for *Double Fantasy,* the same album that had kept *Crimes of Passion* in the number two *Billboard* spot. I was honored to present the award. We talked with a few people—Quincy Jones, Olivia Newton-John, Sheena Easton, and Billy Idol. We didn't go to any of the Grammy parties or socialize with any other artists after the ceremony. I know there was a lot of glitz there at the Shrine Auditorium that night, but we had eyes only for each other, and we just wanted to go home.

DESPITE THE DOM PÉRIGNON served up to celebrate our wedding, the record label's high-handedness did not change. Thankfully we did. Getting married gave us a renewed sense of power and purpose. By the time we went in to record *Get Nervous,* we knew exactly where we stood and where we wanted to be.

As far as *Get Nervous* was concerned, Chrysalis did one good thing at our request: they brought back Peter Coleman, the guy who'd helped start it all by producing "Heartbreaker." As a producer, we knew Peter to be a patient and inspiring teacher. On *In the Heat of the Night,* he'd created an atmosphere of limitless creative freedom and given us confidence in our own abilities. There'd been no worries about looking foolish or making a mistake. Everything was worth trying. Peter had no ego issues, and he was genuinely interested in helping us put on tape what we envisioned. He'd found ways to technically implant what we heard and felt artistically. Spyder, especially, thrived in that element, and this was largely responsible for how he'd been able to step in and save *Crimes of Passion.* In many ways, Peter was the perfect complement to Spyder. Spyder didn't have ego problems, either, and for him producing wasn't about control; it was about making interesting records, going on tour, and having a great time. He never understood the label's misuse of power, the way they treated their artists like they were second-class citizens.

Though Chrysalis brought in a producer whom we were excited to work with, they still kept trying to tell us what to do. For one thing, they argued over what songs we would record. Even with three albums to our name they continued to push us to material that had been written by other songwriters. We weren't opposed to considering outside material, but by this time we were writing a lot of good songs ourselves. Our goal was to keep honing those skills so that we could record songs that had relevance to our situation. We wanted to create art in musical form that belonged to us—not simply embellish someone else's ideas. As far as we were concerned, it was the next logical step. But as usual commerce took precedence over content for Chrysalis. We would never see eye to eye with them; we were artists, *they* were car salesmen.

We started with four of the songs Spyder and Billy Steinberg had written: "Anxiety (Get Nervous)," "Fight It Out," "The Victim," and "I Want Out." Because of the material we were cutting, Spyder decided to change our sound somewhat, following his instincts to wherever they might take him. He was born to produce records—obsessive, but never to a fault, though sometimes producing would take precedence over his playing and I'd have to remind him that he was the guitarist in the band. Still, the breadth of his musicality was staggering. He was like the mad scientist, always looking for new ways to push the envelope, always writing, always arranging. He'd get this look in his eye that asked, *Wanna come with me?* and I'd know there was something exciting up ahead. He never had to ask me twice.

He was constantly picking up influences from things that he was listening to, pushing boundaries and blurring lines together. For him, the only constant in our sound was that it was constantly evolving, growing to encompass more parts yet staying true to itself at the same time. He was a forward-thinker, never content to be in the moment and always curious about where we should go next.

As things progressed on *Get Nervous,* it became clear that several songs needed keyboards, so we made an addition to the band, Charlie Giordano. The vocals, too, were a big part of Spyder's vision for what this new sound would be, and he pushed me every step of the way, keeping my voice high and powerful. *Too* high for the live shows, I kept saying.

"Come on, this is easy in the studio—but what about when I'm running around onstage?" But he liked to test me vocally. I could be lazy, but Spyder knew what my voice was capable of and would not give in to my hesitation. I was always whining about the keys we recorded in and driving him crazy. Sometimes he wanted vocal performances that were so physically difficult I'd cut a session off abruptly and storm out. We'd duke it out, eventually coming to some kind of compromise, but he was always gentle and subtle. He'd coax rather than demand, ever the consummate coach tasked with convincing me that I had it in me all along. He might not have been as stern as my old German vocal teacher, but he definitely got the job done. I came to trust his judgment and made sure I was always ready for the next endeavor. Truthfully, he was usually right; these challenges to my voice were a big part of what made our records so intense.

Chrysalis kept at me, and it seemed like they just never stopped—it was one thing after another. I came to call it the gauntlet, because it felt like that was what I was running through. Every single day there was some new land mine I was dodging. One of the best examples of how off track the label was when it came to songs was the biggest hit from *Get Nervous*, "Shadows of the Night." This was a song that was written by D. L. Byron and first recorded by Rachel Sweet. But Myron and I rewrote many of the lyrics to make it work for me. We did get paid for our work but got none of the credit for being writers on a monstrous hit. That would not happen today. If an artist changes lyrics or adds musical licks, the artist is credited. People demand that.

When the record was nearing completion, I started thinking about the album's cover art. The last three covers had been pictures of me in a sex kitten pose, and *Get Nervous* seemed the perfect time to change all that. Spyder and I were godparents to Myron Grombacher's small daughter, Kiley, whom we all adored. When she was out on the road with us, she'd do this thing that we used to call "getting nervous." She'd clench her fists and strike a little pose. That phrase seemed to work perfectly with one song on the album, "Anxiety." So we not only titled the album *Get Nervous*, but we decided to do a radical cover to illustrate the point.

We scheduled a session, and I was made up to look *anything* but glamorous. The photo shoot took place in a padded room. My hair was really wild, maniacal. I was wearing bright red eye shadow. I looked seriously insane, and we loved the effect. Then we took band photos, with me in the demented mode.

When Terry Ellis saw the cover mock-up, it was his turn to go insane. He called me at the studio and immediately launched into it:

"What are you thinking? There's no way I'm going to accept this."

"Come on. It's great—not to mention different. Can't we just let loose for once, have some fun for a change?"

His response did not surprise me: "No."

I tried to explain to this man that I was sick of some people in the industry saying that my so-called "image" was all I cared about. I was sick of it myself, and this was a perfect opportunity to show some cheekiness. Continuing down the path of sex over substance would come back to bite us in the ass. It was more important to me to stay true to how I was feeling. I was done with the whole sex symbol thing. I wanted to go back to the original plan: playing rock and roll. That argument fell on deaf ears.

After we'd heatedly gone back and forth for a while, he said he was coming over to the studio where we were recording—MCA Whitney on Glenoaks. When he arrived, he didn't miss a beat. He started railing at me, reminding me that my contract said we all had to be in agreement about the cover art. If he wasn't in agreement, then I could not use the photo. And he was *not* in agreement.

He couched all his comments in an overly polite and condescending tone of voice, the kind most people reserve for small children. Watching his mouth move, the words seemed to lose all meaning. The only thing I could focus on was the thought that this guy was one of the most passive-aggressive men I'd ever known. Did other major bands have to put up with this? Somehow I couldn't see Sting or Springsteen having this conversation. What about Stevie Nicks or Ann Wilson? Was it only female artists going through this? I wanted to believe it was happening across the board, but I knew it wasn't true.

Our conversation was creating something of a problem in the studio, because people were trying to record. So, finally, in that same patronizing voice, he said, "My de-ahh. Let's step outside and talk about this."

So we moved the discussion out on the street. In no uncertain terms, he said that if I didn't reshoot the album cover he would shelve the album. And he had the power to do that. He subscribed to the business corollary that it didn't matter how you got there just as long as you got there. The end justified the means. He'd been incredibly successful—not just with me, but with many artists on Chrysalis, such as Billy Idol, Huey Lewis, and of course Blondie—by conducting business like this. Likewise, he'd recognized my potential to be a major star and had worked hard to get me there. All this gave him a lot of latitude and he was unapologetic about it. Terry simply believed he was right and that I should just shut up and get in line.

He let me chew on the thought of shelving the album for a few seconds before looking at me with a haughty expression and beginning a lecture in his severest British accent.

"I don't know what it is with you American women. You're all so beautiful but have such problems using your sexuality to your advantage. It's so provincial. Personally, I think it's a big mistake. And, Pat," he said, adding a slight orchestrated pause, "I hope you don't think people are actually coming to your concerts to listen to you sing."

I let him have it, and God bless America, I slapped him. Right there on Glenoaks Boulevard. That was just too much. Not only had he insulted me on a personal level, but he was doing that patronizing European crap about us "Yanks." He taken this fight to the street, and it had ended up in the gutter. I am not a violent person—that's just how mad I was.

He was stunned. I don't think anyone had ever stood up to him before—let alone slapped him in the face. A look of disbelief hung uneasily across his face like someone had just dropped a bucket of water on his head. Meanwhile all I could do was smile.

He composed himself and continued on as if nothing had happened. And his message remained the same. Either shoot the cover over, or there would be no album. The craziest thing was that Terry Ellis pretended that this incident had never happened. He just continued on with his speech as though nothing had transpired. After it was all over I asked Newman if the man was nuts, or if he thought I was nuts. Did I not just stand out there and slap his face?

"Oh, yes, you slapped his face all right," Newman said matter-of-factly. But there was nothing matter-of-fact about how Newman felt about it. Outwardly, my manager was not happy with these developments. He saw the label as *the* power brokers, the people he depended upon. He couldn't have me going around and hitting them in the face. However, secretly I knew that Newman was pleased that I'd given Terry something that had been a long time coming. Just as I was tired of being pushed around, Newman was tired of being in the middle. We both got some satisfaction from knowing that for at least an afternoon, Terry had been put in his place.

Sadly all that confrontation did was reinforce where the lines had been drawn in the sand. Contractually, I had to compromise. I went back in and took another photo—still in the padded room with me heavily made up, but with a more glammed-up, "presentable" look. The way I wanted to appear on the cover is only seen in the band photo on the back of the album. The entire experience just served to harden me. I felt like a junkyard dog that had been chained up and hit with a stick—only this time I bit back.

CHAPTER SIX

MUSIC VIDEO THEATER

I LOVE DISNEYLAND AND happy endings.

I'm all about white hats and hate to see good lose out in the end.
I've never enjoyed movies or books where good and evil are ambiguous. And I'm not big on antiheroes, either. I don't mind edgy, but don't
think I'm going to be on the side of a bad guy just because he's the protagonist. I like it when the good guys win, and I know who they are. I
have a soft spot for quirky weirdos with hearts of gold being oppressed
by the hypocrite with perfect teeth.

This is probably why the next video I made involved the band and
me fighting Nazis.

MTV was about a year old when *Get Nervous* hit shelves, and despite
the channel's game-changing success, shockingly it had not succumbed
to the trappings of the music industry (no small feat in a business as
cynical as the one we were in). From its inception, MTV had embodied an open-mindedness that had been absent from rock music for too
long, allowing bands to rewrite the stale record company formulas.
Suddenly there were ways to connect with fans beyond just live and recorded music. Bands that record execs never would have given a chance

suddenly found their place because of videos. With its moon-man icon, gritty logo, and hard guitar theme song, everything about it screamed rock and roll, but it was one thing to appear that way, and it was another thing to act like it.

Miraculously, a year into their experiment, their creative vision had not faded. They had changed the industry without compromising their idea of what the channel should be and what everyone wanted it to be. This independence made them an island of experimentation in an otherwise risk-averse musical landscape. Everyone recognized that the medium was still young and the rules were still being written. The network wanted videos that would expand the vision of what a music video could be, and they encouraged artists to take it as far as their imaginations would allow. When it came to videos, everyone—both the network and the artists—felt comfortable taking risks because the risky videos were some of the most interesting to watch. Of course there were critics who held their noses for one reason or another, but it was their job to be the art police. Music videos weren't for them. They were for the masses.

All of our on-camera interviews with MTV were done in studio, so we spent a good amount of time there. Back then, the studio was constantly filled with all kinds of musicians, both famous and unheard of. People were always coming and going. You'd walk around the halls, and there would be young artists chatting with legendary ones. Everywhere you looked, there were people wearing all kinds of outrageous clothes and acting like the parents were away for the weekend. But that was the joke; there never *were* any parents. The kids were in charge and running the show. It was just the private, insulated world of MTV.

Everything was pretty basic, more like shooting in your basement than slick television. The set itself was pretty stripped down and bare. You'd show up, and there'd be a couple of director's chairs for the VJs and the guests along with the two cameras that would shoot the interview. Because we were recording and releasing new music so frequently, I got to know all the VJs really well—especially the original ones: Nina Blackwood, Mark Goodman, Martha Quinn, and the darling JJ Jackson. They weren't the pretentious music journalists you sometimes see today; they were music fans who happened to be journalists. It was all very good-natured, no probing for deep dark secrets, no exposé about your personal life. It was all about music.

It was such a seminal time for all of us. We were embarking on a new and historic venture, but I don't think any of us grasped the significance of those days at the time. We were just having fun.

As for the music video directors, they were fans as well—not just of us, but of the genre. After all, these were rock and roll songs. The directors back then simply saw the music video as a vehicle to do interpretive work. It was such a creative time, and as people would brainstorm and throw out ideas, nothing really seemed too far-fetched or out-there. Compared to a feature film, making a music video was a bargain. It was possible to tell a fascinating story at a fraction of the cost. Everyone was still in awe of video making, and most people simply saw it as something meant to entertain.

Because of this freedom we approached making videos with a blank slate, working with directors to shape the vision that would translate these songs into images. "Shadows of the Night" was going to be our first single on *Get Nervous*, and therefore we were slated to record a video for it. Going into the planning for the "Shadows" video, I was definitely interested in pushing the video farther than what we'd done in the past. After we'd made the video for "You Better Run," we'd done a video for "I'm Gonna Follow You" from *Crimes of Passion*, and then three performance videos for "Fire and Ice," "Promises in the Dark," and "Precious Time." "I'm Gonna Follow You" was the first concept video for us. It had a dark and brooding look to it, with me wandering the desolate cobblestone streets of lower Manhattan and singing the song, menace seemingly hunched around every corner. In that video, the band is nowhere to be seen and there isn't a shot that I'm not in.

I never really liked this style because it seemed like overkill, but for our first foray into the world of concept videos it came out well. When we shot the video for "You Better Run," I'd been angry and self-conscious, but the second time, I knew what to expect. I was much more relaxed and able to enjoy myself, and it showed in the performance. The video itself was beautifully shot, and the locations perfectly suited the tone. There's an element of foreboding that haunts the song, and the video completely captured that feeling of broken glass on the pavement. Ultimately it was a good video, but it was too focused on me—especially considering that it showcased that sultry look Chrysalis continued to emphasize. While I liked the idea of taking a bigger step away from the straight performance video, I didn't want the next video to center on me in the same way. I wanted to be in it, but I didn't want to dominate the action.

When we met with the director for the "Shadows" video, he had the idea of doing a World War II minidrama that involved flying behind enemy lines to sabotage Nazi headquarters. The concept wasn't tied to the song or the message of the song, but that didn't matter. The story was pretty simple, though admittedly unexpected: a factory girl helping the World War II effort on the home front slips into a daydream about flying into Germany to kill a bunch of Nazis. An homage to Rosie the Riveter, there would be airplanes and a chase sequence, and some bad guys would die. It would be a four-minute action flick and I'd get to be the heroine.

As we sat there talking over the director's World War II vision, I loved the idea. It was elaborate, and it definitely didn't scream rock and roll—but that was why I liked it. It was something different. There were a lot of rock fans out there beyond the people wearing black leather jackets and torn jeans. I wanted to make a video that told a universal story. The idea of playing a woman who manned the factories and built munitions for America changing into an undercover agent blowing up Nazis and good triumphing over evil. That's just what I had in mind.

To me it was theater, but it was also rock and roll; it spoke to the blurring of lines that had drawn me to rock music in the first place. In the beginning, I'd idealized rock music and its significance. I was a disciple who believed rock was the place where truth and freedom flourished. Artists were the progressives. Coming from my classical music background, the thought of being able to make music in any form I chose was irresistible.

I soon learned that in rock circles someone with my musical background and more middle-of-the-road outlook was sometimes suspect. There were unspoken rules of behavior, dress, and association. To be considered rock and roll you had to appear like you were always a part of the fringe. Ambition had strict rules as well, and success was to be limited and veiled. No deviation or you'd be seen as a sellout. And women? They weren't equals, they weren't rock stars, they weren't players. Women were girlfriends or groupies.

Early on, I saw a lot of these rules for what they were: bullshit. The clothes were a costume just like on any other stage; the lifestyle was an act that didn't end when people got offstage. Quirkiness was far more interesting to me than being pretentious. What part of constantly being scrutinized and judged was supposed to be attractive? Who were these people who did the judging, and who gave a fuck? These rules were just as confining as those used by the establishment they had so much contempt for. To me, being put into a box meant being put into a box. It didn't matter who stuck you in there.

Not subscribing to these rules gave me the freedom to try things that other people might have thumbed their noses at—especially when it came to videos. I never forgot where I came from or what I was drawn to, and I relished having another arena to create in. I looked at making videos as another way to explore art and express the stories that we were telling with our music.

But this occasionally put me at odds with the band, and this was the case with the "Shadows of the Night" video. On the day we heard the pitch, I was the only one who thought that this World War II idea was the way to go. Everyone else thought the concept was just stupid. These guys were rock and roll musicians. Dressing up in vintage World War II costumes and pretending to fly airplanes was not exactly their thing. The band wanted performance videos. I liked a little theater.

And in this case, Spyder was decidedly with the band. Despite the fact that he knew as well as anyone how vital videos had become, he still didn't approve of them (and doesn't to this day). He understood that they were a crucial marketing tool, but he always felt they corrupted the pure intent of the music. On this issue, our backgrounds were the difference. I had been singing Puccini, Handel, and songs about unrequited love while tap-dancing in a tiara. He had been hanging out with Andy Warhol and Truman Capote. We were the musical odd couple. (To this day we'll be riding together in the car and I'll be singing a show tune, and he'll just shake his head incredulously, saying, "I still can't believe I'm married to a woman who knows all the songs in South Pacific by heart.") But somehow it worked; the contrast was the point.

The difference didn't cause friction between us, but it did complicate the discussion of the video for "Shadows." In the end, I was able to get the band on board, but no one was all that happy about it. I had a good feeling that it would work, that people would embrace it, but the guys couldn't get past the costumes. They hated those costumes more than they hated dressing up for the "Crimes of Fashion" album photo. They finally agreed but told me if I ever wanted to do anything like this again, I was on my own. It became an inside joke and they gave me crap about it all the time. Historical costumes were banned forever.

Compared to the other videos on the air at the time, the production was pretty impressive. The scenes with the Nazis were shot at a mansion the production team found, while the daytime material was filmed at Van Nuys airport, which interestingly enough was a historic place—the spot where Amelia Earhart set a world speed record in 1929 and where parts of *Casablanca* were filmed. The band was spread out throughout the video, and Myron and Zel ended up playing Nazis, which they weren't thrilled about. The funny thing about that video is that Judge Reinhold and Bill Paxton, actors who would later go on to movie careers, were both in it. They were young Screen Actors Guild guys who were brought in for the day, just getting started in the business and taking what jobs they could find. But being there on the video set with them was enlightening. You can tell that the band and I were musicians trying to be actors. Even my background in the theater didn't cover that. Judge and Bill were actors. Maybe they were young and inexperienced, but they were actors. We were just rockers dressed up in funny costumes.

All in all it came together pretty much as we'd envisioned it, and in the end, the director's instincts about the story and the song together were right. The video was a huge MTV success. Moreover, it pointed to the way many would make minimovie-style videos in MTV's future. The network needed a variety of approaches to become the trendsetter that it did. This video had more serious production value to it—a look that made it stand out without overpowering the song. It's such a good example of the genre. Even now, I look back on it and think that it was totally worth it to make the guys dress up.

SPYDER HAD BEEN RIGHT to push me on the vocals while we were recording *Get Nervous,* because they were constantly pointed out by critics when the album was released. One comment by the *Los Angeles Times*'s

Terry Atkinson was particularly perceptive, given my last battle with my label: "Since she's become entrenched in rock, fighting for ground with the opposite sex, [Pat Benatar] has reinforced her position. Her singing has never been more forceful."

That same review also pointed to Spyder's contribution: "The consistent power of *Get Nervous* owes much to the increased role—and increased inventiveness—of her husband, guitarist Neil Giraldo. He has written some strong, if not extraordinary, material. . . . Giraldo's guitar playing has reached a new dimension here, too."

The live show also received kudos for the interplay between guitar, keyboards, and vocals. When we played the Cow Palace in San Francisco, *Billboard* suggested that our tour might well be titled "The Pat and Neil Show." And that's exactly how we saw it.

By the time we went on tour for *Get Nervous,* our tour staff had expanded, but the personal staff was still minimal. The organization started, in addition to lawyers and accountants, with the management company, headed by Rick Newman. We had a tour manager who worked for management, and a booking agency, Premiere Talent, where we were represented by Barbara Skydell and Frank Barcelona. We had a publicist who didn't usually travel with us but with whom we were in constant contact. We had sound and light people and the roadies and drivers—there were three or four buses and some eighteen-wheelers carrying equipment.

On a personal level, it was a more pared-down group. I was blessed to have my brother, Andy, as my personal assistant. Andy and I were so close. Considering how high-maintenance he was as a kid, it was really funny that in the end he worked taking care of things for Spyder and me. Andy was always on a scavenger hunt, more so for Spyder than for me. Spyder was always looking for things that either didn't exist, or if they did exist he couldn't remember the name of the company that made them or where he'd seen them. So every morning Andy would sit down with a pad and paper and say, "What's on the list today?" He also made sure I did all the phone interviews I had scheduled and kept a timeline for photo shoots and that kind of thing. The best thing about working with Andy was that he had a great sense of humor, a quick, dry wit that just doubled me over with laughter.

I never traveled with hair and makeup people. I did my own hair and makeup from the time we started out. There was a valet who took care of all the stage clothes, a necessity on the road with that many people. Wardrobe was a nonissue. I wore what I wanted to, when I wanted to, end of story. Whatever felt right was what I put on. No one, and I mean no one, interfered with how I looked on the road.

One of the most liberating parts of being on the road was that it was entirely our show, the one place where no one outside the band interfered. Live performance was our domain, and no one dared cross the line. We were in charge of everything: what we wore, what we played, how we presented ourselves to the world. There was no pretense, no artifice, no marketing issues, no one's opinions but ours. We played as we always had, with raw abandon. It was the reason we began and it was the reason we continued.

I've long said that the difference between making a record and playing live is that one is forever and the other is in the moment. When you go in and cut a record, you know that you must try to get the perfect sound. It's an act of self-indulgence. You are able to concentrate on every nuance of the song. You can dissect the tracks, the vocals, the arrangement, in an insulated environment, taking things apart and putting them back together in endless combinations. I loved making records. It was intense but Zenlike when it was done right.

Live performance was the antithesis of that—going for the moment with no rules. It was all about the impermanence of the situation. Perfection could be achieved without being perfect, and it was encouraged. Perfection was about that thing in your head needing to get out. When you achieved that, it was done, and you'd live with it. But every night I went onstage it was a new experience. What happened each night of the tour depended on the audience. I had no way of knowing what the crowd would be like on any given night. It was the impulsiveness, the chemistry—the potential for spontaneous combustion between you and the fans. There was nothing more seductive than the shared experience between me and an audience. We made records in a vacuum. Live performance was all about the connection.

And the best part about the live performances on the tour for *Get Nervous* was that for the first time in two years we were able to enjoy ourselves. With my breakup from Spyder a thing of the distant past, we were all able to just relax, play, and enjoy life on the road. It was the biggest relief—for everyone. The band and crew practically threw a party. Without the distraction of fighting, we all had renewed enthusiasm, and it showed in our performance. The record was doing well and we were playing to sold-out venues.

There was one date however, when things got a bit scary. We were playing to a packed house at the Lakeland Civic Center in Florida, when I collapsed on stage—out cold. Newman came rushing up from the sound board because he thought I'd been shot. It turned out it was food poisoning, but I was rushed to the hospital and kept there overnight. The audience had a choice to get a refund for their tickets or come back for the make-up show. An astonishing 98 percent of the ticket holders chose to come back, and we made t-shirts for people who presented their ticket stubs from the original concert that said, "Lakeland . . . You Knock Me Out!"

Food poisoning aside, taking the music from *Get Nervous* on the road was a terrific experience for all of us, especially for Spyder, because he believed it was the best album we'd made so far. He loved the addition of keyboards. Of course, he was a keyboard player himself, but he enjoyed turning that over to someone else so he could concentrate on production. He wanted someone who could play keys as well as he played guitar. For him, the tour was an opportunity to broaden the experience.

He was working on that very thing, expanding the sound, when out of the blue one day, we got a call from Chrysalis demanding we start work immediately on another album. I couldn't believe that once again they were pushing us to record while we were on the road—especially since feelings were still raw from the cover art on *Get Nervous*. The reality was that they didn't want to lose momentum, and as always this was paramount in their minds. It caused them to make poor decisions with no regard to the musical evolution that was so necessary between records. In the end, they demanded another record, and as always, the contract was their trump card.

Even so, I said, "Fuck you." I was *not* ready to record again. The time that we'd been able to take before recording *Get Nervous* had played a key role in allowing us to broaden our sound. We'd had time to experiment and try new things, to see where our sound was heading. To rush back into the studio for a full album might jeopardize all that we'd gained and cause us to fall back into safe patterns rather than push ourselves.

We finally decided that the only way we could meet our nine-month deadline was to record a live album. We pushed for this because it satisfied our contractual obligation while giving us a little breathing room. But we didn't want to cut off our nose to spite our face; a record that didn't sell would hurt us as well as the label. So in a compromise, we decided to include two new songs on the album, which would be called *Live from Earth*: "Lipstick Lies" and "Love Is a Battlefield." This decision would prove to be career and life altering.

We got "Love Is a Battlefield" from our friend Holly Knight. Like me, Holly was a New Yorker who started out in classical music, in her case as a pianist. She made the transition to rock while she was still in high school, and ironically, her band was named Spider. The band signed with Dreamland Records, headed by Mike Chapman at the time. They released two albums in 1980 and '81, and then Holly started writing for Mike's publishing company. The two of them collaborated on "Love Is a Battlefield."

"Battlefield" was originally written as a ballad, unhurried and dreamy. But for some reason, Spyder heard it as a rhythmic anthem, up-tempo and high energy with a beat that was not that of a ballad. Spyder had never liked drum machines; he liked live performances, and trying to create that once-in-a-lifetime moment. But when he was getting ready to work on "Battlefield," he started fooling around with a brand-new drum machine and hearing Bo Diddley in his head. Somehow between the drum machine and Bo Diddley, he came up with an idea for the song. As he described the sound to me, I wasn't sure I understood, but I was intrigued. I was the only one in the band who'd heard the song in any of its incarnations and the only one who knew it was meant to be a very slow piece.

He decided that he wanted the band to experiment on the arrangement, and he called them together at Leeds Rehearsal Studio. Instead of going into the "big room" to rehearse as we normally would, he had them set up in the parking lot. They weren't given any charts, they never heard the demo. He simply gave them random chord changes and the pattern that he'd written on the drum machine. They sat there with curious looks, wondering what he was up to this time.

Everyone in the band was shaking his head. He told them to play the chord changes to the drum loop. They hated that idea!

"Neil, this is nuts! We don't have any idea what we're doing!"

Spyder was in his mad scientist mode. "Never mind. Just play! Just play! Just play!"

Even Peter Coleman was shaking his head. "Okay, I think you're onto something. I'm gonna let you go—but I still think you're nuts."

They recorded every part out in the parking lot; then Spyder took them inside to listen. "All right. Now you've heard what the track should sound like. Play it like you did in the parking lot, and don't screw it up by thinking."

It was from that chaos that Spyder made a song that would be sung in front of bedroom mirrors and at karaoke clubs for years to come. Spyder's talent for seeing where music was headed next was remarkable. He had a gift for anticipating trends and he never let anyone stand in the way of that. The product he made sounded unlike anything else out there. It was its own thing—danceable but still rock. The eighties were still young but they were developing their own sound—and that sound wasn't just about hard-driving guitars anymore. Spyder realized this incredibly early on, and he channeled that instinct into "Love Is a Battlefield." This was where music was headed.

But that was not how Chrysalis saw it. Their reaction wasn't good. They hated *everything.* They didn't like the talking on the front end of the song, the whistling at the end, or the signature drum pattern. To them, the song was far too dance-oriented and not rock-and-roll enough. It moved away from the tried-and-true formula that had been so successful for us. They weren't interested in gambling, especially when it might affect their bottom line. We were a "rock" band. Anything that seemed to deviate from that wasn't acceptable. And Mike Chapman *really* hated it. Though he was usually a forward-thinker, all Chapman could hear was that the song was in no way the one he wrote, and he said we'd ruined it.

As we fought over the song, it became more apparent that these people who in the beginning had been so intimidating in their knowledge of the record business weren't so smart after all. I wasn't sure if it was that they had lost touch with the contemporary music scene, become complacent, or were simply greedy. Whatever it was, they had no idea where music was headed and possessed no vision for how music was changing. In the same way that their confidence in "Heartbreaker" had been tenuous because of disco's popularity, they didn't anticipate the evolution of rock giving rise to something else. It didn't matter to me that they were "lifers"—experienced music industry professionals with an impressive track record. They didn't see where the decade was going. They didn't understand what was happening out there. They had no foresight, no vision. The universe had played its hand, and their time was finished.

Over the period of a few weeks, gradually we began to wear them down. With Peter behind him on everything, Spyder wouldn't back down, because he knew in his heart he was correct. He refused to change one thing. The solid opposition that marked the label's initial reaction gave way and they started warming up to the track. Buzzard was the first to change his mind, and eventually Chrysalis had no choice but to go with it.

It didn't hurt that Bob Giraldi had signed on to direct the video. Bob was fresh from doing the video for Michael Jackson's "Beat It" when he agreed to direct the video for "Battlefield." Everyone knew that he'd put an original, creative spin on the song that would help give it the push it would need. Once again, we went for a story rather than a performance. This time there were no period costumes, though. It was a streetwise tale of alienated youth. A young woman who fights with her parents flees to the big city, only to fall in with its seedy underbelly.

The video as Bob envisioned it would be choreographed and would also have dialogue. Now, anyone who knows me knows I am completely uncoordinated, with two left feet. The thought of doing a dance routine was intimidating, but I figured if I could pretend to fly an airplane, I could probably pretend I knew how to dance. The choreographer was a guy named Michael Peters who was incredibly talented, and the thought of working with a celebrated choreographer made the whole thing even more appealing. If anyone could make a dancer out of me, I figured it was him.

The video was filmed in New York City and there were two days of dance rehearsals before the shoot. The first day of rehearsals started early. We had a lot of work to do. All the dancers were assembled in the dance studio, looking like characters right out of A Chorus Line, beautiful men and women with muscular bodies in skintight outfits, stretching, twirling. As I stood there watching them, I couldn't figure out what exactly I'd been thinking when I signed on to do this. I was in way over my head.

Throughout the day, we danced. Well, *they* danced. I don't know what you'd call what I was doing, but it wasn't dancing. After about seven hours, Michael Peters sent all the dancers home to rest for tomorrow's rehearsal, but he wasn't quite done with me.

He walked over to me and said, "You've never done anything like this before, have you?"

"No," I said sheepishly, as though I'd been caught lying about my homework.

"Don't you worry. By tomorrow night you'll be a pro."

He spent the next five hours breaking down every step, one-on-one, until I got it. The entire time he was sweet and patient, never once making me feel as ridiculous as I probably looked. The next day, while I was not ready for Broadway, I was dancing. That second day, we put in another twelve hours of rehearsal, and I swear even my toenails hurt when we were done. I'd always admired dancers, but I had newfound respect for them after those two days.

With the dance routine as solid as it was ever going to be, we descended into the city for the shoot. We shot all over downtown Manhattan, finding every seamy block that we could. When it came time to film the big dance number, I was more nervous than I'd been in years and flashes of my first performance at Catch were appearing in front of my eyes. I could sing *anything*, anytime, anywhere, but this was a whole new world. It ended up working out well, with everyone being supportive and charitable. The shoot lasted all day, and I was able to convince people that I had some idea of what I was doing.

The combination of the video and the song proved unstoppable, propelling the song to the top of the charts, our highest-ranking single. We'd gone with our gut, and once again it had paid off. The signature dance beat that Chrysalis had hated so much would go on to be imitated by several musicians, including Don Henley for his hit "The Boys of Summer." The different sound to the song expanded our audience yet again, with even younger rock and roll fans beginning to follow us. Of all the surprises that video brought, perhaps the most amusing was that a klutz like me would be forever associated with the iconic dance move the "shoulder shake."

After the song's success, everyone who'd bad-mouthed it in the beginning was suddenly on board, swearing that they'd known it would be a hit all along. Mike Chapman had hated what we'd done with his song at first. After it became a hit, he thought it was a classic. (As a songwriter, Spyder laughingly says that he understands. When a songwriter hears major changes in his music, he or she is often shocked. But you have to learn to let go of that.)

Of course Spyder and I knew better. We'd triumphed. We hadn't given in, and we stayed true to our beliefs. In addition to earning us our fourth Grammy nomination, becoming a top-five single, and inspiring a groundbreaking video, "Battlefield" changed the way we made records. It reinforced the idea that we could tap into something that the label couldn't see. Our instincts were the right ones.

CHAPTER SEVEN

IT'S MY LIFE

AFTER WE GOT MARRIED, Spyder and I lived in the house I'd bought when we separated, but we only stayed a short while. Neither of us felt comfortable there, partly because it reminded us of the time we'd been apart, but also because I'd purchased it myself. That house I owned was beautiful, a midcentury home on a cliff overlooking the lights of the San Fernando Valley. It had a pool and lots of big glass windows so you could see the lights of the valley from almost every room.

Wonderful as that house was, Spyder and I wanted a fresh start. It wasn't *our* home, it was mine. We quickly sold it and bought a house on Rancho Street in Encino. This was a family home with a brick front, shutters, and the all-important white picket fence—literally. It also had a guesthouse in the back, which Spyder promptly turned into a recording studio. I went about decorating and making our house a home while Spyder locked himself away in the studio, happily doing what he did best. He named the studio "Spyder's Soul Kitchen," and it would become integral to our creative process moving forward. For the first time since our relationship began, we had peace.

When I wasn't on the road or recording, I was (and still am) basically a stay-at-home type of person. I preferred cooking in my own kitchen with my family around to being out on the town. The more fame we achieved, the more reclusive I became. I didn't feel that way in the beginning, but as things escalated, I retreated from the spotlight as much as possible when we weren't on the road. Much of this was in response to having a profession that required spending huge amounts of time socializing with people I didn't know. Touring, especially the backstage "meet-and-greets," was like being at a wedding where I was the bride every night. When we were home, my mission was solitude, plain and simple.

That's not to say that I was a shut-in; I simply chose my company carefully. The times that I was able to be home were my refuge, my chance to regain my footing. It's hard to catch up if you never slow down, and those times between tours and albums were the best opportunity to do just that. Because of this, I was never in the whole club scene. Maybe we'd have a few friends over for dinner, but those friends were seldom in the entertainment industry. Spyder and I kept to ourselves and spent most of our time within our inner circle—Myron and his wife, Monica; my assistant, Janie, and her husband, Scotty; my brother, Andy; Newman and his girlfriend, Renee. It wasn't that we didn't enjoy being with our celebrity friends, we just didn't want to talk shop all the time. For four years we'd been on such a ridiculous schedule. We'd been living and breathing the music business so intensely, and we just wanted to have a normal life, with regular people who didn't talk about business all day. Despite the fame, we were still very ordinary people, and this was our chance to act like it, the first time since everything started that we were able to separate our life from our work. Before, our life *was* our work.

For the most part we were just too busy to cultivate friendships with famous people who, like us, were constantly on the go. When you are out on the road, chances are everyone else is as well. In truth, there weren't that many opportunities to socialize with other artists. Music careers don't lend themselves to having lunch with your peers. While we all knew each other and I'd see various people at events, festivals, award shows, or parties, my list of meaningful celebrity encounters was pretty short. I did finally get to meet one of my childhood idols, Robert Plant, once when we played a concert in England. He was backstage, and all I could think of was how crazy life was. I'd spent years listening to him sing, dreaming of being like him when I grew up, and then he was in my dressing room and we were chatting like old friends. I never got to meet John Lennon after being so crazy for the Beatles when I was a kid. But I got to meet Paul McCartney and Ringo Starr on different occasions, which didn't seem odd at all. Bruce Springsteen had a surprisingly unassuming manner—very laid-back, a real down-to-earth guy. Everything you think about Bruce is true—he's a nice person who treats everyone with respect. What you see is what you get.

In the end it wasn't so much a deliberate choice to avoid the various scenes out there. We simply didn't have the time, and when we did, we spent it with our true friends. The only thing that we consciously distanced ourselves from when we were at home was work. One of the things that Spyder and I realized after we got back together was that music had taken over our lives, and more than anything else, this was why we'd broken up. We had allowed music to control every aspect of our earlier life together, and it had almost destroyed us.

We were determined to never let that happen again. If we were going to stay together, we had to set boundaries for ourselves when it came to work, and these boundaries would have to be steadfast. No talking about music, no discussing scheduling, no complaining about the label. We were adamant about not letting music encroach on our private time, and bit by bit, we began to regain control of our lives. We stopped being accessible twenty-four hours a day, ceased planning conference calls after six P.M., refused calls on the weekend unless it was an emergency. We were going to have a life and we strongly encouraged everyone around us to get one as well.

This break after the release of *Live from Earth* was the first time that we really got serious about imposing these rules on ourselves. When we'd had enough of a break that we could start to think about work, we turned our attention to writing, but we would do this in concentrated batches, not all the time. By this point, with several albums under our belt, I had a good sense of what conditions worked best for me when it came to writing songs. I'd written enough to know that it was not something I could just do on command. Songs just didn't hatch fully formed (or at least they never did for me). It was a much more organic process and it was never forced. Words are very important to me and finding the optimum way to say what I'm thinking is paramount. I don't sit with a thesaurus in hand; I want to find the word in the same way you might find an exquisite shell on the beach: by accident.

While Spyder and I were home, we tried to write as much as possible, getting into a pattern that works for us to this day. We would seldom write together. I was actually that way with other writers, too. Over the years I wrote a lot with Myron, and we rarely worked on our songs while we were sitting in the same room. We'd go back and forth on the telephone. The most important thing I needed for writing was solitude. I could begin an idea with Spyder and Myron, but then I'd have to step away and work on it for a while on my own. After I'd gathered my thoughts we could come together again and continue. They didn't like it at first, but after a while we created a rhythm that would be our lifelong writing style.

Furthermore, I didn't like writing for a specific album, preferring a more low-pressure situation when I had time to just flow with the creativity. When Spyder and I felt that we had enough material, we'd start to think more about what might fit together in an album, but creativity would come through the writing and recording process. Sometimes I'd get a burst of energy right at the end of recording, and instead of trying to force it into the record on hand, I'd end up with songs for the next record.

Regardless of where we were in the process, patience and time were key components to getting the right songs on the right albums. This was largely why Chrysalis's incessant requests for new records were so stressful: it was antithetical to my creative process. Some people do their best writing when they're pressed for time, but that was never the case for us.

For the most part, Spyder came up with the melodic stuff and I focused more on writing lyrics, although we would take turns doing both. The times I got into working on a melody were when I heard something in my head that felt good vocally. Then I'd sing it so Spyder could see why that particular melody was best for the composition. We'd do more writing between tours than on the road. When we worked together as writers or in the studio, we each had a spark that the other would ignite. It's a cosmic, spiritual thing—there really isn't any other way to describe it.

Spyder wrote more often than I did—he was constantly working on songs. I think one reason he wrote so much was because of his continuing interest in experimenting with our sound. If we relied on songwriters too much, we'd run the risk of our sound becoming static. We had no interest in receiving unsolicited outside material any longer, and we'd only write with friends or writers whose work we admired. Often, when outside songwriters would bring us material, it would sound like stuff that belonged on our previous record. It would mimic without elaborating. We became insulated, locking ourselves up with the band and maybe Peter Coleman and making music undisturbed. We were always trying to evolve and experiment—it was a very prolific and satisfying time.

Our writing usually went something like this: Spyder would come out in the morning and tell me he had a title. If I hadn't had my coffee yet, I'd wave him away for the time being.

"Get out of my face—it's only six thirty!"

"But I've got a title. I'm gonna leave it on the counter."

He'd put down a little piece of paper with his idea, walk out of the room, and let me wake up, knowing full well that the minute I saw the title I'd start thinking about the lyrics. He knew I'd be compelled no matter what the hour (it's an annoying, dirty little trick that he's played on me throughout our life). He'd come back in an hour or three, ready to work on it again, and by then I usually had the chorus and most of the verses. I'd almost always start by asking him about the melody.

"What's in your head? What chords do you have so far? Give me a hint where you're going with this."

"It doesn't matter," he'd respond. "Just let me see what you've written."

Once he'd read the words, he would sit down at the piano and start working on a melody that he already had in his head. I'd go off and do something else while he worked on that, and after he'd been at it for a bit, I'd come back to see what he'd done. And just like that, it would come together in a very organic way. We'd play off each other, back and forth, even though sometimes to an outsider it might have sounded more like fighting than collaboration, as if we were bickering like the married couple we were.

If he did something I didn't agree with, I never sugarcoated it for him.

"Are you nuts?" I might say. "There's no way that's going to work."

"You're impossible. It *will* work. Don't be so stubborn," he'd shoot back.

"No, it won't. And I'm *not* singing it that way. Pick a key that humans can sing in."

"You're such a pain in the ass. Just sing it, for chrissake."

Or sometimes I'd come to him with an idea that he fought me over

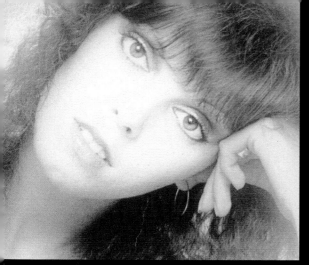

This was my first head shot, taken around the time I first moved to New York and started performing at Rick Newman's club, Catch a Rising Star. *Photograph by Jerry Tyson*

From the very beginning, I loved being in front of a crowd. There was nothing like working the room and keeping the energy high. *Photograph by Joe D'Amato*

In 1979, Mike Chapman introduced me to Neil Giraldo who would soon become "Spyder" to me. It was only a matter of months before we were getting ready for our first tour (*left to right*: Spyder, me, Scott Sheets). *Photograph by Joe D'Amato*

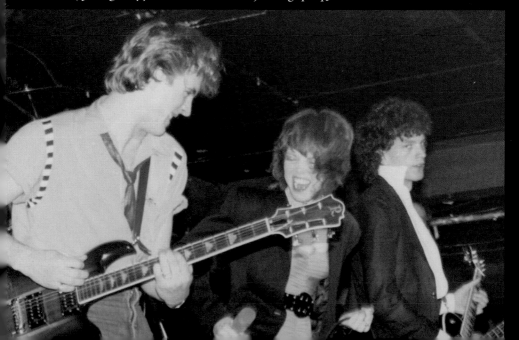

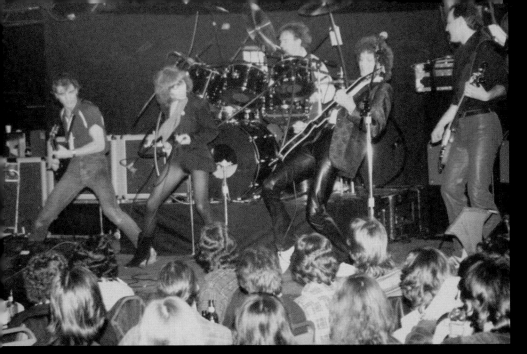

This shot of the band and me was taken at our first gig, at a club called My Father's Place on Long Island (*left to right:* Spyder, me, Myron Grombacher, Scott, and Roger "Zel" Capps). *Photograph by Joe D'Amato*

Spyder and I hit it off right away—musically, we just clicked. He knew exactly what kind of guitar sound I was looking for, but it wasn't until after we'd recorded *In the Heat of the Night* that we became romantically involved. *Photograph from the author's collection*

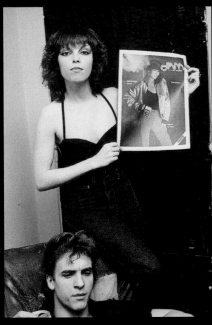

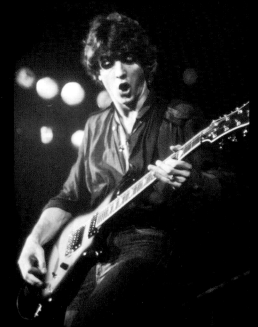

Backstage with Spyder at the Boomer Theater in Norman, Oklahoma. *Photograph by Vernon L. Goudy III*

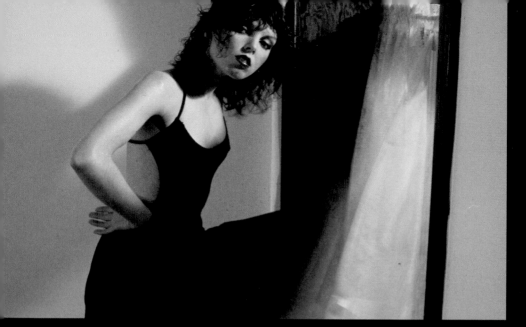

An outtake photograph from the cover shoot for *In the Heat of the Night*. Despite the strength of the song "Heartbreaker," the label hesitated to release it as a single, but once they did, there was no looking back. *Photograph by Alex Chatelain*

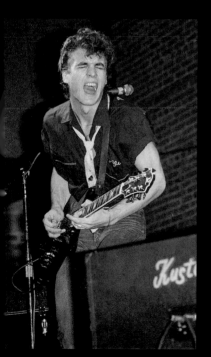

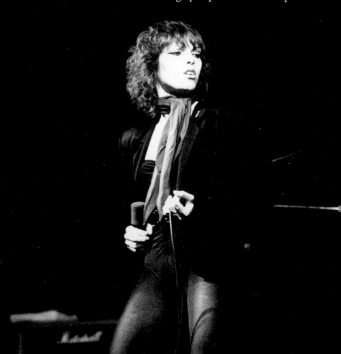

On that first tour for *In the Heat of the Night* in 1979, the crowds were insane. After "Heartbreaker" came out, everything just exploded, convincing Chrysalis, our record company, that they had to push us back into the studio to cut another album. *Photograph by Vernon L. Goudy III*

Spyder tearing it up at the Boomer Theater in December 1979. *Photograph by Vernon L. Goudy III*

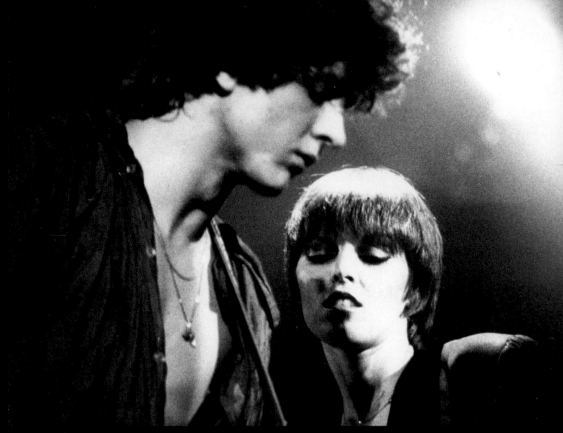

In the fall of 1980, we went on tour to support *Crimes of Passion*. Fueled by the strength of "Hit Me with Your Best Shot," it was mayhem—crowds unlike anything we'd seen before. *Photograph by Fred Joslyn*

Myron Grombacher, Spyder's childhood friend, joined the band for the first tour in 1979 and he's been a vital part of our lives ever since, remaining one of our best friends. He and his wife, Monica, are godparents to our daughters. *Photograph by Neal Preston*

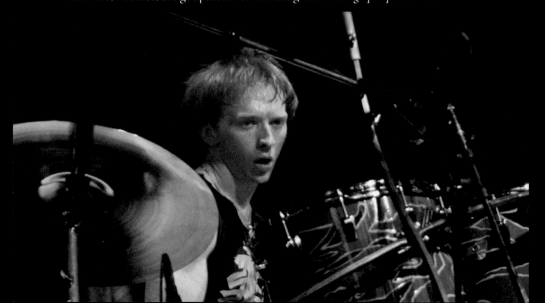

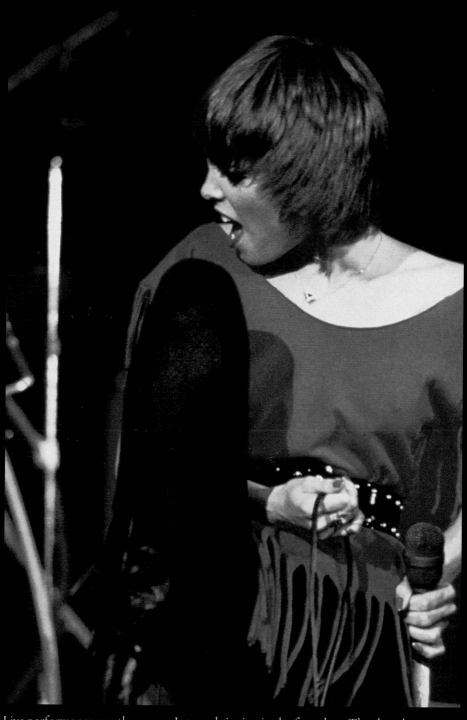

Live performance was the reason I started singing in the first place. The shared

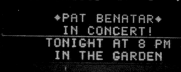
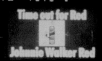

PAT BENATAR
IN CONCERT!
TONIGHT AT 8 PM
IN THE GARDEN

Time out for Red

Johnnie Walker Red

MADISON SQUARE GARDEN CENTER

Peppermint Park

The marquee outside of Madison Square Garden on the *Precious Time* tour.
Photograph by Jeffrey Mayer

It didn't take anyone long to realize what a game-changing phenomenon MTV was.
For the "Promises in the Dark" music video, where this was taken, we rented out a
soundstage in North Hollywood and taped a performance with fan club members,
contest winners, family, and friends as the audience. *Photograph by Neal Preston*

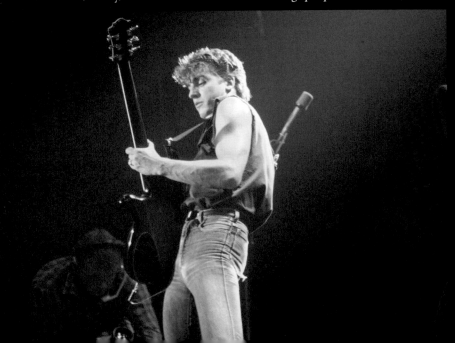

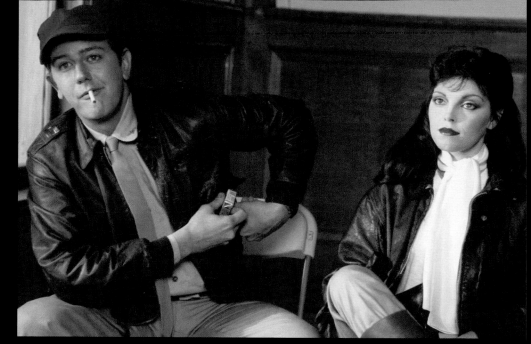

In the beginning, MTV completely encouraged creativity and new ideas. The video for "Shadows in the Night" was unlike any video we'd done to that point. With its story line, elaborate concept about World War II, and professional actors like Judge Reinhold (pictured), I wanted to see just how far we could push the story and still have it work with the song. *Photograph by Jeffrey Mayer*

At the shoot for the "Get Nervous" video. *Photograph by Jeffrey Mayer*

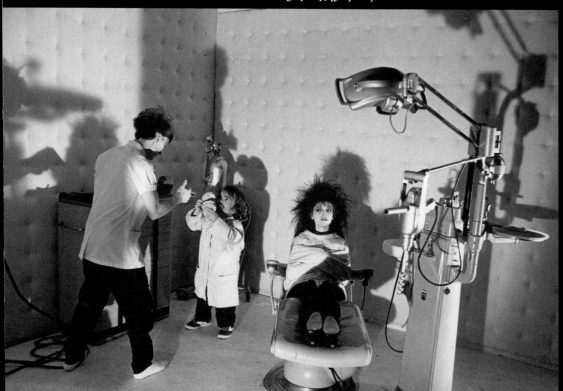

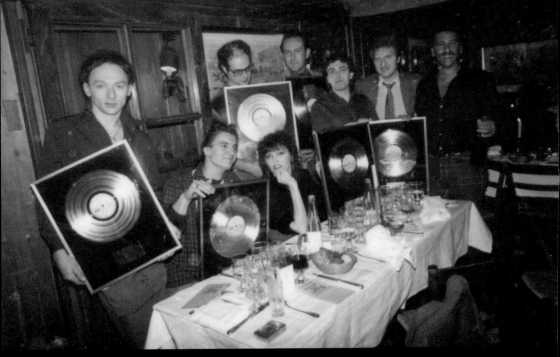

The presentation of quintuple platinum albums for *Crimes of Passion* (*from left to right:* Myron, Spyder, me, Charlie Giordano, Roger, two representatives from Chrysalis, and Newman). *Photograph from the author's collection*

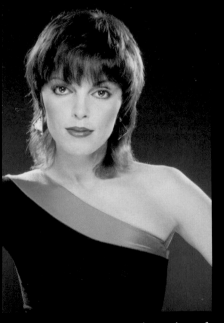

This photograph was taken during an HBO special that we did in New Haven, Connecticut, in 1982. *Photograph by Jeffrey Mayer*

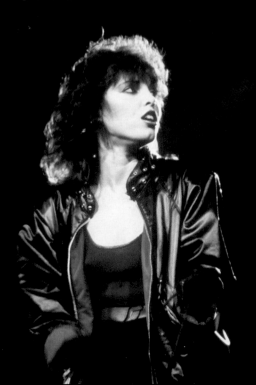

Quintessential '80s: lots of eyeliner and bad clothes. *Photograph by Jeffrey Mayer*

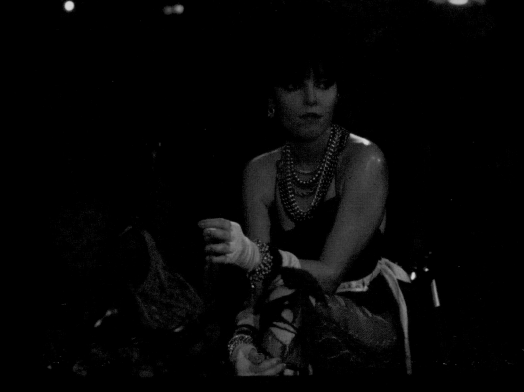

A shot from the set of the video for "Love Is a Battlefield." It took forty-eight hours of intense rehearsal to get ready for the dance sequence in the video. The end results were worth it, but I couldn't walk for days afterward. *Photograph by Misha Erwitt*

During the video shoot for "Lipstick Lies"; this is the band having a laugh between takes. *Photograph by Jeffrey Mayer*

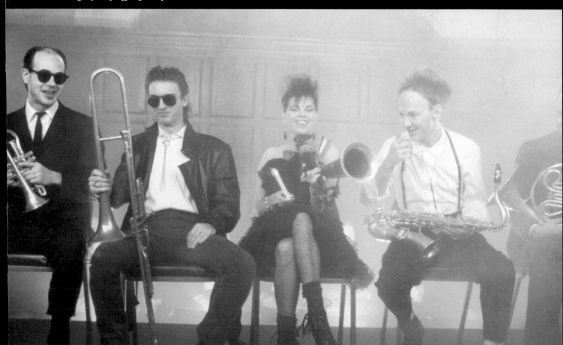

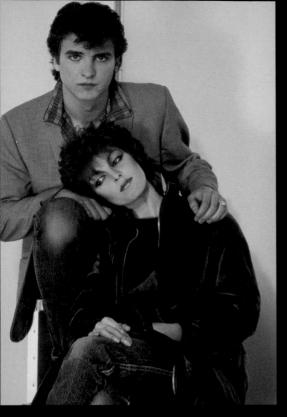

Spyder and me in 1983.
Photograph by Laura Levine

The schedule of touring and promotion was never-ending. When we weren't recording an album, we were either on the road or promoting it with publicity photographs like this one. *Photograph by Mathew Rolston*

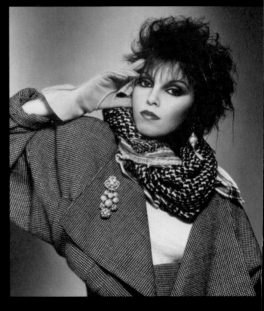

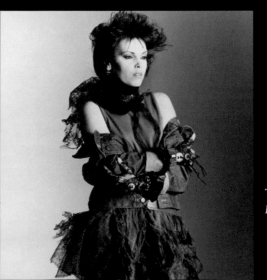

This photograph was from an article in *Harper's Bazaar. Photograph by Mathew Rolston*

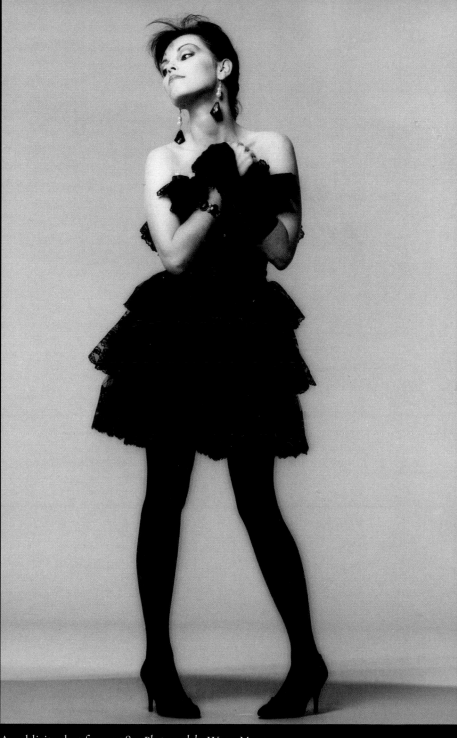

A publicity shot from 1984. *Photograph by Wayne Mazer*

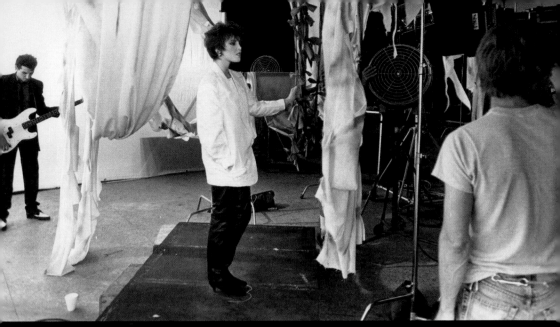

This was taken on the set of the video for "We Belong," which was featured on our album *Tropico*. It was while we were recording this record that I learned I was pregnant with our first daughter. *Photograph by Jeffrey Mayer*

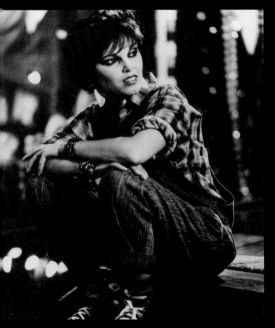

The song and video for "Invincible" were recorded and shot only a few weeks after I gave birth to Haley in 1985. The song was on *Seven the Hard Way* and became a top ten hit for us. *Photograph by Lester Cohen*

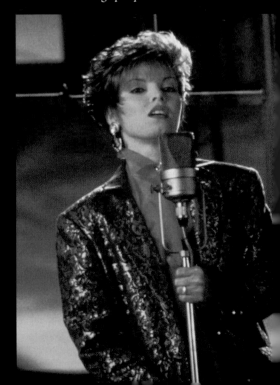

On *Tropico*, we took our sound in a different direction, taking a step away from our signature, electric-guitar-driven sound. This photograph was taken during the video shoot for "Ooh Ooh Song." *Photograph by Jeffrey Mayer*

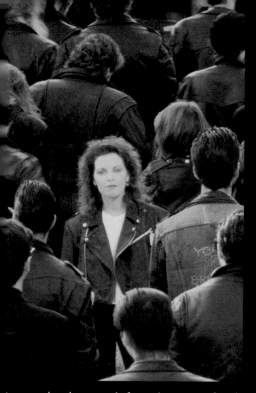

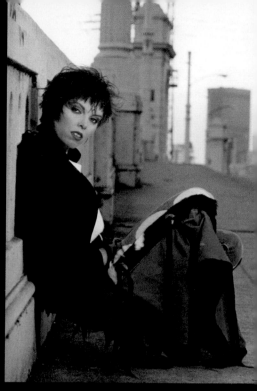

An outtake photograph from the cover of *Wide Awake in Dreamland. Photograph by Moshe Brakha*

This photograph, taken in L.A. in 1988, was a promotional shot for *Wide Awake in Dreamland. Photograph by Moshe Brakha*

A shot from the video for "Let's Stay Together" off of *Wide Awake in Dreamland. Photograph by Lester Cohen*

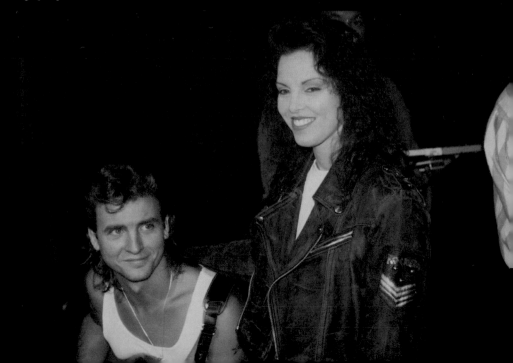

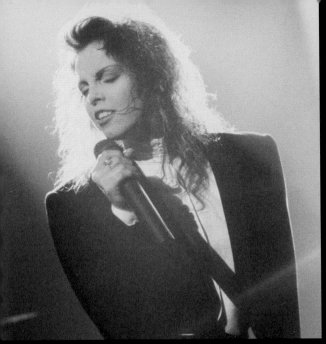

This photograph is from the video for "All Fired Up." Even though the single was a hit, it couldn't save the tour we embarked on in support of *Wide Awake in Dreamland*. *Photograph by Lester Cohen*

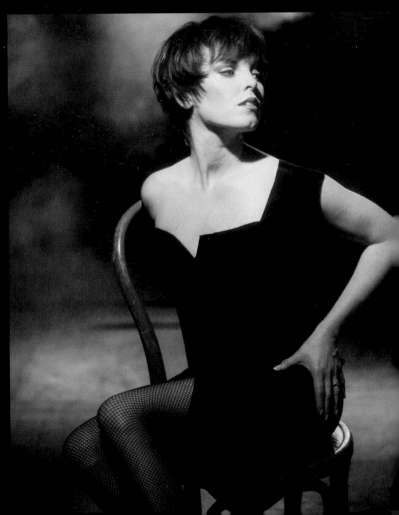

After the fiasco with *Wide Awake in Dreamland*, I was ready to walk away from singing for good. This photograph was taken for the album *True Love*. Spyder's crazy idea. A collection of blues songs that inspired us to continue making music. *Photograph by Randee Saint Nicholas*

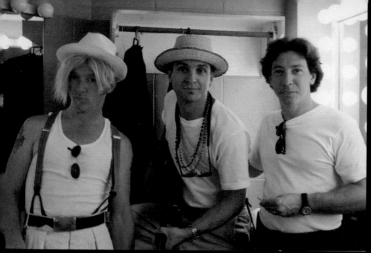

This shot was taken during our Can't Stop Rockin' tour with REO Speedwagon and Fleetwood Mac (*from left to right:* Myron, Spyder, and Mick Mahan). *Photograph by Brigette Leonard*

A photograph from our *Innamorata* cover session. *Photograph by Dennis Keely*

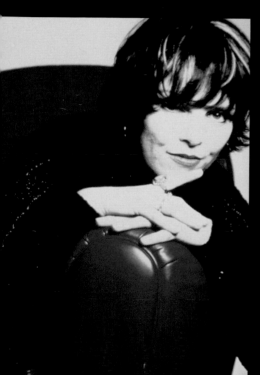

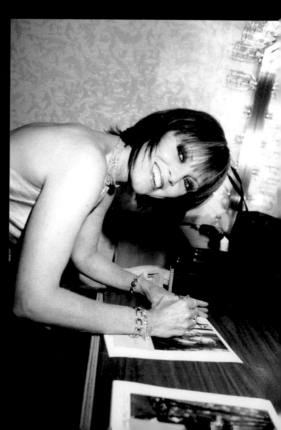

Me signing photographs backstage during the 2001 Summer Vacation tour. We've toured every summer for the past thirteen years. This allows us to be hands-on parents during the school year. *Photograph by Roxanne Lowit*

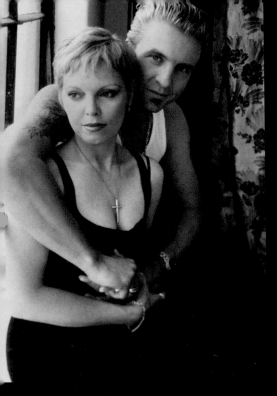

Spyder and I have been together for thirty-one years. Raising kids, making music, it's been an amazing journey. *Photograph by Beth Herzaft*

Our daughters, Hana and Haley. *Photograph by Dana Fineman*

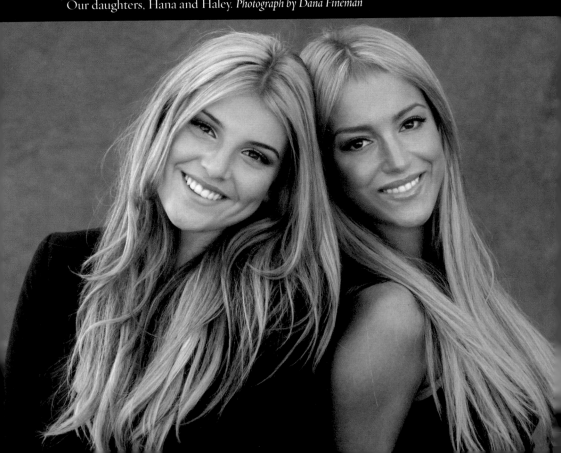

for a time. I remember one time in particular, Spyder was convinced that a song would not work for us, and we argued about it.

"Just listen to the vocal on the chorus. I know I can sing the shit out of that."

"I don't know," he said. "It seems like a predictable love song."

"But you can do your thing, churn it up. Make it sound huge, not like a ballad anymore," I said insistently. "Let me sing it for you."

Then he started warming up to it. In a few days he returned with an epic, beautifully constructed song with an arpeggiated keyboard intro that would become the most identifiable part of the monstrous hit that was "We Belong." By working it out on his own, he'd sold himself on it. Now he was professing his love for the song, to which I promptly responded, "*You're* such a pain in the ass." He smiled back, and said, "Thanks, that's my job." He didn't care how it got done as long as it was great in the end.

"We Belong" was released on *Tropico,* our first full studio album in two years at the time. But that wasn't all that we produced. During the making of *Tropico,* we finally got pregnant.

AFTER THE SUCCESS OF "Love Is a Battlefield," *Live from Earth* went platinum, and I won a Grammy for "Battlefield." The album stayed on the charts nearly three years. Those awards, the twenty-sixth annual Grammy Awards at L.A.'s Shrine Auditorium, on February 28, 1984, marked the reign of Michael Jackson as the King of Pop. Michael won record and album awards in the overall categories for "Beat It" and *Thriller*; Best Pop Performance, Male, for *Thriller*; Best Rock Performance, Male, for "Beat It"; and Best Video for "Thriller."

In my category, Best Rock Performance, Female, I was up against Joan Armatrading for *The Key,* Kim Carnes for "Invisible Hands," Stevie Nicks for "Stand Back," and Bonnie Tyler for *Faster than the Speed of Night.* "Love Is a Battlefield" became my fourth Grammy win. Ironically, we didn't attend the awards show, but they did finally televise the category and someone accepted for me. The video was nominated for an MTV Award. Those were heady days. In the midst of the awards, *Crimes of Passion* went five-times platinum and *Precious Time* was certified double platinum.

Despite everything that was going on, our break from recording emphasized that this was a time of commitment for us. Once we had made the decision to marry, everything had solidified. I was the most important person in his world, and he was the most important in mine. We shared the same goals and aspirations, the same values, and the same professional dedication. One goal in particular that we shared would have caused hysterics at our record label if they'd known about it. Spyder and I were determined to start a family.

Ever since we'd gotten married, we'd both wanted children. We actually started trying right away because we wanted more than one child, and at twenty-nine, I was not getting any younger. But it hadn't been working. Mother Nature played her cruel hand, and after two years we still didn't have a baby. By the time we went into the studio to record the material that would become our fifth studio album, *Tropico,* Spyder and I had just about given up trying to get pregnant.

Thanks in part to our prolonged break, the recording of *Tropico* began without much of the stress that had followed our earlier trips into the studio. We had cultivated some really strong songs and we both felt very optimistic about the ideas we had for "We Belong."

Of course, Chrysalis was still pushing an intense timeline for us, in which we were recording the album and shooting the videos for the singles at the same time. The first video we shot was for the song "Painted Desert," and not surprisingly the shoot took place in the desert outside of L.A. We hired an Italian director and began filming on June 21, which was the summer solstice—the longest day of the year.

It was also the hottest. I remember that the glue that held the soles of my shoes together melted. We had to improvise and make it work, but the heat was making me incredibly sick that day. Normally I'm not affected by warm temperatures, but I felt awful. I stayed in my air-conditioned trailer, only coming out when they needed me in the shot. To make matters worse, my clothes were stretched tight on every part of my body. Two weeks prior to the video, the wardrobe person had done a fitting for the clothes I'd be wearing on camera, but for some reason, now the clothes no longer fit. The pair of black pants she'd fit me for, which were supposed to be tight to begin with, were now cutting off the circulation in my waist and legs.

We filmed all day, and I struggled with my concentration the entire way. I couldn't focus and felt sick. The heat was agony, and my clothes were vacuum-sealed to me. I counted the minutes until it was finally finished.

The next day we went to the post-production site. This director liked to edit on a big screen, and the images from the footage we'd shot were huge. Surprisingly they looked pretty good, considering the main character had been barely able to participate.

At one point I was in the editing room alone with the director; he leaned over and in his thick Italian accent, he quietly asked, "You are with child?"

What a crazy thing to say, out of the blue. I barely know this guy.

"Oh no, no," I responded. "We can't have children."

A shot of me was on the big screen, and he paused the footage, walked over to me, and looked intensely into my eyes. Then he smiled.

"Look here," he said, walking over to the big screen and pointing at my face. "You see there in your eye—a little light. You *are* with child!"

At first, I thought to myself, *Wow, this guy spent way too much time in the sun yesterday.* But then I started thinking about how awful the shoot had been, how sick I'd felt, and how my clothes didn't fit. I didn't want to hope, but immediately I made an appointment to see my ob-gyn the next day. The blood test confirmed what the director had seen in my eyes the day before: I was pregnant.

I couldn't believe it; two years of trying and testing, and suddenly it was a reality. Even the girls in the doctor's office cried. I didn't know how to tell Spyder. I needed something special. On my way to meet him at the MCA Whitney studio, where we were recording, I bought a pair of knitted infant booties.

"Where've you been?" he asked curiously when I finally arrived.

"Editing and the doctor's office."

"The doctor's? How come?"

I placed the gift-wrapped box with the baby shoes inside on the recording console. He opened it and stared down at its contents. For a couple of moments, he froze. He looked up at me, stood, and went straight into the bathroom. He didn't come out for thirty minutes. When he finally came out, he headed straight for me and said, "Is it true?"

I smiled and said, "Yes."

The atmosphere in MCA Whitney shifted immediately. Everyone was overwhelmed by the news. They'd all known how difficult it had been for Spyder and me those last two years. The announcement elicited a collective sigh of relief from everyone in our lives. Immediately all of the nerves and stress that went into recording just melted away. Who had time to fret when we'd been blessed with the seemingly impossible?

And so making *Tropico* became one of the best recording experiences either of us ever had. I was euphoric and felt completely inspired. We felt we were making a record that had been blessed with a miracle. The entire band was so relaxed, and all of us were curious to try new arrangements. Being pregnant permeated the entire process. Pregnancy makes all the long muscles in your body relax, and your vocal cords are a long muscle. Suddenly I found that I could do things vocally that I'd never been able to do before. And once I did, I was able to re-create that sound even without the pregnancy hormones. I've never had an easier time singing than when I was pregnant. To hear Spyder tell it, it was the most cooperative I'd ever been (but it was over as soon as I gave birth).

Unfortunately, our good moods couldn't control the fact that I periodically had to deal with the realities of pregnancy. By the time we were filming the video for "We Belong," I was a few months along and suffering from morning sickness. Throughout the shoot, when I felt sick, I'd run to the bathroom, throw up, brush my teeth, reapply lipstick, and then go back for another take. The whole time I had saltine crackers in the pocket of my jacket, and I'd eat the crackers in the hope that they would curb my queasiness.

Morning sickness aside, I found being pregnant and recording to go pretty well together—that is, until Chrysalis heard about what was going on. When Chrysalis got wind that I was pregnant, they were definitely *not* thrilled. They wanted it to be a guarded secret. They didn't want any photos taken of me once I started to show, and they didn't want me talking about babies in interviews. And of course, they made it clear that they wanted me to go right back to my vixen self as soon as that baby was born and get right back on tour. No time off. Not during the pregnancy and not afterward. I guess they thought the audiences wouldn't notice that I was pregnant and that journalists wouldn't ask about it. I told them that they could kiss my ass.

"This is my life," I told them. And I meant it. I was all about family.

For his part, Newman was happy for us but worried about the impact this would have on my career. It meant we'd have to take time off (what a concept) and that my image would be changed in everyone's eyes.

"Why would you do something like this?"

He was an old friend. So I attempted to explain how unhappy Spyder and I had been when we thought we might never have children and how excited we were to find out that we were finally pregnant.

Newman wanted the best for us, but he was also concerned about how the pregnancy would complicate things.

For the first several months of my pregnancy, I continued to work on *Tropico,* making the video for "Ooh Ooh Song" in addition to the videos for "Painted Desert" and "We Belong." Eventually though, Chrysalis insisted that I rest, not because they cared about my well-being but because they didn't want me to be seen. They were adamant that no one get a shot of me when I was pregnant. I wore big coats and loose clothing to hide it. At one point, I was actually chased by the paparazzi, which was unusual in those days, as I was coming out of a movie theater on Fifty-seventh Street in New York. Luckily I was with my old friend Cynthia Zimmer, who proceeded to chase away the photographers with her gigantic Louis Vuitton bag. Needless to say, no one ever saw a photo of me pregnant.

It may sound amusing, not to mention ridiculous, but it wasn't funny at the time. In fact, it was terribly upsetting. This was the 1980s and I was a married woman, yet Chrysalis treated me like some Hollywood starlet from the fifties who'd been knocked up out of wedlock. My pregnancy was something to be ashamed of instead of celebrated. It was insulting, not to mention sexist. It was discrimination in the workplace, plain and simple. I shouldn't have been shocked, but I was. They had spent years objectifying me, but somehow I thought pregnancy would be different. This was about the beauty of childbirth; this was about my life, my family. This should have been off-limits.

Of course all of these frustrations evaporated with the birth of our beautiful daughter Haley on February 16, 1985. She came into the world demurely, no crying, no purple baby skin. Just beautiful eyes shining and bright, with a full head of black hair and eyelashes that looked like caterpillars draped over her eyelids. Spyder and I were overjoyed. At last, we were a family. Everything about our lives was changed the second she drew her first breath. It was a new day. The playing field was about to be leveled, by a seven-pound infant.

⌘

FOR EVERY DAY SINCE I was old enough to think, I've considered myself a feminist. Even before I knew what that word meant, I was one. From early on, I believed that it was my job to advocate for women's rights in every context because we were equal to men in every way. I believed that if you protected the rights of one group, all groups' rights would be protected. It was simple, it was pure, and as a young girl grow-ing up in the sixties, it was my mantra.

In my parents' house, feminism wasn't theoretical; it was being practiced every day. Everyone's paycheck counted and everyone was expected to do their share of child rearing, grocery shopping, and dish washing. My parents did this without debate or bitterness. It was simply their way of life. They loved each other and respected the contribution each of them made to the family. This was the atmosphere that I grew up in. It never occurred to me that women could be regarded as inferior.

I could have been the poster child for feminism in America. I read everything I could get my hands on, attended rallies at school, and protested discrimination against women on the railroad tracks in the middle of town. As I got older, squishing all those worms on my bare legs to prove myself to the boys paid off big-time, helping me scrape my way through high school, life as a military wife, the South, and the boys' club of rock and roll. I forged a path for myself where there wasn't one before, putting up with lecherous radio program directors, sexist record executives, and all their sleazy brethren. Now, at long last, I was someone's mother. My life—both professional and personal—would never be the same.

From the first moment I held that baby in my arms, I knew things would be different. For all my blustering and battling, I'd spent six long years being vetoed or coerced into doing things I didn't want to do. I'd made concessions because I didn't want to be a bitch or cause problems for the band or upset Newman, or because of whatever stupid reason I used to rationalize allowing them. With Haley in my arms, I knew those days were over. I had something to protect that trumped all else: my daughter's future. Now every artistic and financial decision would impact her life. It wasn't just about Spyder and me anymore.

Of course just because Haley was born didn't mean that Chrysalis was about to change their ways. They hadn't had much regard for our personal lives before, and they sure as hell didn't after. It was difficult enough being a first-time mother without their hassling. Ask any new mom how ominous it is to suddenly be responsible for the care and well-being of an exquisite little creature whom you love more than your own life. It's terrifying. Complicating things for me was the fact that when Haley was born I knew *nothing*. I'd never even babysat when I was a young girl. I had no idea what I was doing. Not to mention that being an entertainer brought a whole new set of problems. I knew women who were married to rock stars and who had their babies with them when they traveled. But when I had Haley, I knew few female rock stars to begin with, let alone female rock stars with babies. There's no handbook for being a rocker girl with a newborn baby.

At heart, though, I was simply a working mother, and working mothers are all pretty much the same. Our profession is incidental. We all feel like we have no grip, like there aren't enough hands or hours in the day. Every one of us has to choose between our child and our job every day—and it sucks. There's absolutely nothing worse than having to pry the fingers of your sick-with-a-101-degree-temperature toddler off your body and walk out the door to go to work. It's horrible, even when "work" is performing at Madison Square Garden.

One of the most reassuring things I heard around that time was something Chrissie Hynde told me when I ran into her at an event where she had brought her little girl, who was born about six months before Haley. I'd met Chrissie a couple of times while we were on the road. I'd long admired her work. I loved her voice and I appreciated her unorthodox attitude. But she was dark and moody. There was a distance she possessed. We never really connected, but we were acquaintances and new mothers. I asked her how it was going, being a new mother and a rocker. I hoped maybe, since she was six months ahead of me in the mom department, she would have some good advice or insight.

"How are you doing this?" I asked in desperation. She shook her head.

"I'm not doing it! I'm *not doing it*! I'm just trying to get through the day—*every* day."

Oh, crap! I couldn't believe that she was telling me it didn't get any easier. But once I thought it over, I realized that what she'd said was priceless. I knew that I was no different than anyone else. It's the hardest job that you'll ever love. And it *is* your job. I'll never try to perpetuate the big lie—that you can do it all easily. But I will tell you that it's worth every minute of it.

I started being very honest about what being a new mom on the road was like, and I never stopped telling people the truth. Years later, when I had my second daughter, Hana, I remember a young journalist explaining how other singers readied themselves for their shows.

"I've heard that Mariah Carey lies down in the back of the bus and doesn't take her head off the pillow," the woman said. "Her assistants bring her a warm liquid that she sips through a straw to keep her vocal cords loose."

I nodded. Okay.

"And Céline Dion doesn't speak for twenty-four hours before a concert," the woman continued. "How is it with you?"

So I told her how it was with me.

"Here's what I do. I'm standing in the bathroom on the bus trying to put on mascara for the show. My two-year-old is sitting on the potty saying, 'Mommy, wipe me!' That's how I get ready."

The young woman, who was only twenty-three years old, was horrified. *Horrified!*

"Oh . . ." was about all she managed to get out. I just smiled. I didn't say anything. I didn't need to.

I'm not sure she got it, unless maybe the day came when she went to a meeting with baby puke on her blouse or had to wipe a child's bottom while trying to get ready for something. As for me, I decided that to be a parent is to develop your sense of humor. I decided I rather liked the idea of being Erma Bombeck with an edge.

Ultimately, what I discovered with Haley was a hard lesson that many women, before and after, have been forced to confront: no matter how wonderful having your baby is, there is a big lie about how you can easily have it all as a working mother. The truth is, you can have it all, but it ain't gonna be easy. It's not like they told you—they lied about motherhood and careers. It's harder than you think it's gonna be. You can do it, and I think you should do it. But go in with your eyes wide open, and know that sometimes people won't try to make it easier for you. They won't realize that your children—your family—must come first, and the career second.

And *that* was the part the feminists conveniently left out. There was no mention of how the scent of a newborn could render you incapable of making a clear decision. No explanation of how love-drunk you would be because of baby spit and chubby little fingers. No sense of how some primal bond hard-wired in your brain could cause you to do unthinkable things—like want to stay home and be a wife and mother.

But that's exactly what happened. In the weeks and months immediately after Haley's birth, my brain went smooth. I couldn't write, I didn't want to sing—I just wanted to be with my baby. "We Belong" had missed the deadline to be nominated for a Grammy, and so for the first time in four years, I didn't win one. That wasn't the strange part, though. The strange part was that I didn't even care.

CHAPTER EIGHT

THE HARD WAY

THE DISTANCE THAT HALEY'S birth put between my music and me quickly became a problem. I had a bunch of dudes around me who wanted to continue with the status quo. Keeping things as they had been was their goal, and they did not want to negotiate this next chapter.

Almost immediately after I'd given birth to Haley, a litany of comments from Chrysalis began in an attempt to motivate me back to work by warning me that there could be backlash about me having a baby.

"No one wants to see a rocker who's someone's mother. Mothers aren't sexy."

"You downplay this; no talking about the baby, no photos with the baby."

"You need to make everyone forget it ever happened. You need to assure them that nothing's changed. That you're still the hard-core rocker girl you've always been."

At first I dismissed all this as their typical insulting bullshit, but after hearing this chorus for long enough, I started to believe it. They made me feel that by becoming a mother, I'd risked my entire career. It got under my skin. I started to convince myself that the only way to stay on top was to rush back into things. I became panicked. What if they were even half-right? I didn't want to make a mistake and mess everything up for our future, for Haley's future. So I did what needed to be done: I pulled my new mother self together and went to work. And that was how in 1985, approximately three months after giving birth to Haley, I found myself recording the song "Invincible."

"Invincible" had come to us through our friend Holly Knight, who'd also written "Love Is a Battlefield." She'd written the song for a film called *The Legend of Billie Jean,* and not long after Haley was born, she approached us to see if we were interested in recording it. In a perfect world this opportunity would have come six months later, allowing me to settle into motherhood, but unfortunately it didn't. I really wasn't ready on any level. I was just beginning to get a routine with Haley, figuring out how to avoid falling asleep on my feet. But there I was back in the studio laying down vocals. When it came time to shoot the video, I hadn't even lost all my pregnancy weight, and we ended up incorporating live performance footage with scenes from the film.

Even though the movie "Invincible" was made for ended up being a bit forgettable, the song itself was a smash, a top-ten song in the U.S. It was the hit that everyone had wanted to keep us visible, but it also had another consequence: it whetted Chrysalis's appetite. They didn't want just one hit single—they wanted a full album.

With the success of "Invincible" fresh in their minds, everyone pushed us to go back into the studio. This time, though, it was clear this wasn't about my career and staying in the game, it was about their bottom line plain and simple. What they didn't understand was how not ready we were for undertaking an entire album. It was one thing to bang out one song, but to craft an entire album so soon after having a baby was unfathomable.

When Chrysalis started making noise about a full album, our entire world was consumed by Haley—as it should have been. We knew we didn't have the focus necessary to get the job done. At that point, the most important thing on our agenda was trying to figure out how to achieve something resembling a sustainable routine. Haley wasn't even sleeping through the night. I was up and down at all hours breast-feeding her and living in a perpetual state of exhaustion. I was in no position to do much of anything, let alone write, rehearse, and record an album.

In most professional musical families, the husband and wife don't usually work together, and this means they have different schedules, making it easier to take turns caring for their kids. Alternatively, one of them is a layperson who can stay at home while the other is off touring or recording. In our case, we had the same schedule. If I was working, Spyder was working. It was a logistical challenge. We didn't want to hire a nanny to take care of this baby we'd waited so long to have. We wanted to do it. It's the same struggle all working parents go through. I wanted to stay home, but I knew that would be a mistake professionally, and Chrysalis did not waste an opportunity to remind me of that.

In truth, Chrysalis had bigger problems than dealing with me. The infrastructure of the record company was in the process of a major transition. Over the course of 1985, Terry made it clear that he wanted out, and eventually he sold his share of the company to his cofounder, Chris Wright. This was a stunning, jaw-dropping change. As much as Terry was a pain in the ass, the man knew the record business. He knew how to bring an album to market and how to get it sold. We weren't so sure how things would go with Chris, but the immediate result of Terry's departure was disarray.

Still, the shakeup with Terry and Chris didn't stop Chrysalis from demanding a new album. On the contrary, the banging only got louder as it became clear they needed another hit record as soon as possible. When I told everyone—including my management—about the realities of having a three-week-old baby, the men made light of it, shrugged it off. I begged Chrysalis for a little more time, but they wouldn't go for it. They didn't want to lose the momentum created by "Invincible." Strategically, I couldn't argue with them—they were dead right—but on a human level, it couldn't have been more callous. As always, they retreated behind their contract and used that to get what they wanted— no matter how unreasonable it was.

Their shortsightedness was staggering. They were willing to sacrifice all of our futures for one more shot at making some money. Meanwhile the record label as we knew it was disintegrating around us, and the new record that they so desperately wanted us to record would suffer for it. But everyone continued with the same lines they'd been using for years: "You gotta get in the studio. You gotta get in there." We had no choice; we packed up the baby, got my parents to babysit, and went in to record.

In gambling, craps to be specific, the term "the hard way" refers to rolling doubles to get four, six, eight, or ten. It's difficult. Since you can't roll doubles and get an odd number, "seven, the hard way" is slang for an impossible bet. That's what this record was all about, an impossibility—seven albums in seven years. Hence the eventual title of the album, *Seven the Hard Way*.

Life in the studio on *Seven the Hard Way* was a cruel comedown from the emotional high we'd felt making *Tropico*. There was none of the smoothness or ease that we'd encountered with *Tropico*. This time, everything was a struggle, everybody was agitated, and all of that showed in the final product. There was bickering and fried nerves—not to mention a general lack of cohesion between us and between the cuts themselves. By the end of it, everyone just wanted me to go back to being pregnant.

Attitude was only one part of the problem. Simply put, we didn't have any songs ready. We'd always gone in to make a record with at least half of it written. This time we had nothing. Nothing! And Chrysalis shrugged that off as well. *Just write something.* So while we were trying to record, we were also trying to write the songs. We knew all too well what our process was for writing songs, and writing with the clock ticking in the back of our minds was not a good way to unleash our best material. During the recording, we ended up writing a few good songs that would have become great songs had we been able to work in our usual way, but there was no time. Instead, we recorded songs that hadn't fully evolved, songs that never should have been released. Songs that we weren't even finished writing, for God's sake! We accepted outside material because we had to, but even then the album only contained nine songs, which was ridiculous because normally we had twenty or so contenders from which we'd choose ten to fourteen tracks.

Perhaps the most frustrating aspect of all this was that many of the tracks were almost there, and knowing that felt so much worse than if we'd missed the mark altogether. It was heartbreaking that we'd spent our whole career striving for such a high level of integrity in everything we did, only to have it end up here. More than ever we saw ourselves for the commodities that we were to the label. They didn't care about us, they didn't care about our future, and they sure as shit didn't care about our family.

I kept lecturing myself to get a grip, but when you are a first-time mother you can't get a grip. You're doing well if you can hang on, feed and change the baby, and maybe—just maybe—get a little sleep. I was always very picky about recording. I wanted everything and everybody to be the best possible. I wanted to work my butt off and have everyone else doing the same. And I didn't want to hear any sissy crying about hard work, either. But there were not enough hours in the day to pull that off this time.

I was so exhausted and distracted that I couldn't do my job, and Spyder was so worried about me that he couldn't do his. I'd be ready to sing and Haley would start crying. We took a Winnebago to the studio every day, and we set up a porta-crib in the studio. Between recording sessions, Haley and I retreated to the RV, but when I was singing, I was often distractedly worrying that Haley was hungry or wanting her mama. The problem was, I couldn't just run back in and check on her. It's virtually impossible to get a cohesive vocal if you're constantly starting and stopping, because you lose all your momentum. This meant I had to continue singing until we got the take. That was just how it had to work. By the time I'd get back to Haley, we were both crying.

In the end, only *Crimes of Passion* surpassed this record in terms of difficulty and tension. Of all our albums, *Seven the Hard Way* cost the most to make and sold the least. The record came out in November 1985, but it was not a huge success, peaking at number 26 and only achieving gold record status, with 500,000 copies sold. It was the first time in seven years that we'd made a record that didn't sell a least a million copies. I was stunned but not surprised. We'd made a record we had no business making, at a time when the record company had no business selling it.

Perhaps the worst part of all this was that making this album at this pace was completely unnecessary. Even just a little sensitivity on their part, a little flexibility in scheduling, would have made all the difference in the world. (Spyder still dreams of taking all of our original songs from that record and crafting them into their true potential. It would be closure—maybe one day.) If they'd been willing to give us just a couple of more months and a bit more space, we would have returned to the studio ready to do what needed to be done. After all, making records was our job, and we knew as well as anyone that we weren't ready to stop doing what we loved. We just needed time to achieve a balance between being parents and being musicians. But that kind of latitude was not in the cards.

The hardest thing to stomach was that I knew they were manipulating me. All of the clarity I'd experienced in the immediate aftermath of becoming a mother was still present, but I was simply too beaten down by exhaustion and fear of making the wrong decision to do anything about it. They knew all of this. They could see it in my face and hear it in my voice. They knew I was struggling, and they used it against us.

Ironically, despite our dissatisfaction with the final result and the lower sales figures, the reviews were good. *Rolling Stone*'s Tim Holmes wrote: "Behind the scenes, producer-guitarist-songwriter Neil Giraldo uses the studio like a machete to help Pat slice through the thorny entanglements of relationships. Pat and Neil seem to be a match made in AOR heaven. Their approach combines the sonic bombast of yarbling metal with the intelligence and compassion of feminism. Railing against the constraints of male-dominated power rock, Pat Benatar sings her lungs out with the kind of sentiments that the rock boize might address if only they had the balls. The album is an emotional combat zone."

Interestingly, without any inside information, Holmes made a shrewd observation:

"Luck has little to do with [Benatar's] position as the apotheosis of Eighties American womanhood—she got there through experience."

Damn straight.

THE MINUTE THE RECORD was released in early 1986, we went out on the road. Naturally, this time out everything about touring changed. With a young baby in tow, life on the bus would never be the same.

Strangely enough, Haley seemed to love all the traveling, and in fact touring with her was easier than it had been to record with her. During the recording, we'd been working twelve-to-sixteen-hour days with hours on end spent apart from her, but in our insulated world on the road, the schedule was much more manageable, not to mention predictable. Kids thrive on routine, and because of the strict schedule that touring requires, routine was the one thing we had plenty of. I only had two responsibilities every day: be with Haley and perform. Of course, there were also press events and photo sessions, but for the most part my schedule eased up much more than in the past. With Haley around, it was impossible for me to go to radio stations and do endless press like I'd done in the past, so a lot of those options were simply taken off the table. While this gave us more time to be together as a family, it was definitely part of what hurt record sales. It was, however, a price we were willing to pay.

The entire day was organized around naps and feedings. Calling ahead to promoters to find out the best restaurant in town was replaced with locating the closest Chuck E. Cheese or playground. We carted a ton of crap with us—cribs, playpens, strollers, anything and everything we thought we might need. Haley even had her own Anvil cases for toys. (Later on when our second daughter, Hana, was small and I had learned not to drag around so much stuff, we were in a hotel lobby in New York when a tour bus pulled up. Some crew people got out and proceeded to unload a ton of baby gear. It turned out to be Bruce Springsteen's bus, and his wife Patti was there with their kids. Spyder and I just chuckled, remembering the days when we did the same.)

Even though we'd been touring for years and had played in these cities hundreds of times before, this time was different. We got to explore cities through Haley's eyes, creating wonderful memories along the way. She learned to walk in Minneapolis and had her first birthday in Detroit. She loved the bus. It made her sleep better, which was a blessing because I needed to sleep in order to sing. When she wasn't sleeping on the bus, she was taking in the outside world as it flew by the oversized glass of the tinted windows.

On that tour, my philosophy about many things changed. I didn't want to put on an outrageous show. I wanted to give the audience a layered offering of our music. It was less about the act, more about the music. While this shift made sense for a lot of reasons, my voice paid the toll for that road, too. Because my vocal cords had gotten no rest, I started having throat problems for the first time in my life. I truly felt like I was the caboose of this train, being pulled along with no chance to ever catch up to the rest of it. Doctors were brought in, but all they could do was tell me to take a break from singing and shoot cortisone in my throat.

The whole tour was supposed to stretch out over a period of a few months without interruption. We didn't even have a chance to come home. All this would have been fine if I'd been in great physical shape, but I wasn't. Of course, when I asked them if I could take a few dates off so that my voice could recover, their answer was a resounding no.

"Look, if you don't do these five shows, here's how much we'll lose. You've got to look at the bottom line. You may want a day off, but we're still paying the crew. Look how much that costs!"

When I'd resist, which was most of the time, they'd bring out the big gun: "You've got forty employees who depend on you. Do you want to be responsible for them not getting paid? Those people have families."

That was what always got me. They used my nature against me. Those guys all knew that I was a straight shooter, always the good girl trying to do the right thing. I was a conscientious, ethical person. And they knew that talking about people depending on me would bring me around every time. It's my worst character flaw—not so much guilt as it is that I simply cannot quit. No matter the circumstance, I will be compelled to complete something if I've committed to it—regardless of whether or not I should. The knowledge that people were depending on me only exacerbated this personality trait, pushing aside what was right for me in favor of what was right for others.

I let them bully me into doing what they asked and I stayed out on tour. I couldn't quit and they knew it. Each time they pulled that I said to myself: *This is sickening! They are just playing you, figuring out the way to make you do something that is not in your best interest. Not if you want to keep your voice, anyway.*

But instead of telling them I was onto their tricks, I usually said, "Okay. I can do it. I can do it."

And I did.

WHEN THE TOUR WAS finally over, we returned home and at last got some time off. It was the first time in seven years that we were home and *not* working in some capacity. This was a wonderful period for our family. We were basically having a "normal" life—eating dinner at home and putting our child to sleep in a bed, not a bunk. We had barbecues, saw our family and friends, went to the park—all the things we'd never been able to do before.

Being home felt so good that it overshadowed the fact that a month earlier I'd been handed my first Grammy loss. "Invincible" had been nominated, but I lost to Tina Turner. It was a disappointing end to a disappointing year, and we were ready to put the whole mess behind us. I remember making a note to myself that it seemed unfair that your professional life had to suffer in order for your personal life to thrive. I'd have to work on that.

That balance was something that I thought a lot about when we started talking about the next album. The time off allowed Spyder and Myron to write songs at their own pace, and as that happened we collectively began to figure out where we'd go from there. Long ago, I'd stopped worrying about whether each record outsold the last one; I understood that careers don't work that way. And I wanted my career to work my way. But that didn't mean that I shrugged off my frustration with *Seven the Hard Way*.

In 1987, we finally took the material we'd been working on into Spyder's Soul Kitchen, setting out to record what would become *Wide Awake in Dreamland,* and from the outset, things went incredibly well— the best they'd been since *Tropico.* The difference between recording at a huge studio and doing it at home was like night and day. There was a relaxation to everything we did, an ease to our approach that none of us had felt in years. It didn't hurt that Haley was a couple of years older now, and appropriately, she was more independent.

Being in our own studio emphasized that this was *our* record we were making. It was more on our terms than anything we'd done in years. With *Wide Awake,* the music took the listener into our world both sonically and personally. We recorded what would become our first single from the album, "All Fired Up," as the last song for the record. Peter Coleman and Spyder produced all of *Wide Awake* except for this song, which Spyder and Keith Forsey produced. We were actually enjoying the process again. We were happily doing what we'd always done: creating, writing, and recording. I had gotten motherhood under control. Our personal lives were in order. I was ready to go back to being a rock star in a big way, but what I didn't fully understand was just how screwed up things had become at Chrysalis.

Despite the fact that the album was progressing nicely, Chrysalis was collapsing around us. Before his departure, Terry had been in charge of the U.S. portion of the company and Chris had run the UK and international divisions. As a result of this hierarchy, we hadn't dealt much with Chris. We had a more casual relationship with him. Chris was more of a businessman, whereas Terry worked a lot on developing talent and promoting records.

All that changed when Terry left and Chris was forced to take a more active role in the U.S. business. Chris didn't seem that interested in the day-to-day running of the American company, so he hired an endless stream of "presidents" to do the hands-on work—some good, some not so good. It was a revolving door, with people only staying a short time, which made doing business with them chaotic and disorganized.

This turmoil at the label ended up having a disastrous impact on the release of *Wide Awake in Dreamland* and the subsequent tour supporting it. When the record came out, we went out on tour, but for the first time since 1979, we weren't selling out venues. Right away we could see that this tour was a bust. This was partially due to audience fatigue. Our ridiculous schedule of an album and tour every nine months had officially come back to bite us in the ass. The audience had seen us a lot. We had saturated the market, and this backlash was a direct result. Tours were supposed to be special, unique experiences, and there were very few audiences that were truly insatiable for them. After a certain point, they've had enough, and it seemed we'd reached that point. Our career was slowing down.

But while there was no doubt that we'd been on the road too much, it was the confusion at the label that really sank the record and the tour. Chrysalis was in transition; they didn't focus on marketing and promoting the record as much as they should have or as much as they had with past records. This combination proved fatal to the album and the tour.

Of course we didn't realize this until it was too late, and we started off the tour feeling as confident as ever. At first we simply kicked back and had a great time with Haley on the road. She loved it—and the "house-bus" was her favorite part. She decorated her bunk and was the little queen with an extended family totaling nearly forty people. Her parents and godparents were with her every day. Before she was born, I'd sleep until one P.M. when we were on the road, usually because I'd been up 'til four A.M. the previous night. Now, we were up and out the door first thing in the morning, always looking for ways to entertain an energetic three-year-old. Up until this point, I'd led a pretty insulated and reclusive life, but with Haley we had lots of visits to museums, parks, kid movies—even the dreaded mall.

Though only three, Haley was an avid shopper, and I found myself traipsing through places like the Mall of America with a huge African American bodyguard and a three-year-old decked out in a Disney Princess costume (complete with tiara and "sparkle shoes") and trying to blend in. Women would stop us, oblivious to me, but dazzled by the child and say, "Oh! Isn't she adorable? Is it her birthday?"

I'd smile and say, "Yes. . . . Yes it is," and then I'd get the hell out of there.

We spent many days teaching Haley how to swim in pools across America. Spyder taught her how to play baseball in the artist's parking lot of Pine Knob Music Theater outside of Detroit. Eventually Haley became such an experienced traveler that she would walk into our hotel suite, go straight to the phone and say, "Mommy, I'm going to call room service and see if they have crème brûlée." She was incredibly precocious and sweet, and we adored her.

While all this was fun for us, it was not exactly the rock star life that most people imagined. When I was plugging the new record, I went on Howard Stern, who was in L.A. promoting his new radio show. I had met Howard years back in New York before he became the shock jock he is today. I did my interview first; we were talking about how normal my life was, considering my profession. You know, no trips to rehab, actually married to my daughter's father—the usual. Between takes we talked about having kids, and he asked me where he could get a Disney princess costume for his little girl while he was in L.A.

Also on the show was Robin Leach, who was the host of the show *Lifestyles of the Rich and Famous*, and when Howard started interviewing Robin, Robin launched into his stable of great stories about the excesses of the wealthy. When Robin's aristocratic British voice came to a break, Howard chimed in: "Robin, you should have Pat on the show sometime."

Robin deadpanned, "She just spent twenty minutes telling you how boring she is. Why would I do *that*?" All I could do was laugh, but I had to admit, the man had a point.

But as much fun as we were having, the actual shows themselves became increasingly lackluster. Venues were undersold; the crowds weren't showing up in the same numbers. "All Fired Up" was flying up the charts, but even that wasn't enough to stop the tour's break-neck downward spiral. Promoters began panicking, and before long, our booking agents for the tour were suggesting that we cancel the tour and cut our losses before there was any more bloodletting. We had to protect our relationship with the promoters for future touring. Spyder and I were reeling; we immediately went into survival mode. Our first priority was salvaging everything we could. We'd put our heart, soul, and blood into this for the last nine years. After all the shit and sacrifices we'd made in our personal life there was no way we were going to sit idly as it all went up in flames.

We met with our attorneys and business manager and proceeded with triage. Besides all the damage that had been done to our reputation, there was one truly terrible question to face: we had a crew of forty people who depended on us for their livelihood and if we canceled the tour, what would happen to all of them? The very thing that they'd used to manipulate me on the *Seven the Hard Way* tour was about to come to pass. I was sick. We had to do the right thing. Some of these people had been with us since the beginning. Everyone was paid a severance and released from their obligation to us so that they could work elsewhere.

In the aftermath, I was furious. How had no one seen this coming? The label alone was not to blame. What had our side been doing? Where were our people? How had things gotten so bad? It seemed incredible that everyone was so complacent and hesitant to take a proactive approach to protect all of our interests. We were rife with questions and had very few answers.

GETTING OUR FIRST TASTE of real failure was eye-opening, but we didn't come back from the *Wide Awake* tour to feel sorry for ourselves. We were eager to pick ourselves up and figure out where we'd go from there. As luck would have it, a peculiar chain of events led to a dramatic turn that would reshape our entire career and impact the rest of our lives.

It all began shortly after we returned home from our aborted tour for *Wide Awake,* when our attorney, Owen Epstein, died of a brain tumor. Newman and Owen had been best friends, and for years he'd represented Newman with the club and many of his comedy acts. Our A&R guy, Buzzard, was close with Owen as well. This strange triangle was a little too cozy for comfort, and it inevitably created a conflict of interest for Newman and Owen. Where did their allegiance lie—with us or the label? For years, we'd looked the other way, but the combination of the *Wide Awake* disaster and Owen's death meant that we had new incentive to take hold of the situation.

After Owen died, I retained new counsel, a man named Gerry Margolis who had been Spyder's original attorney for a short time in the very beginning, and the first thing Gerry did was clean house. He examined all of our current contracts and associations, and as we sorted through the documents, it immediately became clear that we had major problems with how our management had been handling things. He sat me down and said it simply and clearly: "The bad news is that there are a lot of problems here. The good news is that they are all fixable."

And then he laid it out for me in no uncertain terms: there were large-scale issues with how our affairs were being handled. For a couple years some things had been going on that we hadn't bothered to take control of; now all that had to change. These problems began with

Newman but they didn't end there. Because money was always an issue and Newman was pretty overwhelmed with his various responsibilities to us as well as the club, he eventually took on a partner, a guy named Richard Fields.

Appropriately, this had all started around the time we made *Get Nervous*. At first Fields didn't actually work with us—he worked with Newman. Fields's job was to help Newman run the business of the club and the comedians that Newman managed, and we were adamant that it stay that way. But Fields wasn't content doing that. All the fun stuff was happening in our world, and slowly he began to infiltrate it. That was when we learned one of the ugly axioms of the entertainment business: if someone works directly with your manager, they are also working with you. Don't dream that they're not.

Spyder and I protested his involvement. We didn't want this guy to just waltz in after all of us had worked so hard together to achieve what we had. But Fields was crafty, making us feel at ease and showing us how much this would help Rick out. Little by little he worked his way in, and we started to see the impact here and there. When we filmed an HBO special, his name appeared as a producer. When decisions were made, he was always there. And he seemed to think he was a Rockefeller. The next thing I knew, our most trusted business manager had been let go. Fields became more involved in everything. Suddenly we had Dom Pérignon in the dressing room. We had fleets of limos taking us around town. We were staying at the St. Regis. We were encouraged to spend money as well. At Fields's suggestion I once bought our attorney Owen a DeLorean, as compensation for doing such a good job on the renegotiation of our record contract. Money was being pissed away moment by moment.

Millions of dollars were coming in the door, and a lot of it was going out for no good reason. We weren't completely oblivious and we didn't go broke, but we weren't in control as much as we needed to be because everything was channeled through my management. I kept feeling like something was very wrong, that what had basically become a show-business empire was in danger of going in the dumper. The money we got from our writing, for example, we protected. But there was money coming in that we couldn't even track. My management even took out a million-dollar life insurance policy on me, using power of attorney. Apparently this was not illegal, but crazy, nonetheless.

There were other reasons that some of this maneuvering slid past us at first. Fame brought more than money in the door. For a while I had a Winnebago full of FBI agents protecting me from a stalker. Out of the blue one day, some crazy guy's parents contacted our office. It seemed their son had just been released from a mental hospital in Georgia because of some loophole that prevented the hospital from keeping him. During his time there he'd written threatening letters saying that *he* was the real Neil Giraldo and that Spyder was an imposter living in his home with his wife and child. The letters claimed he was going to California to set it all straight, even if it meant killing Spyder. Now, I've been around weird people all my life, but the crazies, they're scary. So the FBI was brought in and they lived in our driveway, in a Winnebago, for six months. They finally caught the guy; he'd made it all the way to Denver.

In the end, between the fleets of limos and expensive hotel suites, I would guess that the new partner cost us about half a million dollars. We probably wouldn't have ever discovered the full extent of what was going on if it hadn't been for Owen's death.

As Gerry laid everything out for me, I felt like I'd come out from inside a cave. This had all been happening under our noses. We took a serious look around us, and it wasn't pretty. With the exception of everything surrounding *Wide Awake,* the last few years had been incredibly good to us professionally and financially, but the rate at which everything had unfolded caused us to commit to things without fully understanding what we were getting ourselves into and what the consequences might be. The music business is littered with these situations.

If I was going to be the mother I wanted to be, I needed to be protective. I began to see the future in terms of taking care of a family, of providing for a family's future. All of a sudden it wasn't our money, it was for our daughter, and that realization helped me to see I didn't have to be so nice about things anymore. If I questioned what people were doing, I wasn't being a selfish pig. I was looking out for my child. I became a viper. I ended up marching in and saying, "What the hell do you people think you've been doing? I want an accounting. I want to know where every dime is. And if you don't know where it is, you better be able to explain why."

It was like day and night. I'd drawn a line in the sand. I called each and every asshole on the carpet and started heads rolling. People got fired. People got scared off. People realized that we were done bankrolling whatever they wanted. It was a beautiful thing to see.

While it felt good to take control, in reality this turn brought about one of the saddest points in my professional career. All of the aggravating and tedious experiences we'd been through with the label paled in comparison to what it felt like when we finally had to confront Newman about what had been going on. Newman was one of my oldest friends, going back even farther than Spyder. From the first moment that I stepped off the stage at Catch, he'd been there, listening to my crazy ideas and helping me make them realities. Even when he wasn't sure he agreed or understood what I was talking about, he'd cheered me on. He was my confidante, my manager, and my friend.

Even today, I don't *really* know what happened, and I'm not sure I want to. Somewhere, as things progressed, boundaries became blurred, ethics were pushed aside. People justified their actions and codes of conduct were relaxed in the name of compromise. Being forced to see it all in the daylight hurt immensely. Newman didn't do anything out of malice; that much I knew for sure. His intentions were good and his heart was always in the right place, but he was in the horrible position of keeping the peace between all the parties. Something had to give, and unfortunately that something turned out to be us.

To some extent, I think he and I were both naïve and trusting, and people took advantage of that. I took full responsibility for my part in all of this, but I held everyone else accountable as well. Newman had allowed Richard Fields to play far too prominent a role in our affairs. Fields's actions may have hurt us, but they destroyed Newman.

We parted ways "amicably." It broke our hearts, because Newman was a friend, but for both our sakes, we had to sever the old tie. It was 1988, and I'd been with him for over ten years. Now for the first time in my professional career, I didn't have a manager.

As if that weren't a sea change in itself, there was still one surprise waiting for us. As big as Gerry's discovery about our managerial problems had been, it was not the most shocking thing that he had uncovered when he went through Owen's paperwork. Rustling through the reams of contracts and decade-old documents, he made the most important finding of all: our contract with Chrysalis was no longer legally binding.

It seemed that under California law, a person could not legally be bound to a personal service contract for more than seven years. Though the original document was signed in New York, which didn't have that law, when we had renegotiated our contract with them in 1980, it was done in California, so the law applied. It was now 1988, meaning that more than seven years had elapsed. They had been so caught up with everything happening in their company and focused on pushing us back into the studio that they hadn't realized their mistake until we brought it to their attention. Just like that, we could walk—no lawsuit, no lawyers. We simply could walk away with no repercussions. It was crystal clear; we were *free*.

CHAPTER NINE

ALMOST OUT

THE NEWS THAT WE were no longer obligated to Chrysalis came as a complete shock. We'd been waiting for this moment for so long, we almost didn't know what to do with it. But as monumental as it was, it was almost overshadowed by another, equally dramatic development.

Unbeknownst to us, while we'd been on our problematic tour for *Wide Awake,* Chris Wright had been busy laying the groundwork for a deal that would give the international record giant EMI full control of the U.S. division of Chrysalis, with Chrysalis selling 50 percent of the company to EMI/Capitol. Chris never discussed his plans with anyone from our camp, and we didn't know what was happening until it already had. When the news was announced, we were in disbelief. As bad as things had been, after ten years of being with one company, we were being sold to a group of strangers.

At this point, we were without a manager, and while it was extremely liberating, it was a little unnerving as well. We weren't set up to take care of the huge responsibility of running our careers. We went on the hunt, interviewing several people for the job and ultimately deciding on Danny Goldberg. Danny was well respected in the industry and had an eclectic roster of successful artists such as Nirvana, Bonnie Raitt, and the Allman Brothers. He was a talented, decent man, which was crucial because he had a challenging job ahead of him: fixing the mess we were in and restoring our status.

With Danny signed on, we all went to work repairing the damage that had been done. The first order of business was straightening out our relationship with the record company, and we went in with every intention of crucifying them. As free agents we were in a position to decide if we even wanted a relationship with them anymore. We went with a hard line: *If* we decided to work with them, *we'd* choose the kind of record we were going to make, and it would occur under the conditions and terms that *we* dictated. It was a very big "if." It was unfortunate, but they were going to pay for the sins of their predecessors.

Once the deal was finalized, the two new presidents—Joe Kiener, who was the former vice president of A&R and marketing for Adidas, and Jim Fifield, who was with EMI—came to L.A. to meet with us. The company was "under new management" and they wanted to show us this by having our first face-to-face sit-down. Right away, it was clear Kiener and Fifield were both affable, decent people—a far cry from the people we had grown so used to dealing with. These new executives were actually gracious and amiable people, but they clearly had no idea about our history with the label. They were completely unaware of how contentious things had been and the hell we'd been put through. Chris Wright hadn't bothered to fill them in on our turbulent relationship. Neither of them knew about the discovery Gerry had made about our contracts. They had signed on to Chrysalis thinking that they were getting us along with the company, and I was all too happy to tell them this was not the case.

When we finally got down to business, I was incredibly blunt. I told them in no uncertain terms that we did not owe them another record, and that if we decided to do anything with them in the future, it would be on our terms. We were free to dictate everything that we wanted. They were not going to tell us how to make records.

They were stunned. Not surprisingly, they had no idea our contract was up. They'd assumed we were locked in and were astonished to learn we were no longer under contract. While our last two albums had not measured up to our previous sales and Chrysalis had recently hit it big with Sinéad O'Connor, we still had a history as one of the original artists on the roster. We were no longer the lead artist, but we had been responsible for much of the earlier success that had helped build the label into what it was.

Regardless of what our recent sales had been, they made it clear that they wanted us to be a part of the label going forward, and speaking to our specific concerns, they made it clear that they'd never even thought about interfering creatively. "We would never tell you how to make a record," they told us. "We're businessmen. You make it, we'll sell it."

THOUGH MY GUT REACTION was skepticism, their overtures seemed genuine. There was nothing about their approach that seemed calculated to placate us or kiss our ass so that we'd stay and they could screw us over later. Still, we proceeded with caution, agreeing to do another album with them, but only *one*. We had options for more albums, but those would only happen if we all agreed to continue. Spyder and I would wait and see how well they did their job, then we'd decide whether more albums were in the cards. On this next album as well as any subsequent albums, they increased our advance and royalty rate. Going forward, we would now own 100 percent of our publishing, beginning with our next album, which would be called *True Love*. There was also a provision that increased the royalty rate for all our previous records, both retroactively and on any future sales, to make up for the increased rates that our previous attorney had failed to negotiate on our behalf.

As we signed our names to the new deal, I felt the most tremendous sense of freedom. At last it was there in writing. We'd won. We were calling the shots. We were the ones making informed decisions based on personal comfort and artistic merit as opposed to financial gain. We were finally able to put our best interests, desires, and passions above all. Our contract gave us complete creative control. We could play whatever we wanted, do whatever we wanted, tour whenever we wanted—and there wasn't a damn thing anyone could do about it.

THE IMMEDIATE IMPACT OF our new deal with Chrysalis was that we had downtime. There was no one rushing us back into the studio, no one asking when we were going to get back on the road. With the fallout from the *Wide Awake in Dreamland* tour still fresh in our minds, we knew that we had to be shrewd about where we went from here. We wanted to tread carefully, but we also were not interested in recording anything right away.

This break enabled me to donate some of my time to things I really cared about—children and family. Ever since writing "Hell Is for Children," I had been advocating for children. Controversy aside, the song and its response had a profound impact on my life, leading me to do whatever I could to improve the lives of children. Becoming a mother myself only deepened my commitment. Any time an event, benefit, or recording that was attached to a children's organization came our way, we participated.

It was around this time that we were approached to participate on the second record of Marlo Thomas's *Free to Be . . .* series. The original *Free to Be You and Me* came out in the early seventies, and it used songs, poetry, and sketches to teach kids essential values. This sequel, *Free to Be a Family,* was in much the same vein, but for an entirely new generation of children—Haley's generation.

Growing up, I loved Marlo Thomas. I was a devotee of her TV show *That Girl,* and I'm pretty sure my rabid affection for heavy, long bangs can be attributed to her. I also had fond memories of her dad from *Make Room for Daddy,* and I'd always loved the story of how he created St. Jude's Hospital, where no sick child is ever turned away for the inability to pay. The idea that one man's heartfelt prayer turned into a safe haven and lifesaving facility for the world's children touched my soul.

Because of all this, the prospect of working with Marlo Thomas on *Free to Be a Family* was incredibly appealing, and we happily signed on. The album consisted of material taken from the book of the same name, and like the first one, it empowered children by tearing down the stereotypes about boys and girls. Marlo asked us to record "Jimmy Says"; we'd never done anything like that before, and it was a great experience and a positive message for kids.

Another project I worked on during this time was especially important to me, because it gave me the opportunity to meet one of my inspirations, Elizabeth Glaser. It's been so long now since Elizabeth died in 1994, and I hope people haven't forgotten her and the important work she did. She was the wife of actor Paul Michael Glaser and was one of the first and most visible victims of the AIDS epidemic. In 1981, while receiving a blood transfusion during childbirth, Elizabeth was infected with the HIV virus. Her newborn daughter, Ariel, contracted the virus through breast milk, and the Glasers' son Jake, born in 1984, was also infected. It was not until 1985 that any of the family underwent testing and learned they were HIV positive.

In 1987 the Food and Drug Administration approved AZT as a treatment, but only for adult patients. Elizabeth and Paul fought to get Ariel the drug that might have made a difference, but it was too late, and Ariel died in 1988. Elizabeth then founded the Elizabeth Glaser Pediatric AIDS Foundation, working to raise awareness and research funds. Her story is heartbreaking and heroic. She told it in her 1991 book, *In the Absence of Angels*.

I had just read this gut-wrenching book and was still reeling with emotion when I was approached to participate on the album *Disney for Our Children: To Benefit the Pediatric AIDS Foundation*. We could choose any song that we wanted, and I remembered that a dear friend of mine, Michita, who was a fellow mom at Haley's school, had once mentioned that she'd love to hear me record the hymn "Tell Me Why." When they asked us to do the record, I immediately thought of Michita's suggestion; it was perfect. Spyder and I decided to record the song in its simplest and purest form, like a lullaby.

All the artists who had signed on to do the record were invited to New York to hear Elizabeth speak, and when I met her in person, it was almost spiritual. I don't have a lot of experience with the metaphysical side of this world. I haven't had those kinds of encounters. I don't even know how I feel about them, although I do keep an open mind. But on that day, I felt like I was seeing another plane of existence.

I walked into the large banquet hall that had been set up with a podium and rows of chairs. It was packed with people mingling before it was time to take their seats, but I could see Elizabeth at the far end of the room. We had spoken on the phone but never met each other in person. I made my way to where she was standing. I could see this glow around her. I kept thinking, *What is that? My God, this woman is surrounded by light*. It was truly astonishing, and I couldn't figure out if I was hallucinating. I found myself staring around at other people to see if they were seeing the same thing. Did anyone else see it?

It was a beautiful, soft, warm light. It made you want to be closer to it. Not only that, but there was a powerful vibration coming off her body that was so intense I could actually feel and hear it. It made a humming sound, a low *mmmmmm*. When I finally reached her and we said our hellos, I took her hand, and it was like an electric shock, a jolt—the most wonderful feeling. Her very being simply radiated energy. We both looked at each other and smiled. I knew I was in the presence of an angel. I felt blessed to be there with her, to stand in a space close to her.

And I was blessed again when they asked me to come back so that along with former president Reagan, I could present a check to the foundation. Spyder and I went with Danny Goldberg. While we were waiting in the greenroom for the presentation, President Reagan, the former first lady Nancy Reagan, and a bunch of Secret Service people were there with us. The two of them were just a darling old married couple. As we waited, President Reagan perused the dessert table and he grabbed a couple of chocolate-chip cookies. He began eating them and turned to Nancy, saying, "Aren't these delicious?" with chocolate all over his mouth. Just then Nancy noticed his face and looked like she was ready to faint. She rushed over to wipe his face with a napkin.

I've never been one to be starstruck, but I had never been near a former president before and I figured I might never be this close again, so even though it was completely out of character for me, I walked over to him and said, "Mr. President, would you sign an autograph for me?"

"Sure, sure," he said with a smile. "What's your name, dear?"

"Pat," I replied. I knew he had no idea who I was, so I said, "Just sign it to Pat, please."

"What?" he asked.

"Pat."

"Cat?"

"No, Pat!"

The first lady chimed in with a little frustration in her voice. "Pat! P-A-T!"

You just had to smile because she was both exasperated and pro-tective. It reminded me of the kind of exchanges Spyder and I, and most married couples, have from time to time. It made them human to me. It substantiated what I'd always thought—that people are all the same. I don't care what heights you get to—you're not that much different from the next guy. We all get chocolate on our face sometimes.

I did a few other public-service and charity type things during that time, but mostly we kept out of the public eye and out of the recording studio. The bottom line was that everything from the last few years had caused a lot of emotional stress. Between the problems with *Wide Awake in Dreamland,* the backlash from our tour, the messy end to our relationship with Newman, and the management change at Chrysalis, I just didn't know how much more I had in me. This downtime allowed me to feel that recording was something I could live without. The cumulative effect of ten years of shit had taken its toll. I began thinking that I was ready to hang up my tights and throw in the musical towel for good.

The more I considered it, the more I realized this wasn't just something I was kicking around in my head. This was real, and I meant it. Finally I told Spyder in no uncertain terms that I intended to quit. He could continue on his own—producing, writing, and playing—but I was finished. I was going to stay home and raise our daughter. A few years earlier I would have been shocked to think those words, let alone say them out loud or actually mean them. But I meant them. I meant every syllable. I was exhausted physically and emotionally. For a decade, I'd given my career everything I had—twenty-four hours a day, seven days week. In that time we'd accomplished more than most artists do in their entire career. We didn't have to prove anything to anyone, least of all ourselves, and it wasn't enough fun anymore to do it for its own sake. It hadn't been for a long time.

In many ways, the final straw had been the way everything ended with Newman. To know that the team that had helped make it all happen had also played a role in its near destruction was difficult to face. The people who'd shared our success had managed to taint the experience so badly that retirement seemed to be the only logical solution. There was too much in the way, too many obstacles that overshadowed the joy of making music. To have worked so hard, to have struggled with the rampant sexism, to have kept a marriage intact when everyone was hell-bent on destroying it, to have found a way to balance motherhood and a career—to have done all that only to be done in by my own camp was heartbreaking. I didn't see any way to salvage it once that had happened. It simply wasn't worth it. I was done.

AND THAT WOULD HAVE been the end of it. Truly, the story would have ended right there if it hadn't been for the man I married, the man who always knew how to push me into ideas that initially seemed completely ridiculous and probably were. But he also knew how to be pretty persistent.

One day in 1990, he came to me with exactly this kind of idea: he wanted to make a jump blues album. I was incredulous.

"Absolutely not," I told him. "There's no way we're doing that."

Spyder and I had loved the blues all our lives. It was the music we played at home, for personal enjoyment. Big Maybelle and Sonny Boy Williamson are my absolute favorite singers. Spyder knew that. And he also knew enjoying that music as a listener was one thing, but singing it was something else entirely. He was convinced we would make an amazing record, but I was pretty sure that he'd lost his mind. I didn't want to be one more white chick trying to sing the blues, and Christ, who was whiter than me? It seemed like a recipe for disaster, but Spyder was adamant—just like he always is when he knows he's right about something.

He was right about one thing: with total creative control, now was as good a time as any to roll the dice. I mean, honestly, since I was already thinking about quitting, what difference would it really make? We had a chance to make whatever record we wanted to make. Why not use that to try to remember why the hell we were even making records in the first place? I wasn't completely sold, but Spyder has this wonderfully annoying habit of never totally hearing me, especially when he's trying to persuade me to challenge myself. In the end, even though I wasn't 100 percent convinced, he'd planted the seed in my head, and he knew that was all he needed.

He set out to find the people who could make it work. He started out by approaching our friend Chuck Domanico, a great upright bass session player. Chuck was unbelievable and had played with everyone, including Frank Sinatra and many of the blues players we loved. He was a big guy with this big belly and masses of curly black hair. He was Italian, but he definitely sported an Afro. And he was constantly smoking, coughing, and telling stories. We knew that with Chuck, not only would we make some great music, we'd have a great time in the process.

With Chuckie on board, Spyder then went about putting the rest of the band together, eventually securing the group Roomful of Blues. They were tremendous players out of Providence, Rhode Island. They'd released their debut album in 1977 and had been playing constantly ever since. Respected and revered, they're widely considered to be responsible for paving the way for artists like the Fabulous Thunderbirds and Stevie Ray Vaughan. Spyder loved their work and knew they were exactly who we needed to make this record swing.

"I'll just cut some tracks," he said, trying to entice me. "Then you can see what you think."

"Okay. Just a few tracks, though."

"Right, first we need to pick some songs."

And so we listened and listened. I picked some of my favorites and he picked some of his. The band came to Spyder's Soul Kitchen, and in eighteen days we ended up making a record. The recording was unlike anything we'd done before, a completely unique experience. With few exceptions we recorded without overdubbing, and if something was messed up, we went in and redid the whole thing. Everyone was in a terrific mood all the time, and Chuck set the tone. He was an endless source of irreverent humor that came out no matter what was going on. And he was strictly a union guy. We'd be on a roll recording, and then out of the blue, he'd stop us and say, "Lunch break!" We'd do two or three takes at a time, and then he'd stop us again and say, "That's enough." He'd then blow on his hands, kiss each of his fingers, and say, "You gotta let 'em know when they done good," before laughing uproariously. There wasn't a single moment during the making of that record that wasn't pure delight.

The last song we planned to record for *True Love* was "I Feel Lucky," which was going to be an up-tempo, swinging rave in the style of Louis Prima. Spyder and Myron had written the lyrics, and when it came time to write the music for the song, to get in the mood, Spyder would start drinking coffee and smoking cigarettes first thing in the morning. He never was much of a coffee drinker because it just made him a wired maniac. He'd have an occasional espresso after dinner, but that was the extent of it. But when he was creating the music for "I Feel Lucky," I'd find him at the piano, jacked up on caffeine, working out this *boom, boom, boom* progression. He was the Mad Hatter on steroids, but he wrote one hell of a song.

"You are nuts!" I'd tell him. "You're flying! What do you think you are doing?"

"You gotta hear this song! It's gonna be great!"

The song was this fast-paced swing number that was unrelenting from the first note. He showed the horn guys what he was doing, and they jumped all over it. Those guys just rocked it. When they finished I shook my head and said, "Spyder, you are a maniac. I hope you know that."

"Oh yeah, I know it," he said with coffee-induced glee.

You can hear the fun we were having in every bar of *True Love*. This recording was joyous for many reasons, not the least of which was that we felt like we were being reborn. Spyder called it a *cleanse,* an event that turned the tables on the old mistakes and grievances.

When it came time to do the video for the title track, "True Love," the idea was to show the beauty in all the ways that people experience love. That included the love between a parent and a child, between brothers and sisters, between a preacher and his congregation, between friends. This was about true love in its many forms. We filmed scenes of a young couple holding an infant, beautiful laughing children—and the label wanted it all cut out and replaced with me . . . being sexy. Yawn. It was ridiculous. And it didn't happen; in the end they came around and the result was a tender, beautiful, and sensual video. Compared to our past dealings on creative issues, their initial opposition to the video ended up being just a small bump in the road.

We did a short tour to promote the record, convincing Chuckie and the entire Roomful of Blues band to go with us. Unfortunately promoters were still a little nervous after the disastrous *Wide Awake* tour. Rather than take the chance that audiences might not want to hear us playing the blues, they covered their butts by billing the show with the ambiguous moniker "An Evening with Pat Benatar." As a result, there were occasionally disgruntled audience members who'd come to hear us play our bigger hits and would get unruly from time to time.

"Play 'Heartbreaker'!" they'd call out.

"Darlin', you're at the wrong show," I'd call back.

We were playing songs off the record, like B. B. King's "Payin' the Cost to Be the Boss" and "I've Got Papers on You," and Albert King's "I Get Evil." There was no question we rocked, but there was also no mistaking the fact that "Hit Me with Your Best Shot" was not happening at these shows. We tried to get the advance promotion changed so that people knew what they were going to be hearing, but there wasn't enough time. The main thing that happened was that a few marquees read "Rock and Soul."

Even with that small glitch, we had a blast. Chuckie entertained us with his endless stories, and traveling with Roomful was like having all your crazy brothers over for Sunday dinner at once. We had a lot of laughs, but most important, it wiped the tour slate clean. It was like starting over; we'd been given a gift, a second chance.

There's no doubt that as an album *True Love* wasn't as commercially successful as the earlier records, but it was a completely different genre. It had absolutely no radio support. It was like comparing apples and oranges. Blues records can't be held to the same sales standards as pop and rock records. *True Love* sold 339,000 copies in the U.S., and for the blues, that's a damn good showing.

In the end, making *True Love* turned out to be the most important decision of our career. Spyder's idea to create a record that had a completely different direction was brilliant and fateful—exactly what we needed to conjure the spark that had brought us together in the first place. *True Love* was a labor of love from two people who couldn't bear the thought of a life without music. When it was finished it had surpassed all that we hoped for. We were newly inspired and ready to begin the next phase of our musical life together. *True Love* was God's gift to us for sticking it out.

WITH *TRUE LOVE*, we'd put the new Chrysalis's pledge to give us creative control to the test, so we decided to sign on for another record, *Gravity's Rainbow*. It would be our last with them.

From the start, we were looking to make this album something that was more traditional for us, but the impact that *True Love* had on our psyches was apparent. The high from *True Love* carried over to *Gravity's Rainbow,* making the atmosphere positive and optimistic. We were all happy to be there. Don Gehman was co-producing with Spyder, and he was a mellow, upbeat guy. He brought along his engineer, Rick Will, who we could tell right away was born under the same "I'm a bent, lovable lunatic" sign that Spyder was. We had some fun. We were happy to be back playing the kind of music that had been our signature sound. Seeing all those amps again and hearing that wailing guitar just made me smile. I had tucked my love for all of this away in a safe place and it had survived. In spite of everything, I still loved my job.

By the time we recorded *Gravity's Rainbow*, Spyder and I had given up trying to have another child. We'd been trying for almost nine years—ever since Haley had been born. In 1988, I'd had an ectopic pregnancy and lost the baby very early on, and that was enough to make us feel that we were not destined to have another child. We desperately wanted one, but it just wasn't going to happen.

One weekend while we were making *Gravity's Rainbow*, we went away—just on a little getaway to decompress from recording since I had to be back on Monday to shoot the cover for the record. That weekend, Spyder and I talked about how we really needed to stop trying for another baby. Obviously God had a different plan for us, and we were so grateful to have Haley, who was now eight years old. We made a pact to give up the hope of having another child and simply live in the present, enjoying our family the way it was.

On Monday after the relaxing trip, I went to the studio where the shoot would take place. I got my hair and makeup done, and then it was time to go to work with the stylist. She'd put together a bunch of outfits for me to try on, but I always hated this part, dressing and undressing—the whole thing was so tedious. On this particular day, it was especially awful because apparently she'd gotten all the wrong sizes. Everything was uncomfortably snug.

"I don't understand it. I know I took the correct measurements," she said, exasperated.

"Don't worry about it," I said, trying to adjust the seams on my clothes. "Let's just get it over with."

We tried on several outfits and took Polaroids to preview how they looked before we started the actual shoot. One of the photos in the pile was a close-up of my face to check the lighting. I picked it up to see if I liked the makeup, and looking closely at my face, I stopped dead: there, in my eyes, was the light I'd seen before, in the footage from the "Painted Desert" video.

I couldn't believe what I was seeing. I told myself not to get my hopes up. I didn't say a word to anyone, and I finished the shoot. On the way home I had the limo driver stop at an all-night pharmacy, where I bought a pregnancy test. This was back when you had to wait to do the test in the morning, so when I got home, I hid the test and set my alarm to get up before Spyder. I got up the next morning and took the test. The line was blue. It was a miracle. Nearly nine years of trying and finally, a baby. I ran into the bedroom and jumped on my sleeping husband, waking him out of a dead sleep.

"Spyder, wake up! We're pregnant!"

"What? What? What are you talking about?"

"I took the test, it's blue, I'm pregnant."

He just stared at me. "Nope. I don't believe it. You did it wrong. I'm going to the drugstore and getting another test."

It was six-thirty in the morning and the closest pharmacy didn't open until seven A.M. He sat there waiting, and when it finally opened, he bought $150 worth of tests. We spent the next hour turning sticks blue. Oh yeah, we were definitely pregnant, and we had a pile of blue plastic sticks scattered across our bathroom floor to prove it. The next day I went to the doctor, and it was verified—we were having another baby.

The knowledge that I was pregnant again made the release of *Gravity's Rainbow* a particularly joyous occasion. This album was back in the AOR pocket and contained a big hit with "Everybody Lay Down," which reached number 3 on the album rock chart. A second single, "Somebody's Baby," was released with a beautiful and compelling video.

Of course, when it came to the label's reaction to my pregnancy, old habits die hard, even when the old habits are being perpetrated by new people. This was partly because by the time we found out I was pregnant, the reasonable and rational team of Joe Kiener and Jim Fifield was gone and Chrysalis had been completely absorbed into EMI. Now we were EMI artists under the direction of Charles Koppleman, CEO, and Ron Fair, the head of A&R, part of a monstrous company with their fingers in every pie, from music publishing to electronics. With all that the folks at EMI had going on, you would have thought they'd have better things to worry about than my pregnancy. Apparently not. They shouldn't have cared but they did. While they didn't put us through the hell that we went through with Haley, they were clearly displeased and made no attempt to hide their dissatisfaction.

Gravity's Rainbow came out, and though I was pregnant, we still went on tour. From the start, though, the performances were tough. I had terrible morning sickness that made it really difficult to focus. Eventually it got bad enough that we had to cut the tour short after three or four weeks. Our decision didn't go over well at the label, and there was no doubt that the premature ending hurt sales. While it was disappointing, we made no apologies about where our priorities were. We didn't forget how blessed we were to be in the situation we were in, and how careful we needed to be in order to preserve it.

Whether the record execs they liked it or not, Hana Juliana was coming, and she arrived in the world on March 12, 1994, screaming her head off. She was so loud that Spyder and I started laughing and her godparents, Moni and Myron, jumped up and peered through the delivery room windows to make sure everything was okay. She was a force of nature from the moment she arrived. She was beautiful, with twinkling eyes. As for Haley, all of her sisterly instincts came out, and she doted on Hana night and day. We worried about her having been an only child for so long and thought maybe she'd resent this new little creature, but if she felt any of that, she never showed it. She adored her baby sister. Our lives were officially on our terms, and we were going to do whatever we could to keep them that way.

CHAPTER TEN

ALL'S FAIR IN ROCK AND MUSIC

AFTER *GRAVITY'S RAINBOW*, WE made the decision, once and for all, to leave Capitol/EMI. The decision was mutual and without any big fireworks. The timing just seemed right to go our separate ways. Though we'd grown up there, it was not the label it once was, and it hadn't been for years. The record business was made up of too many bean counters and not enough guitar players. Just watching what had happened to Chrysalis after the EMI merger was disheartening. Artists were considered roster "prizes" to be included in money deals, stock values, and corporate wheeling and dealing. While we were treated much better than we had been in the 1980s, it came at the expense of marketing and promotion. Simply put, they weren't supporting our records as they once had, and we were ready to move on to whatever the next phase of our career would be. EMI wasn't exactly crying to see us go.

Not long after our departure, they put together a hits package, *All Fired Up: The Very Best of Pat Benatar*. Now that we were gone, they didn't have to pay us advances or consult us on artwork, content, or release dates. In fact, when it came to our catalog, they could do pretty much whatever they wanted. Since these were songs that already existed and they owned the masters, they could decide things unilaterally. They could package and repackage them as many times as they wanted with barely any overhead. For a while, they seemed to put out a compilation every year—with no input from us whatsoever. They'd pick some producer who'd go in and hack up our original recordings and make a record out of it. It was just put out there with no promotion. Throw it against the wall and see if it sticks.

I knew it was "just business," but I felt used anyway. While in the short term their efforts didn't hurt us financially, if they got greedy and saturated the market, it would make selling new product difficult. We had to make sure this didn't happen. They didn't care how this would impact our future, because they didn't have any claim to our future. It was shortsighted and mercenary, and of course, it was all about the bottom line.

But not for us. We weren't shortsighted. In the end, the EMI product was very profitable for us, but we knew we had to become better businesspeople. We began to look at ourselves as a brand. We had worked long and hard to establish what we were. We were unique; no one else could do what we did. That had to be worth something. We still had a lot of music in us and we weren't about to let anyone screw that up. Figuring out our next step was crucial, and it was made more complicated by the fact that we also had to find new management. After *Gravity's Rainbow*, Danny Goldberg had decided to take a hiatus from his management company, going instead to Atlantic Records as president. We started looking and had a few short-lived relationships but finally decided on the team of Elliot Roberts and Frank Gironda, who went right to work getting us back out in the public eye.

Right away they approached us with an idea for a tour package: Fleetwood Mac, REO Speedwagon, and us. My initial response was "Absolutely not." I had nothing against those other bands, but we'd never been part of a package before. I was used to headlining on our own. However, I also knew we were in transition and without a record label. After much discussion, Spyder, Elliot, and Frank convinced me that it was a good idea, a way to see where we stood with audiences with minimal risk. We signed on.

And so we spent the summer of 1995 traveling the U.S. as part of the Can't Stop Rockin' tour. It ended up being a great experience, a little like being in the circus. It was a huge operation with three bands, three road crews, and an endless parade of buses and semis. We forged friendships with everyone on the tour and had a great time. We played baseball and had barbecues while our kids hung out together. All in all it was just a great group of people.

This was Hana's first tour, and she was fourteen months old when it began. Like her sister, she was a wonderful traveler who loved the road, the bus, and swimming every day. She learned to swim in the pool at the Arizona Biltmore, and she loved being onstage, something that Haley didn't care too much about. Haley was a little shy when she was small, but Hana wanted to go out onstage all the time. In general it had been our policy to keep the girls out of the public eye, but Hana would wait in the wings every night hoping one of us would scoop her up and bring her out. I remember taking her with me one night; I had her in my arms, and I introduced her to the audience:

"Hey, everyone, say hello to our youngest, Hana." They all cheered, and Hana had a huge grin on her face. The crowd was yelling pretty loudly, and I asked her, "Are you scared?"

"Noooo, I like it," she said happily. After that we had to find ways to distract her during the performance or she'd cry to go out. We'd station crew members in the wings, because she'd always try to escape from her babysitter and sneak onstage during the show to get bubblegum from Spyder's onstage stash. We'd be deep into the set and this baby would calmly walk out onstage and grab a handful of bubblegum off of Spyder's stool. The audience would go crazy, and of course that only encouraged her to do it again at the next show.

Overall the tour was a success for us. Throughout that summer the reception we got from the crowd was encouraging—strong enough to show us that there was plenty of support for us all around the country. There were still a lot of people who would show up to hear us, and that was an important confidence boost that would help dictate our next step.

Now that we knew there was still goodwill out there toward us, it was time to try putting out a record. Tours were good but they weren't enough to keep us relevant. To do that, we needed to record new music. We'd have been delusional to think that once we left a major label, we could just sit back and hope people remembered us. Without the exposure that new material generated, we could do ourselves long-term damage. We stood at a crossroads, knowing that if we didn't step up and make a new CD, we might never again be in the position to do so with any fanfare.

We could have easily signed with another major label, but why? Fifteen years of being big on a big record label had left us feeling exhausted and demoralized. The label had helped us to tremendous success but at a huge psychological cost. Our goal now was not to replicate that success, but to find ways to continue to do what we loved and make money in the process. And so instead of jumping right back in with another major, we set off on a different journey.

Around the time that we split with EMI, I read an interesting article about the singer-songwriter Ani DiFranco. At the time, I wasn't all that familiar with her music, but I was instantly fascinated by what she was doing. In 1990, she'd started her own record label called Righteous Records (later changed to Righteous Babe Records), and through this label, she had financed, produced, and distributed her own records. This was something that Spyder and I had been talking about for years—creating an independent label that would give us complete artistic freedom to do whatever we wanted at our own pace.

What seemed like far-fetched crazy talk started to make sense after I read about what Ani DiFranco was doing. The recording industry has long had a rich history of independent labels. Let's face it: Jac Holzman founded Elektra Records in his dorm room in 1950. Sun Records in Memphis launched Elvis Presley. Motown. The list goes on. These were historic labels, and if Ani could do it, so could we. I always say, "God bless Ani DiFranco," because she was my inspiration to stop thinking about being independent and actually start doing something about it.

As it turned out, this intense interest in going independent combined with another trend; by the midnineties, we could see that digital music would soon be forcing change on the recording industry. For a few years digital technology had been slowly seeping into the music business, and we'd been keeping an eye on how it was changing things. *Gravity's Rainbow* was the first recording we edited and mastered digitally. Spyder loved the technical aspect of recording, and he embraced digital advances with enthusiasm. As producer he was constantly looking for new ways to push the boundaries of what he could do in the studio, and the digital world held all kinds of possibilities, many of which he utilized on *Gravity's Rainbow*. Its value was undeniable, and in the years since *Gravity's Rainbow*, Spyder had been steadily incorporating digital methods into his recording process whenever he was playing around in his Soul Kitchen. At first it was simply digital editing and mastering, but then he moved on to digital recording and mixing.

While Spyder was fixated on the new studio experimentation that digital made possible, my goals were different. The way I saw it, digitally recorded music opened up a whole new way to get music to the masses. No more large manufacturing costs, no expensive album art—it might not even be necessary to make actual CDs if we didn't want to. All these ideas crystallized in 1994, when Spyder and I read an article about an innovative new concept called "file sharing." Learning about this process helped me visualize how we could actually implement this new distribution to the consumer while cutting production and manufacturing costs. Basically we'd be eliminating the middlemen, who of course were the record companies. It would no longer be necessary to have their money or muscle to get product made and sent out to the public. Distribution would be simple and cost-effective. The playing field would be level: artists and small labels would have the same access and clout as the majors.

Spyder and I each had our own vision for the future significance of digital music, differences that mirrored our original disagreement over the role of music videos. Spyder was fascinated by the impact on the actual music and the limitless creative possibilities that the digital age ushered into the studio. My interests were not so lofty. I was a businesswoman first and foremost, and though the artist inside me saw what technology could do for recording, I was more drawn to how it could prevent the financial turmoil that we'd experienced at the hands of the record label throughout our career. It was true digital was untested and uncertain, but if it worked, it would return the power to the artists, where it belonged. As with music videos, we recognized the game-changing promotional power that existed in digital music if we used it to meet our own needs.

What I was after was simple: the end of the record industry as we knew it. I wanted to see the collapse of the major labels' stronghold on music. Consolidation had both strengthened and weakened the majors. They had more money and clout, but they often lacked innovation. If the labels didn't get on board with the digital age, they would implode. And since we despised the way they did business, we figured we'd be only too happy to stand by and watch it happen. The digital age was going to shake them up and change everything, and I wanted us to be part of it. That said, we didn't want to be moguls and we were not looking to build an empire. This wasn't about creating a label that had dozens of bands on it and being able to control other people's careers; it was about controlling our own.

The environment seemed ripe for us to take advantage of the digital advances and strike out on our own, but as prepared as we were mentally, we still had reservations. We could finance a record ourselves, take our time making it, put together a distribution deal, and retain control over everything. We could afford to do it. Each time we met with accountants, we were pleasantly surprised at how much money we had managed to keep over the years. It's frightening to see the money lost by musicians through personal lifestyle choices, bad management, and record company rip-offs. But our years of being basically frugal people and homebodies had paid off. Even so, financing a record ourselves would be taking a huge chance. We had the money, but we didn't have unlimited funds. We weren't set up like corporations that could leverage one loss against other wins. If we rolled the dice and lost, we could lose everything. We'd be putting not only our career but our children's futures on the line.

Spyder and I had never been impetuous people when it came to finances, so we decided to move ahead with caution. We wanted to test the waters without diving in completely. Rather than simply launch into our own indie venture, we made the calculated decision to sign with an indie label for one record, so that we could learn the business model and see if it was something that we could make work on our own.

With this specific goal of learning in mind, we started searching for an independent label that would meet our needs, and in the process we met a man named Tom Lipsky who ran an independent label called CMC International Records. A really dedicated guy, Tom loved rock and roll, and his only goal was to create an environment for artists to make the best music they could. And he was a character! A gregarious Southerner, he only wore shorts—no long pants ever. He said that he'd been denied entrance to some of the finest restaurants because he refused to change those shorts. You just had to love him.

Tom spelled out the deal, telling us exactly what he could do and what he could not do. And he hired the best people available (including people stolen right out from under moguls like Clive Davis) to do those things he couldn't. He told us exactly what kind of money he'd put into the recording and promotion. He believed we needed to have a new record out there and he was willing to put his money where his heart was. What he asked was that we make the record we wanted to make, with no thought to what might play on radio or what might be written about it. He wanted our music as we saw it. Moreover, there was a level of artistic respect we'd never before felt. He didn't see us as product to simply be packaged or manipulated. His philosophy was that people who'd made great strides in the industry should have the opportunity to make the music they wanted, to keep producing, keep being creative—but on a different level.

From our first conversations with Tom, it was clear that he understood exactly what we wanted to do with this record. Neither one of us had any big expectations about what this deal would do. There was no bullshit talk of platinum sales or aspirations of returning us to our former glory. And quite frankly, we didn't want either of those things. I'd been a rock star, I'd sold out stadium shows, I'd been chased by paparazzi. I had no interest in any of that. What we wanted was to figure out how we could keep our personal life intact, make money, and still have fun. I wanted to be a badass mother who could rock and make a living doing it.

This arrangement met those needs, while also having the added benefit of getting a new album out to help us keep a toe in the water from a recording standpoint. I didn't want my career to disappear, but I did want it to belong to me, not some record stooge. Regardless of how the record performed this would be a win-win situation for us. The deal with CMC was a means to an end, satisfying our need to keep recording while also giving us the chance to learn the business of running a label. Once we accomplished that, we'd be able to branch out on our own.

The result of all this was *Innamorata,* a record we made under some of the most peaceful circumstances we'd ever worked in. The record is one of my favorites; it was the beginning of the artistic experimentation we'd been missing for so long. Sure, we'd had freedom with our last two records on Chrysalis, but there was always pressure to sell. They went along with our plans because they had to by contract, not necessarily because they wanted to. There's such freedom in creating when you aren't concerned with critics or people trying to make your life miserable.

From the beginning, Spyder wanted to mix the tone up a bit. He wanted to make an electric/acoustic record, bring a viola in—keep the vocals aggressive but make the bed a bit different. The only electric guitar is actually on "River of Love," and even that felt a little odd at first because we were going in another direction. The title cut, "Innamorata," was the first song we recorded, where we got the technique down. Once again, we made it live with very few overdubs. One of the songs, "Papa's Roses," was inspired by Katherine Dunn's provocative novel *Geek Love,* about a traveling carnival and the crazy family that runs it. It's quirky and fascinating, and it encourages a great deal of interpretive thought. We ended up making a beautiful video for the song "Strawberry Wine," which we shot in Dallas with two very young directors. It was simple but innovative, and, most important, it was peaceful. I was sad more people didn't get to see it, so we included it on a video compilation we later did called *Choice Cuts.*

In the end, *Innamorata* sold a respectable amount of records, but that wasn't the point. We'd accomplished what we'd set out to do, and that convinced us we were ready to go independent and start our own record label. Though it wasn't nearly our most successful record sales-wise, we made more money on that record than on any other we'd done simply because we owned everything—all the publishing was ours. Even when you're a major star and selling millions of albums, you're still only making less than a dollar on each record you sell (in some cases it's *a lot* less than a dollar). While we were making more than that in our most recent deal with EMI, in comparison it was still terrible.

Almost all the money from each record sold would go into the pocket of the label. But with CMC, we took home about 40 percent of the revenue from every record sold, a number that presumably would be even higher if we had our own label. So even though we were selling less, we were making more, and we were doing it all without having to put up with any crap from the record company. This was a revelation. Not only was this going to give us the creative freedom we craved, it was going to be lucrative as well.

Seeing the money we could make combined with our gut feelings about the fundamental shifts digital technology was bringing to the industry. After years of having other people tell us what to do, being independent just felt right. We could put aside the commercialism, and the charts, and even the profits. I'd get to make the music I felt like making and have a wonderful time doing it. Nobody would be saying "You need to cut this song because so-and-so has publishing." Or "This one's a radio-friendly record." Or "You need to get in the studio today no matter what because the schedule is everything." I would make music at my own pace and not think about hits. If one or two squeaked out onto the airwaves, it would be great. It would be gravy. But my lifestyle didn't have to change. I could still have time to be with my family and friends. I could have a life.

We played a few dates with Steve Miller, who was quite the gentleman, and tried some of the *Innamorata* music out. On the whole, it was received enthusiastically, enough so that we put together a nationwide club tour that took us from St. Louis to Chicago, Cleveland, Scranton, New Haven, Norfolk, Phoenix, and Las Vegas. We played Tramps in New York and the House of Blues in New Orleans. Of course the crowds loved hearing our older hits, but we were pleased that some of the biggest ovations came from performances from *Innamorata*, including "Only You," "River of Love," and an acoustic version of "Papa's Roses" that Spyder and I did.

Musically this tour was exciting. Switching from electric to acoustic performances was great for contrast, and I believe it added some fascinating texture to the shows. We also opened shows for Styx during that time. It was one of the best ways to showcase the music for a big crowd yet not have to work on a grueling eighteen-month tour. Again, these decisions were ours to make. No record company was telling us we *had* to do something.

I never again wanted to work for a company that *got inside my head.* I didn't want some guy in a suit invading my brain and rattling around in there. Almost from the beginning I'd been saying that I wanted a situation where *everybody did their job.* My job is to make music; the label's job is to sell it. How hard is that to figure out?

AROUND THE TIME THAT we'd been preparing to take *Innamorata* on the road, I was approached about participating in an upstart new traveling tour that was beginning that summer, something called Lilith Fair.

On its face, the pitch was quite a concept: an all-female festival tour celebrating women in music. Grammy-winning singer-songwriter Sarah McLachlan came up with the idea, not as a political statement, but to showcase the wonderful music that women continue to contribute to the culture. But political or not, Lilith Fair grew out of Sarah's refusal to accept stereotypes about female artists. I had always loved Sarah's voice and songwriting, but her business sense and entrepreneurial spirit were equally admirable. First, she was fighting stigmas like the decades-old idea that radio listeners wouldn't stay tuned to a station that played two female artists in a row. Then, of course, there were the concert promoters who remained skeptical about booking too many women on the summer tour schedule.

To counter the portrayal of women as bad business, Sarah and her friend (and fellow Grammy-winning singer-songwriter) Paula Cole booked a summer tour in 1996. One of their shows was called "Lilith Fair," after the biblical Lilith who refused to obey Adam and exited Eden for parts unknown. The shows were so successful that in 1997, Sarah launched a wider Lilith Fair tour, playing thirty-five cities, with a variety of female musicians, and it became the top festival tour of the year. I already had our *Innamorata* tour booked, so when I was approached about playing Lilith Fair, I found I only had two dates available. But you couldn't have kept me away from those two. It was such an honor not only to be asked to participate in this groundbreaking event, but to be told that I had been an inspiration for many of the young women involved.

Some people questioned whether this "all-chick-singer" tour could work. Would this end up being a bunch of divas fighting over dressing areas? Would egos spin out of control? Could that many women actually be trusted to *get along*? At the press conference just prior to my August 19 appearance in Milwaukee, I told people exactly how I felt about all that kind of talk:

My first impression [on being asked] was that I was so happy. I've waited twenty years for this. I stood there in 1978 in front of a bunch of people who patted me on the head and said "That's nice" and "We don't think that can ever happen." They were convinced that women would never be able to compete with their male counterparts regarding record sales and concert attendance. So for me to be here with all of them [the female artists], I could just cry. It's so emotional. It's fantastic. I've heard really great things; I haven't heard any bad things.

This is my first day here so I'm here with a lot of enthusiasm and am honored to be with all of you [the other women on the tour]—who I know were about five or ten when I was beginning! So, it makes me feel like the grandma, which is kind of nice. The important thing is that it isn't about divisiveness—that's what I don't see. I see that it's about a celebration of being female, not about separatism or any negative things about being female, but the good things that we are. Everyone is looking for dirt, but I haven't heard any.

I played two nights and truthfully they were the best forty-eight tour hours onstage I'd ever had. Standing up there with all those successful, capable young women made me think of the early years when every day was a fight just to be a woman in the man's world of rock and roll. I thought back to all the radio promoters and record men. The guys who'd said things just to try to make me feel uncomfortable and the guys who told me I didn't know what I was talking about. I thought about wearing baggy clothes to hide my round pregnant body and having the program directors at the radio stations lick their lips as they asked me to take a seat on their laps. I thought about the extra five layers of skin I'd had to grow just to be standing on that stage two decades after that lunatic songwriter had chased me around a piano.

While times had changed, I knew that none of those problems had gone away completely. I knew that all those women—both those onstage and those in the crowd—had to contend with these issues in one way or another, usually on a daily basis. But the most important thing was that all of us kept going. We'd be damned if we were going to let bullshit get in the way of our vision for the future, our plan for life. I'd spent my entire career being the only female in a sea of guys. Now I was surrounded by women who, like me, couldn't resist the call to perform. I watched them up there, confident and in control. Seeing all of those young women enjoying each other's musical talent, supporting each other, warmed my heart. Women like Sarah McLachlan, Paula Cole, Meredith Brooks, Jewel, Shawn Colvin, and the Indigo Girls were playing their music, interacting with each other, being treated with respect, and proving once and for all that an all-female lineup could sell out festivals.

The best part was that their shows were all spectacular. That was what made me almost cry with happiness. I'd felt like I was constantly out there fending off the lions with a baseball bat. I kept thinking what a struggle it had been and how far we'd come as female performers. Just like me, they had a sound in their heads that they had to follow;

they had to put their voices out there. And it made me so proud to know that without even realizing what I was fighting for, I'd been on the front lines on behalf of young, strong women like the ones I witnessed onstage those nights. I'd signed on with big hopes, but even those hopes couldn't prepare me for the atmosphere of beauty that permeated the entire tour. It was an uplifting and emotional experience. It was an incredible sisterhood. It was the Estrogen Express.

On the second of my two nights, we sang an ensemble number together, Joni Mitchell's "Big Yellow Taxi." I got the fun line, "Late last night, heard the screen door slam / And the big yellow taxi took away my old man." Earlier that day, we'd done another press conference at a big long table with all the ladies. I'll admit I got teary eyed when each of them spoke about the sacrifices that those of us who'd gone before had made and how grateful they were for what we'd done. I'd never been prouder to be part of a group of women who forged a path where none had been before so that future generations of women could walk unencumbered in pursuit of their dreams.

The next day, Lilith Fair's website said: "Pat Benatar rocked the house."

IN MY HEAD, THE strength that I gathered from Lilith Fair mingled with my newfound understanding that I could be successful and independent. Together they solidified my resolve that whenever we were ready to release another album, we would do so on our own. Bold vision required bold moves.

This resolve was aided by a rather serendipitous encounter after the tour. For years we'd been scouting land in Hawaii, near where we married in Hana. We could see how wonderful life on that island could be, the privacy and the inspiration of the surroundings. Now we could afford to consider buying the land, building a house, and living there part of each year. The problem, of course, was the very thing we loved about the area: its remoteness. This is the jungle. If you don't build close enough to a populated area, you will never get the power and water hooked up. You have to start from absolutely nothing. We had looked every year for just the right place.

It got crazy. It seemed like every year we went to Hana for vacation and spent the whole time looking for a place to one day build a house. We'd drive here and there, look at some piece of property that was too far into the jungle and another that was too close to the neighbors. It ended up taking up all the hours out of what was to have been time off!

Finally, in 1998 we found a piece of property that was just what we wanted. It was on a street in Hana that had houses, but they were not so close to each other that anyone felt they lived "in town." It was also right on the ocean, up on a bluff where you could look out over the water. The place we found was connected to the family of Paul Fagan, the man who saved Hana by building the original Ka'uiki Inn and opening up tourist trade.

The first Paul Fagan had purchased five parcels of land that were now owned by his grandchildren. Spyder fell in love with a parcel on a little strip of the family's land. He wanted to build there *so* badly! But there had seemed to be no way to do it. "No, no, no! That's Fagan land. You'll never be able to buy that."

One day, after we'd been looking for about twenty years, we said, "Enough is enough." This time when we went for our vacation, we decided that it would be a vacation, not a site search. We told our real estate representatives, Carl and Rae Lindquist, who were also our good friends, that maybe we should just look elsewhere.

"Wait!" Carl said. "You won't believe this—I think I may have something you'll want to see."

He took us for a short ride, and there it was—the very place Spyder had loved since we'd first started coming to Hana! As fate would have it, one of the grandchildren needed to sell his land. I guess he hadn't wanted to let his family know he needed to sell, because as I understood it, none of his brothers and sisters knew that it was on the market. He'd approached Carl privately.

We bought it that very day.

It took several years before we started, but we did build a home in Hana. It's not a big house, but it is beautiful—a lovely plantation-style house with a view of the ocean. It's a home where I can sit with a cup of coffee and watch the waves crashing against the cliffs, the Ewa birds, and the turtles that come into the cove to lie on their backs and float in the water. It's paradise.

Hana is a very tiny, close-knit community, a place where you don't "talk stink," 'cause you never know who you're talking to. Almost everyone in Hana is related in some way. It's also a sanctuary of sorts for some celebrities because it's isolated and the folks in Hana are immune to the modern fascination with famous people. They simply don't care about it. They're much more interested in whether you are a good person and you respect the *aina* (land). A perfect example is Kris Kristofferson and his wife, Lisa, who are responsible for our finding Hana in the first place. We've known each other for years; Haley went to Our Lady of Malibu school with their sons Jesse and Jody, and Hana later went to Hana School with their youngest son, Blake. Kris and Lisa are our neighbors and good friends. The thing I love about them is they're straight shooters, no pretense; what you see is what you get. They're tireless activists, hands-on parents, and good people.

Everyone in Hana calls me CP; our dear friend Pinky gave me the name after he heard my mother call me "Patti." There are a lot of cattle in Hana, so there are a lot of cow pies and patties around. Pinky thought it would be "cute" to call me "Cow Patti," abbreviated later to "CP." Spyder is known to everyone as either "Coach Spyduh," because he was the soccer coach for two years, or "Paisan."

In a lot of ways, the Hana property coming along when it did seemed to represent much more than just our finding a home away from home. For years we'd been wandering, searching for a path that was truly ours. Now, in this town that meant so much to us, we'd found what we'd been looking for all those years. Coming at the same time as our epiphany about going independent, the symbolism was too clear to deny. We had found our way out, our way to happiness. We didn't belong to anyone but ourselves. We knew what we had to do.

CHAPTER ELEVEN

IN THE BALANCE

IN 1999, EMI RELEASED *Synchronistic Wanderings: Recorded Anthology 1979–1999,* a three-CD box set of our music to mark the twentieth anniversary of our first release, 1979's *In the Heat of the Night.*

This was a project we believed important after several years of EMI putting out one compilation after another. Sometimes the songs were put together in an inappropriate sequence, and sometimes the song choices were just *off.* But to the company's credit, EMI approached us about how we'd like to be represented for a twentieth-anniversary release. As long as we had some say in it, we were on board. One thing we insisted on was the use of certain material we'd done that they didn't own and had no access to. That way we could show the entire career and not just what Chrysalis had been involved with.

To celebrate the milestone we set out on another big tour and made a few changes in our usual set. During the mideighties we'd cut back on doing so many of our oldest hits. I believed in looking forward, in playing new music and trying new styles. Also, it gets old singing the hits like "Hit Me with Your Best Shot" every night. But now we brought back the whole hit parade, and the audiences loved it.

The box set was a collector's item. For example, the box-set version of "I Need a Lover," from 1979, was recorded at the Bottom Line just a couple of weeks after we put the live band together. It wasn't the best version of that song in existence, but it was raw and authentic, which is what we wanted. "Love Is a Battlefield" is an original demo version with only one vocal, whereas in the final version, I recorded several. We included some things no one had heard. "New Dream Islands" was an unreleased outtake from *Seven the Hard Way*, the first song Spyder and I wrote for the album. But in the end, it did not make the cut. "Run Between the Raindrops" was recorded live in Philadelphia in 1988 and had been used only in one radio show. "True Hearts" was another previously unreleased recording, as was 1978's "Crying," the Roy Orbison song that I'd performed at my first (and only) showcase. I found an old cassette tape of "Crying" in a box of material that I used to take around to pitch myself to labels before I ever got a deal. It was amazing to find it and to be able to let the fans hear what had initially been turned down! We also included a song I'd done for an Edith Piaf tribute, "The Effect You Have on Me," and "Rescue Me" from the *Speed* soundtrack.

There was talk of adding some of the old material I'd recorded with Coxon's Army, but in the end we decided it was just too different from our music's evolution. It was definitely cabaret-type music, and even though it played a role in my getting started, it had never been a part of my ultimate career.

Unlike the earlier retrospectives that EMI had issued, this process felt cathartic and well produced. It was a good encapsulation of everything that we'd done—everything that we were proud of. In talking about the record it was also a chance to clear the air about the vital contribution that Spyder had been making since day one. As we looked back at twenty years, it was the perfect time to eliminate the long-held misconceptions about how our collaboration functioned. When Jim Moret of CNN interviewed us about *Synchronistic Wanderings,* he introduced Spyder as "producer/collaborator/songwriter/guitarist and hus-band."

"That's too many titles," Spyder said.

"You just have 'entertainer,' Pat," Moret said to me.

"That's because I'm smart," I said with a laugh. "I've got one job. I like it. It's good."

AFTER FINISHING OUR LEARNING experience with CMC International, we thanked Tom Lipsky for the caring job he'd done and we moved on. We began writing material at our own pace. Eventually we'd put out another new album, but in the meantime, we would concentrate on touring, merchandise, and brand extension—all building up to the launch of an independent record label for our albums. Since 1995, we'd been touring consistently every summer, but now the goal was to raise our profile, increase our exposure, and rekindle the love affair with our fan base. The diehards were loyal (God bless 'em) and they never strayed, but looking to the future, we also wanted to capture a new audience.

With this in mind, we refined our set lists and made it a point to play songs that would get different kinds of listeners out to the shows. We wanted to focus in on the sound that had helped get us to where we were in the first place. The tour wasn't a way to help sell millions of records or sell out the biggest venue in every city we went to. We wanted to play to audiences that knew us and give them a show that they wouldn't forget.

And every summer without fail our kids came with us, along for the ride no matter where we were. It turned into a family tradition—every summer was a two-month-long road trip. And while being rock stars didn't preclude being parents, ever, it did help when you had girls who were obsessed with teen bands. Just because we were rockers didn't mean that we were above aiding and abetting our daughters' teen pop obsessions. Every summer Haley and Hana would get on the bus armed with their favorite bands' touring schedules, our itinerary, and an atlas, and then proceed to map out the number of shows they could attend while we were touring. Spyder and I each had to pay our parental dues, accompanying both girls to see everyone from Hansen and N★SYNC (Haley) to Miley Cyrus and the Jonas Brothers (Hana). Only kids can make you grovel to get backstage passes. We both spent many of our evenings off during those summers being trampled by hormonal, squealing twelve-year-olds.

For a short time during the boy band craze, Haley and two of her friends, Erin Potter and Molly Torrance, thought it would be great to have an all-girl band à la N★SYNC, so they formed a group called GLO. Molly was later replaced by Natasha Porlas. Spyder wrote a couple of songs for them, they got a choreographer, and they practiced day and night. After a little bit they got really good and we decided they should open for us in the summer. It would be a gentle introduction; they'd perform about three songs. They were always working on their stage personas, changing hairstyles and outfits constantly. They all wore those low-cut jeans; I always said that during that tour I saw more butt crack than there was at a plumber's convention.

These consecutive summers on the road had exactly the kind of impact that we'd hoped for, so much so that by the time the millennium began, we were ready to be on our own completely, and we formally parted ways with our manager. From now on, we would be self-managed. We felt that after twenty-one years of making music there was no point to having someone guiding us. If we weren't able to take charge of things after all this time, then we had no reason to be in the business anymore.

Armed with that, in 2001 we set out to change the way we did business. We would now take an active role in every aspect of our professional career. Back in 1993, we'd formed a company called Bel Chiasso to handle our eventual publishing program. Now that would become the name of our new label. "*Chiasso*" in Italian means "noise," "uproar," and "*bel chiasso*" means "beautiful noise," which was what we planned on making after *Innamorata*. We had our business manager Gary Haber and our agent Brad Goodman to help us navigate. Spyder and I would be the CEOs of the company, and our trusted friend and tour manager John Malta would oversee to the day-to-day. The plan was to grow the brand that was Pat Benatar and Neil Giraldo.

And throughout 2001, that plan was in place and moving forward, but like most of America, all that we were doing came to a screeching halt for us on the morning of September 11, 2001.

We were on the road and had a gig up in Napa Valley that night. We were staying at an area hotel to be ready for an early sound check, and I woke up to a frantic call from my mother: "Patti, wake up, we're under attack! Turn on the TV!"

It was one of those moments in everyone's life where you never forget where you were when it happened, like Pearl Harbor or Kennedy's assassination, pivotal moments in history that impact your life forever. We woke up, turned on the television—and were horrified at what we saw. It still seems surreal to think back on it all. There was my city—New York—attacked, smoke billowing from the streets, people screaming. How was this possible? I was trying to calm down our crying daughters and their friends who were traveling with us. I stared in disbelief at the images of the city I'd grown up in. Half of my family lived less than two miles from Ground Zero. It was too much to comprehend. We sat glued to the television, listening to the reports, trying to make sense of what had happened. As terrifying as it was, I felt, as many people did, a camaraderie with all Americans that morning. I knew we were all feeling the same shock, fear, revulsion, anger. It was one of those things that are so huge, so horrific, that you feel like the entire world has just been stopped in its tracks. I assumed everything *would* stop, including the concert. Surely the show was canceled.

The phone rang; it was John Malta telling us the promoter still planned on doing the show that night. Were they insane? How could they possibly think it was appropriate to go on with a planned performance in light of what had happened? Our country had been attacked! I went crazy.

"Absolutely not! There is no way that I'm going to perform after all this; it's disrespectful! And who would come anyway? The answer is no!"

It made no sense to me that anyone would hold a concert on this of all nights. They had to cancel. Everyone was going to stop doing everything. But the promoter had a list of reasons why the show had to go on, none of which made a goddamn bit of difference to me.

"It's completely inappropriate," I told him. "I won't participate."

When the follow-up call came, the answer was the same. The show was going on.

"The guy says he'll sue you if you don't play."

"So many Americans have died today! How can he do this?"

I didn't know what to do and still hadn't decided when I got another call. This time the tone had changed. The promoter had had a change of heart, and he was about to cancel the show when the phones started ringing off the hook. People were calling and asking if the show was still on, because they wanted to come. They wanted to be out together with other Americans; they didn't want to go through what they were feeling alone. They wanted to mourn together, even if it was only for a few hours.

While a part of me thought he was full of shit and making it up so I'd play, if there was even a remote chance that what he'd said was true, I couldn't walk away from people in need. I agreed to go on. Once the decision was made, I had to figure out how I was going to manage this. I was heartbroken, sickened by what had happened, and I was afraid. I was afraid for the people of New York, my family, America, and the impact of this on the world. How on earth was I supposed to justify something so trivial in the face of something so profound? How was I going to go out there and jump around and sing stupid love songs? I still couldn't believe it. I kept thinking, *Oh my God, don't make me do this. I'm not that cool, not that good. Don't give this to me while I'm feeling so torn apart.* I just shook involuntarily at the thought of what I had to do.

I still hadn't pulled myself together by the time I got to my dressing room. I paced and paced, praying I could make it through this show and trying to figure out how. What about the set list? Christ, every song seemed to have a reference to either war ("Love Is a Battlefield," "Hit Me with Your Best Shot") or fire ("Fire and Ice," "All Fired Up"). I'd have to take everything out. But then I started thinking, *What about "Invincible" and "We Belong"? These are positive songs about survival and brotherhood. What about "All Fired Up"? If this was done by terrorists, well, they can just kiss my ass. They can kiss all of our asses. You bet I'll do "All Fired Up."*

Then I started to think maybe I *could* do it. It wouldn't be business as usual; I'd have to talk to the audience first, get a few things worked out. We'd do this show together: if I felt uncomfortable with a song I'd stop; if they did, they could ask us to stop. We would go one step at a time and see how far we'd get. Maybe this could work after all.

I am never nervous about shows, but when I walked on the stage that night I was shaking. My teeth were chattering so bad I didn't know if I could talk. I went to center stage and sat down on the stool I'd requested. It was a beautiful night. The stars were out. It was in a vineyard in Napa Valley—one of the most beautiful places. I'd played it so many times, and it had never looked any more spectacular. I asked that they turn the lights up at the venue, so I could see the audience better. I needed to see their faces.

When I looked out my heart broke, for all of us, for America. People had brought flags, hundreds of them in all sizes, and they waved furiously. They'd made banners out of sheets and spray paint that said

"God Bless America." I could see people in the front rows, and they had tears running down their faces. There was a collective weep that went out across the crowd. People were sobbing, and so was I. We all were.

The hairs rose on my arms and even more than ever, I believed I might not be able to speak to them or sing. My emotions were wound too tight. When I finally pulled myself together, I began to talk to them. I was so upset and worried that I wouldn't be able to say anything that would be relevant or sufficient. I felt so anxious that I wasn't up to the task at hand. Knowing how awkward I probably appeared only made me feel even worse—how could I let an audience see me like this? I normally have a boundary line that I keep between an audience and me so that I don't get too emotional and lose control of the situation. In order to take them on a journey, someone has to be able to steer the boat, and that someone was always me. That night, I crossed the line. We sat there, the band, the crew, the waitstaff, and the audience, and we put our trust in each other and tried to make sense out of a senseless act.

I should also say here that I am personally a pretty political person. I have strongly held political beliefs. But I don't talk about them publicly, and I certainly don't try to influence anyone to think like I do. For one thing, I don't want to put people off just because we think differently on one thing or another. For a second thing, it's not my job to go onstage and be political. I don't like the idea of people picking their politics because of a favorite star. For me to give a speech was the most remote of possibilities.

But this was not about politics; this was about the collective loss that America had just suffered. When I spoke, I tried to be as honest as I could. I'm not a big talker onstage. I'll introduce songs and tell a story now and then, but I'd much rather be singing. I told them that I didn't know what to say. I didn't have a plan. I was feeling just like they were—shocked, confused, and afraid. I told them that doing this show was going to be very difficult for us, but we would do our best. We might make mistakes, choose songs that might be inappropriate, and that we'd stop if we felt weird.

We began the show with "America the Beautiful"; they all joined in, and the words never seemed more fitting. As I looked at their up-turned faces on that pristine early fall evening, I began to feel strong and defiant. I was sad but I was angry. Who were these people who did this, who'd murdered civilians? I told them we must stand up against the ones who did this. People who threatened democracy and free-dom. This was the United States of America and we would not stand down. That our forefathers had a dream of freedom for all and *nobody* was going to destroy that. They could crash planes and knock down buildings but not our spirit. The people who died that day didn't die for nothing.

As I said the words, I could feel a shift taking hold. Everyone started to rally; the energy was changing and we were moving from fear to pride. And just as the transformation of the crowd seemed at its pinnacle, we launched into "Invincible," and the lyrics took on a whole new meaning: "We can't afford to be innocent / Stand up and face the enemy / It's a do or die situation / We will be invincible."

We continued in that way for the rest of the evening, playing songs and discussing how everyone was feeling. So many of them worried that we wouldn't be able to get back to normalcy any time soon. They worried about the upcoming holidays, Thanksgiving, Hanukkah, Christmas, and whether we'd be able to celebrate as a country.

"How are we gonna have Christmas? How will anyone feel like celebrating?" one person called out.

"Oh, we're gonna have Christmas," I shouted back. "We're going to do what we do best: pick ourselves up and move forward. We are *going* to have Christmas!"

That night, when we got back to the hotel, the genesis of a song started rolling around in my head. The lyrics would come from the conversations we had with the audience at the Napa show. I would call it "Christmas in America." Part of the song goes like this:

> So keep your babies close tonight
> Hug your husband, kiss your wife
> Be thankful for this way of life,
> We're fortunate to share
> And not forget the ones we've lost
> Their memory lives on in our hearts
> They'll be forever in our thoughts
> And always in our prayers
> Unto this world a child is born
> His gift was meant for everyone
> The light of peace shines on and on
> And never fades away
> America, America indivisible we are
> One nation under God
> And that will never change
> Coz it's Christmas in America
> Let the angels sing
> It's Christmas in America
> Let freedom ring
> Let peace resound throughout the world
> Especially on this day
> It's Christmas in America
> God bless the USA

That night, I was awed by the healing power of music. It wasn't so much anything I had done as it was the crowd's willingness to go along with me, to open and come together. Standing up there that night, I felt an intense sense of pride that our music had helped ease the pain of a terrible situation, if even for just a couple of hours. The whole thing was cathartic. I had never done any kind of a sit-down with an audience. To have that conversation on that night was exhilarating and healing.

As fate would have it, we played four more shows in quick succession, and for each of those shows, I repeated the give-and-take. I needed it and the audiences needed it. Every time it was the same, an audience filled with flag-waving, heartbroken Americans who rallied and stood strong as the night went on. What those shows taught me is that we do have a collective American soul. It was important for that audience to have a place to come on the night of 9/11, a place where they could interact and show their love of their country. Even as I write this almost nine years later, the memory of those days is so vivid and uplifting.

Most Americans acted with grace and exemplary behavior in the face of this tragedy, but there is always a group who just can't seem to get with the program. This group usually needs a two-by-four across the face to get the point, and the promoter of our final show was precisely one of these people.

One of the conditions of our summer tours is that we always have to be home and off tour by September 15, because that's when school starts. I'm a hands-on mom when it comes to the girls' schools and so I'd always made that a priority. After those four dates following September 11, we had gone home to California so Hana would be there for the first day of school. We had a few days to unwind, and then we were scheduled for a final show in Florida that would have required us to fly. Of course, after 9/11 there was a ban on flying for several days. This fact was publicized in every newspaper and on every TV and radio station. You would have had to have been living underground *not* to know about it. It was assumed we would not perform, because no one was flying, the skies were not safe, and there wasn't enough time to drive across the country and make the show.

Well, apparently the promoter in Florida didn't care about any of that. The moment the ban was lifted, he demanded we do the gig. When John called me to tell me the news, I was incredulous.

"No way. You tell the promoter we fly with our children, and I'm not getting on a plane with them a week after terrorists attacked our country. Tell him we'll reschedule when things calm down. When we can be sure it's safe to fly. We'll honor the contract and make up the date. This guy has to understand the situation."

He didn't. He was adamant that we play and threatened to sue us if we didn't fulfill our obligation. What is it about human beings? Disasters either bring out the best in us or show the ugliness that we're capable of. I was stunned but not surprised. So I decided what I *was* willing to do. I told our agent Brad Goodman to call the promoter and ask him if he had children. If he did, I asked him to put his wife and *one* child on a plane, not a private jet but a commercial airliner, so they could fly across the country to California to pick me and my family up. If he was willing to do that, then I would fly to Florida and do the gig.

You know what happened then. That was the end of it. He didn't ask again, nor did he sue me.

One thing that I believe 9/11 did for people was to make them see just how precious and fragile life is, and to make family a priority. At least I hope it did. We'd tried hard to put our family first, and 9/11 simply reinforced the importance of those choices.

WHILE 9/11 LEFT EVERYONE reeling in emotion, I had no doubt that we would all emerge a stronger, more resilient country as a result of what we'd been through. But as it turned out, it wouldn't be long until my personal resilience was tested again by tragedy.

On December 2, 2002, my brother, Andy, died suddenly of a heart attack at the young age of forty-six. He was driving my father-in-law and Haley when it happened, and even in the middle of it, he had the wherewithal to slow down the car so they wouldn't crash. The instant Spyder and I heard what had happened, we sped over to my parents' house and told them there'd been an accident. We all rushed to the hospital. I can still see the emergency doors swinging open and Haley leaning forward and shaking her head no. He didn't make it.

My family was heartbroken. Andy had been my best friend since childhood. He was one of the great joys of my life—his humor, his gentle demeanor, his love of family. Just because we were all grown up didn't mean that I'd lost my feelings of responsibility toward him. I was still on the lookout for him at all times, and now he was gone in an instant. Even now, all these years later, I still have dreams about Andy. In my dreams he's alive and laughs at my surprise at seeing him. He's still the joker, still my baby brother. He tells me that he is fine. I miss him every day.

In the aftermath, I just couldn't stand it. Nor could my parents. It nearly killed them. I couldn't make sense of how something like this could happen, how someone so special could be taken from me with such swift resolution. It was so awful that I found myself wanting to spend more time in Hawaii, wanting to get as far from the familiar as possible. When he died we were still building our house there, and though initially it was just meant to be a getaway, it was our dream to live there full-time. After Andy died, I started thinking a lot about the impermanence of life, and eventually Spyder and I agreed that we should stop talking about living in Hana and actually do it. And after all that happened, we decided that it would be the right time to just do it. We ended up staying for four glorious years.

Perhaps it was partly because we were looking for a way to channel our sadness over Andy's death into our music, but in the year following his death, Spyder started wanting to get in the studio again. We hadn't made a studio album since 1997's *Innamorata*. So he said, "Why don't we make a record?"

"I don't know," I said. "I'm feeling kind of lazy."

"Come on, come on."

"I don't know. I've decided now that I'm an old woman in my fifties, I'm just gonna be opinionated and lazy."

"You were a pain in the ass when you were young! Now you want to be an *old* pain in the ass?"

And so we ended up laughing and making a record titled Go. It's a guitar-driven record, something we'd moved away from on *Innamorata*. It was great to be bashing again. It was the first album that we recorded completely digitally—no tape whatsoever. While I was intrigued by the new process, I was a little freaked out as well. All the tracks, all the vocals, weren't on the twenty-four-track tape; they were numbers stored on air. It was strange to think that there was nothing physical that existed to prove what we'd actually made. It was all just space on a computer.

Making Go was a unique experience. It was the first time after twenty-four years of recording that we would make a record totally unencumbered. We weren't just musicians anymore. Of course, the workload was enormous at times. There was no strolling into the studio at one P.M., Starbucks in hand. We were in charge of financing, distribution, marketing artwork, and while it was a daunting responsibility, it was exciting to finally realize the goal we'd been working toward for so long. All of the lessons we'd learned from our experience with *Innamorata* were put to incredibly good use, and they really supported our decision to learn the indie business from the outside before diving in ourselves.

We worked round the clock, and when we weren't recording, we were doing any number of other necessary tasks, from writing to choosing artwork for the cover to making distribution deals. It was busy but gratifying. The idea that we were responsible for our own destiny was extraordinary. If things went south it was our doing. Likewise, if things were a success, that would be our fault too. Either way, it was so much easier to live our fate knowing that we weren't at the mercy of someone else's whim.

Recording was fun for me, although Spyder says that he got too deep into making it and couldn't climb out—couldn't wrap it up. Then when he *did* finish it, he scrapped parts and redid them. Consequently, he's not a big fan of *Go,* but I think this all happened in part because our focus was spread out into so many areas. A big part of that record was learning how to manage and delegate duties when we were running the whole show. With a lot of that learning done, we'd have a better sense of things next time. In the end I think we made a good, solid record with some great stuff on it, but more important, we created the model for all future projects. We put "Christmas in America" on as a bonus track, and all the proceeds from the sale of the single were donated to a 9/11 charity organization.

After *Go,* we went on our annual summer tour, of course, but we also took on other projects as we kept ourselves visible. Of these, my absolute favorite was *CMT Crossroads,* a show on Country Music Television that pairs country artists with artists from other genres, and the two come together for a performance. We were set up with Martina McBride, whose work I was familiar with and had high regard for because of her vocal talent. As it turned out, I was even more impressed by her down-to-earth, no-nonsense personality. This was a woman I could relate to. She was much younger than me but was basically dealing with all the issues I'd dealt with throughout my career, save the sleazy program directors (there were laws against that now). But she, too, would pack up her daughters and take them with her, and she reminded me that juggling home, family, and career was alive and well. We spent an interesting and enlightening weekend together, comparing notes and swapping tips. The close bond that we shared ended up coming through in our performance, which went better than I could have ever anticipated, becoming the second-highest rated in the show's history.

COMING OFF THE POSITIVE experience of the *Crossroads* performance, during the next several years, we concentrated on one thing: achieving balance. Discovering and then implementing a schedule that worked for us instead of against us. It was important to stay in the public's consciousness and we had to stockpile cash to fund future projects. We knew what we wanted and that was to not have to deal with the pressure to record. If wanted to record, great, but if not, we wanted that to be great too. So we went about implementing a strategy that could help us achieve that.

The cornerstone of this plan was rethinking the way we toured in the summer. Touring would become the financial anchor subsidizing all our creative projects, but it would be done in a time frame that benefited our family life. It needed to be on an annual basis, but on our terms. And with kids in school that meant the summer—every summer. It wasn't easy at first; agents and promoters balked, saying it couldn't be done, that neither we nor anyone else would make any money. But in the end, it did work, and everyone profited both financially and on a much more basic level.

Part of the key to touring was making sure that my voice could go the distance. If touring was going to be the centerpiece of our plan, I needed to make sure my voice could make it. I didn't want to be one of those singers who had to create totally new arrangements of her songs just so she could hit the notes. I knew that people came out to shows to hear their favorite songs, and while it's one thing to inject new life into those songs, it's another to revamp them completely. I wanted these songs to take people back. To remind them of what rock and roll sounds like. To do that I would have to take care of my vocal cords.

My classical voice training and my discipline over the years had given my voice longevity, and of course not smoking and not drinking had only helped my chances. (Not partying may have made me boring by rock star standards, but at least I could still sing.) While we always packed the tour schedule to the brim, we also made sure to build in days off so that I could give my throat a rest. I knew I had the stamina to keep singing like I wanted to. I just needed to be smart about it.

Touring by itself, though, would not be enough. We had to diversify, and so we branched out, doing more TV and more endorsements. A couple of years ago we'd shot an episode of *Dharma and Greg*, playing ourselves. We get stranded in an airport with Dharma and Greg and a couple that is going to get married. Dharma decides to throw a wedding for them, so Spyder and I perform the Carpenters' "We've Only Just Begun." Spyder got a kick out of the fact that the only other music person who'd appeared on the show was Bob Dylan. It was fun working with Jenna Elfman because she was such a nut, just as funny offstage as she is in character.

That experience went well enough that I thought I should do some more—not because I was looking to transition into an acting career at age fifty, but because it was an easy way to show people that I was out there. If they saw my face on VH1's *Behind the Music* or A&E's *Biography*, there wouldn't be that same question mark about what I was up to now the next time they looked in the local paper and saw that I was coming to town.

We ended up doing a bunch of TV guest spots, usually playing ourselves. We were guests on *The Ellen DeGeneres Show* and on an episode of *Charmed*, with an assortment of music specials mixed in. Spyder and I also appeared as ourselves in a 2008 episode of *The Young and the Restless*, singing at the Indigo Club. Our buddy David Kurtz writes the music for Y&R (as it's affectionately known) and he'd been asking us to come on the show for years. Finally, we agreed to do it. TV is such a strange medium, not really my thing. But everyone in the cast and crew was very sweet, and we did have a good time.

When we weren't making assorted TV appearances, we were cross-marketing our recorded music, live performances, merchandise, and anything else we could throw in the pot. I let my entrepreneurial spirit take over and just ran wild with the possibilities now that we were calling the shots. We licensed our music, and looked for new ways to put it out there. With total power, I could keep the reins as slack or tight as I wanted. I soon discovered that while I made a pretty good rock star, I made an even better businesswoman.

All sorts of different opportunities popped up. We put out a few different video retrospectives that contained all of the videos we'd released. "Love Is a Battlefield" was featured in the movie *13 Going on 30*, much to the delight of Hana, who was nine at the time. In 2007, we heard about an interesting opportunity coming our way: a video game called Guitar Hero wanted to use "Hit Me with Your Best Shot." Never one to shun new ways to promote and market, I was excited not only that a whole new generation of fans would be listening to our song, but that for four minutes, everyone would get to be Spyder, playing onstage at one of our shows. I must say, it was not what either of us envisioned when we first sat down in that studio together, but it was pretty damn cool.

Spyder also started to branch out beyond music, beginning a new business venture, On the Rock Nutrition. Spyder is Sicilian and most Italians have terrible stomach issues; "*acido*" is a common ailment. After years of searching for a natural remedy, he decided to make one himself. His mission was to improve his health and vitality, which years of touring had compromised. He hired a group of chemists and they began formulating, under his guidance, a natural, food-based product that supports energy and digestion. The product Burn Out was born.

Spyder currently runs a brisk and successful online site for his products and this year will begin retail distribution.

This wasn't about squeezing every last drop out of our career; it was about making smart business decisions so that we could continue to create music out of passion, not necessity. A lot of people who've been in the music business as long as we have don't always have the luxury of that choice. Sometimes it's because of mismanagement, sometimes it's because of recklessness, and sometimes it's because of addiction, but more often than not, it's simply that even with all the money you can make as a top-selling musician, a lifetime is a long thing to prepare for. Combine that with pop culture's notoriously fickle nature, and it's rare for any musician, save those in the absolute top tier, to simply kick back and rest on their laurels once their heyday has come and gone.

Since Spyder and I view our body of work as something that will provide for our family for years, we have long told our girls that when we're gone from this world, they must look on what we've accomplished as their future. We've worked incredibly hard to establish a sound and image that are unique to us. If Haley and Hana are smart they will perpetuate that for their children. They should always have integrity about their choices for our music, but they should not be afraid to create new ways to expand access to our music for the public.

I often refer to Priscilla Presley and her brilliant reconstruction of Elvis's legacy as an example for how to handle these things correctly. Priscilla, concerned for their daughter Lisa Marie's future, took a hands-on approach to managing the estate. When Elvis Presley died in 1977, his estate was worth $4.9 million. Last year, Elvis Presley Enterprises generated $55 million. She was a mother who saw the potential for huge financial success that would benefit her child and made it happen. This is the model I use to teach our girls about business. I tell them, "Make it bigger than it was while protecting and preserving everything your father and I worked for."

Years ago, when I first met Priscilla, I told her she was my hero. As it turned out, I was Lisa Marie's favorite singer when she was growing up. Every now and then an interviewer will ask me to name some of the cool and crazy things that have happened to me over the years and I always tell them that being the King's daughter's favorite singer ranks right at the top.

Ultimately our plan was simple: to take our career and turn it into a successful family business, one we could pass on to our children and their children. As the decade came to close, it became increasingly clear that we'd not only met but exceeded this goal. And we'd accomplished this *because* we'd put our family first, not in spite of it. Our values and our love for each other had made everything possible. We'd picked our priorities and stuck with them. In Anna Quindlen's book *A Short Guide to a Happy Life,* she says, "Don't ever confuse the two, your life and your work . . . get a life, a real one." And that's what we did. We got a real life, one with time for barbecues, birthday parties, soccer games, and of course breathing.

CHAPTER TWELVE

MY WAY

I HADN'T SEEN DEBBIE Harry in twenty-five years, and then out of the blue—a phone call. Not from her, but from my agent asking me if I wanted to go on tour with Blondie.

Some of my earliest memories in the record business are of Debbie, since hanging out with her on the set of *Union City* was one of the first things Chrysalis had me do after I signed with them. She and I were old friends, label mates who went all the way back, but it had been such a long time since we'd seen each other—largely because we were both so busy and we lived on opposite coasts. Though we hadn't spoken in ages, I still looked back fondly on the time we'd spent together, so it was only fitting that after everything I'd find myself back with her again.

Debbie called me up that March, before we started out in July. She wanted to coordinate our wardrobe choices. That just killed me because I hadn't given it a thought at that point. My real life took every minute of every day. I figured that I'd decide what to wear on stage the week before I packed to go.

"Well, all right," she said. "But I wanted to make sure we wouldn't be wearing the same thing."

I started laughing so hard I thought I'd fall off my chair.

"Oh, Debbie—I can pretty much guarantee that we won't be wearing the same thing."

And sure enough, when we got on tour Debbie showed up wearing red high tops and crazy outfits. *Great* outfits—but crazy.

Debbie was just one of the things that made the 2009 tour, "Call Me Invincible," a blast—even better than I could have imaged. It was amazing that in all the years she and I had been around we'd never done this together before, and as it turned out, it was a little like rock and roll summer camp. We all hung out together during sound checks and knocked on each other's dressing room doors to borrow hair dryers or mascara. The Donnas joined us on the tour as well, and those girls seriously know how to rock. I love, love, love those girls. We had a ton of laughs, they played great, and were just crazy, fun to be around. As it turned out, those brats were all born the year *In the Heat of the Night* came out.

Between the Donnas, Blondie, my family, and me, there were a lot of women around, and I mean a lot! Spyder went nuts. Sure, he was used to having a lot of girls in our house, but this was something else entirely; and while there'd been a lot of women on Lilith Fair, we were only there for a couple of dates. This time he was spending an entire summer surrounded by even more women. He hid away on the band bus, where Myron was also looking for sanctuary. Occasionally Clem Burke, Blondie's drummer, would join them when he'd had enough too.

While Debbie and I were old hands at this stuff, it was interesting for me to watch how the Donnas carried themselves. No matter where we were, what city we were playing in, they just went about their business confidently, like it was the most natural thing in the world to be four girls, in a rock band, touring America. It was one of those moments where you feel like you're seeing progress in motion, and suddenly everything sort of adds up, why we all bother to put one foot in front of the other and keep pushing ourselves forward.

In a lot of ways that tour just made sense—a unique combination of my past and my present, but also with a glimpse of my future. Or maybe not my future, but our future. Like everything I'd experienced at Lilith Fair, it left me inspired with hope about what women in this business could accomplish and their ability to achieve whatever the hell they wanted to. I like the idea that we're living in a world where four girls who were high school friends can just start a band and keep rocking until someone starts to pay attention. And when they hit it, and it's time for them to travel the country, they don't think twice about it—they just go and do their job, no compromising.

The situations that girls who want to rock face today are both easier and harder than what I was up against. In many ways the playing fields have been leveled; certainly digital music has put a lot more power into the hands of young women everywhere who are looking to make the record they want. At the same time, there are some things that will never change. There will always be sleazy guys looking to take advantage—guys looking to use sex as power and capitalize on an industry that is fundamentally superficial.

But still, I see women everywhere doing their thing and throwing themselves into situations headfirst, and not taking shit from anyone— man or woman—who tells them how they should be doing things. It's empowering to watch, and to know that, perhaps in some way, I made the hard path that they still have to walk just a little bit easier. To know that all those arguments about image and attitude weren't for nothing, and as a result, it's simpler for someone else to walk out onstage.

Music can be a very shallow business, and if you're not careful, it's easy to get sucked into the cesspool. People are constantly telling you what's wrong with your looks or your age, and learning how to ignore them is an acquired skill. I live in Los Angeles and Hana, and I can't think of two places that are more diametrically opposed. While L.A. seems completely consumed with perfecting one's physical appearance, Hana is all about beautifying the spirit. Living in both gives me a unique perspective. Any time I get too hung up on wrinkles or weight or age, I only have to think of the amazing beauty of the Kupuna (the elders) in Hana. They are a living example of grace and wisdom with a twinkle in their eyes that shines out of their leathery, browned skin. I've enjoyed every age I've been, and each has had its own individual merit. Every laugh line, every scar, is a badge I wear to show I've been present, the inner rings of my personal tree trunk that I display proudly for all to see. Nowadays, I don't want a "perfect" face and body; I want to wear the life I've lived.

Superficial things become less important when you suffer the loss of a parent. That was driven home to me when my father died on January 2, 2009. He'd been sick for about five years, suffering with diabetes and heart problems. Dad never took care of himself—he didn't exercise, never ate a vegetable, and paid little attention to his health. He was a hardworking man who loved his family. Dad and Mom remained like teenagers in love until the very end. When it became obvious his time was close, we brought him home and took care of him in-house, which is how he wanted it. He watched television, ate exactly what he wanted, and enjoyed having his family around him. Mom was an amazing caretaker. I know that he waited until the holiday season was over before he peacefully passed away. That was the way he was—thinking of us first, even in death.

I DON'T APOLOGIZE FOR much anymore, and I certainly don't feel bad about doing what I need to do for my family. To say I listen to my gut is an understatement—I hang onto my gut's every word.

My world now is a lot smaller than it once was, and that's just fine with me. I'm a mother and a singer—in that order. The music is important, but a distant second to family. While I still love performing, I don't yearn for the spotlight. I love the feeling of stepping on the stage and interacting with the audience, but that craving comes from my desire for a shared musical experience with the audience. It's about taking them somewhere and having them do the same to me, not about being a rock star. I don't miss dressing up every single day or putting on makeup for a show each night. (Well, maybe the eyeliner.)

I don't have an overwhelming passion to record new music. If I never win another award or have another gold record on the wall, that's okay. It would be a fun but not a necessary addition to my life. Recording and making music as often as possible is more important to Spyder. He plays in a little Italian band called the New Sicilians. They do contemporary Italian songs and some traditional, while also composing new music too. He plays some accordion and bandolino. They have great fun. And they just might go into the studio and record some of it one of these days. Me? Unless I am out on a tour, I'm happy singing Broadway show tunes in the car on my way to pick up my daughter and her friends. My dream is to end up in the islands, sitting on the side of the Hana Highway wearing a muumuu, selling leis and pineapples.

That's not to say that I take for granted what music has done for my life. On the contrary, I'm incredibly grateful for everything music has given me, but music has its place as does everything else. Hana is still in high school, and I am an involved parent. It makes me happy to be Haley and Hana's mom, who also happens to sing. And because I know that I like that, because I know that's enough for me, I'm a much saner person than if I were trying to relive the glory days. At least now I know where I stand. I've put everything in the place where it needs to be. I'm not reliant on anyone, and I'm living the life that I want to live.

We'll keep touring for as long as fans will have us. In 2009, Spyder ran into REO Speedwagon's Kevin Cronin, and the two of them started talking about how much fun we'd had working together during 1995's *Can't Stop Rockin'* tour. REO had come on the rock scene the same time as we did, with their 1980 number 1 hit, "Keep On Loving You," as well as so many others including "Can't Fight the Feeling." Out of Spyder's random encounter, 2010's *Love On the Run* tour was born. I've been looking forward to it because I really did enjoy *Can't Stop Rockin'* and the fans—old and new—that came out to hear us. And I'm sure next summer we'll be right back out there, on the road ready to do it all over again.

Sometimes, when I have a moment to catch my breath, I'll flip on the TV and scroll past MTV. There's little today about the channel that resembles the one that we helped launch, and I'd be lying if I said that there wasn't a part of me that gets nostalgic for that aspect of the way things were. It's cliché but true that MTV has little or nothing to do with music anymore. Videos were such a positive extension of the music, and things haven't been the same since they pulled them off the air for reality programming. It's too bad, but it's not something that I dwell on. Just another way in which this continues to be one of the most frustrating and fascinating businesses to watch. Nothing lasts for long.

I continue to be amazed by how technology has the capacity to change the way that people find and listen to music. The transformation that started with MTV morphed into digital music, and has now become having a song on the Guitar Hero video game. But while the machinery for distributing music and attracting fans has changed, the actual art of making music still remains very much the same. For all the technological marvels that exist, the basic ingredients that go into creating a song have stayed constant. Ultimately there is something so human and so special about making music, and this will forever make it a far greater force than any technological advance—no matter how impressive.

The digital music revolution has accomplished a lot of what we hoped it would when we first started thinking about it in the nineties.

While it hasn't done away with the record labels altogether yet, it has gnawed away at their ironclad grasp on power. But for all that digital music has eroded the centralized control of the record label, it's also had an impact far greater than anything we could have anticipated, upending not just record companies but the entire power structure of the music business. It's not just the label execs who are fighting for dear life—nothing in the music business functions as it did twenty years ago. Online radio, music journalism—everything has changed, returning much of the power to the artist, where it belongs. Ever since our decision to leave EMI, we've never looked back, never regretted our choice. Even when we were in the throes of doing all the work, we had the satisfaction of knowing that we were doing it all for us.

Thinking about how music has changed in the last ten years, I am reminded of how important it is to be unafraid. That's not an easy thing to do, because there are times you just want to give up. I know I came damn close to it after the disaster of the *Wide Awake in Dreamland* fiasco. Getting off the ground after that was probably one of the hardest things I've ever had to do. It would have been so much easier just to throw in the towel. And I'm sure in some alternate reality that's just what might have happened—my career would have ended late in that summer of 1988.

But like so much in my life, it was Spyder who set me straight and pushed me over the next hill. I had many terrific years left in me, and just as I never would have found my sound in the first place if it hadn't been for Spyder, I never would have kept it going without him either. Perhaps one day I'll decide to hang up my mic for good, and when that happens, at least I'll know that the time is right, because my chance to end it early came and went a long time ago. Until then, Spyder keeps me going, keeps me grounded. Every day I look at him and I'm reminded of how I got to where I am and why I'm even still doing this in the first place. And every day I get up and love the life that we've built together.

There are lots of famously over-the-top ways for rock careers to end, but seeing as how I've never been one to follow in anyone's footsteps, I'm not about to start now. As the producer for VH1's show *Behind the Music* once told me—mine is one of the only stories that doesn't involve at least one trip to rehab. I'm proud to say that like a lot of rock and roll truisms, that whole debate about burning out or fading away is bullshit—the same crap music execs kick up to sell records and make you think that rock music only belongs to people under thirty. A true rocker is going to do whatever the hell she wants to, whether she's a school teacher, a CEO of a large corporation, or someone's mommy. Because that's what rock and roll is really about: following your passion with no apologies. Following that sound in your head that only you can hear.

And that's what I tell young musicians—female or male—who are trying to make it today: create your own music. Don't listen too much to what's out there. Don't try to follow a trend or fit in with what's selling. It may not be fashionable next week. Don't try to sing like anybody else but yourself. Hone your songwriting skills. Practice those guitars. Practice your instruments. Make sure that you're the best you can possibly be at what you do. And own *everything*! I'm proud that we made our music and never tried to remake the previous record. Don't be afraid of criticism. Don't be afraid of taking a chance, of switching your musical direction. One of the greatest things about getting older is that you care far less when someone uses you as a target. Stay open to the world around you. You never know where inspiration will come from, or what form it will take. It may be a journal or a blog entry—or it may turn into a song.

And girls—stand up for yourselves. Demand respect and then return it. The world has changed, but not all that much. Evolution is a slow process, but that's what intellect is for. You can bypass what's been hardwired in by being smart. You'll still screw up here and there, but at least you'll know what to do afterward. No one made more mistakes than me, but sometimes I think that was the point. I believe that every step, good or bad, has been a step forward. People much smarter than I am have long agreed life's not meant to be perfect.

I've nothing left to prove, which is probably the most liberating feeling in the world. I'm not holding on for dear life, trying to recapture some fleeting moment that's long since evaporated. Over the past thirty-one years I have been a singer, a lover, a businesswoman, a daughter, a friend, a wife, a mother, and yes, sometimes even a rock star. In my journey I tried my best to honor all of these things. In the end, I suppose that's all that's really required.

At night when I close my eyes, I don't see myself back onstage at Catch, thinking back to where it all began or some romanticized version of that past. I don't revise history that way, and I don't forget that the great times were never as great as they seem in the rearview mirror. Instead I see the road that's led me here to this moment, and how now after thirty-one years, I am exactly where I want to be. The only clock that I punch is the one that I built myself.

ACKNOWLEDGMENTS

Thank you—to all my friends who cheered me on and to my family for putting up with my absence, and take-out.

To my assistant, Lindsay, who found the answers to all the questions and still laughed every day. To Brad, Gary G., Gary H., Clair, and Johnny M. for taking care of business. To the countless fans around the world, new and old, you're the reason we're still here. To Newman, in the end a leap of faith is still a beautiful thing. To my bandmates for every note, we've had some fun, haven't we? To my crew for making it all roll. To Georgia, in your loving care I learned to fly. To my parents, for bringing me into this world and teaching me all about unconditional love. To God—for trusting me to be the steward of this amazing gift. To Andy—boy, crazy, huh? Miss you, every day. To Matt, editor extraordinaire, for wrangling all my thoughts and turning them into a wonderful book. You Rock. To Patsi, for being such a gentle teacher, your humor and talent inspired me every step of the way. To everyone at William Morrow, I'm thrilled to be working with such an amazing team . . . Shelby, you're a doll!

To my darling daughters, Haley and Hana, your beauty is surpassed only by your loving hearts. Being your mother has been the greatest pleasure of my life. And finally, to my husband, the best man I know . . . A lifetime will not be enough. *Ti amo.*